THE LEGEND OF

GENGHIS KHAN

SUTAPA BASU

Readomania

Readomania Publishing
A division of Kurious Kind Media Private Limited
466, DDA SFS Apartments, Pocket 1, Sector 22, Dwarka,
New Delhi – 110077
books.readomania.com
email: support@readomania.com
Facebook: facebook.com/iamreadomania
Twitter: twitter.com/iamreadomania

First Published in 2018 by Readomania

ISBN: 978-93-858547-0-5

Typeset in Palatino Linotype by Shine Graphics
Printed and bound in India by Thomson Press India Ltd.

Readomania

India has traditionally been the land of storytellers and a lot of us have an inherent skill of creating good plots, good stories and good narrations. With a little encouragement and support, many more authors will be widely read and attain a place in the sun. This is the essence of *Readomania*—an initiative that nurtures emerging stars of the literary world.

It would not be an exaggeration to say that *Readomania* is the talent hunt in fiction. It goes a step beyond by not just identifying the talent but also nurturing it and showcasing it to the world. In the process, we have created a powerhouse of content.

Readomania has four principle interest areas—traditional print publishing, online library of short stories and poetry, literary events and products.

The print publishing works towards delivering good quality content to the readers. We publish good authors in meaningful anthologies, novels and works of narrative non-fiction. Our books stand out for their perspectives, the plots, the language and most importantly their ability to enrich lives.

Take a break, read something nice, write something beautiful. Read our books or visit us at www.readomania.com and enjoy a whole new world of literature.

For

Dr John Anthony Garnet Man
Writer, Traveller, Mongolist.

Mentor and Guide
to me.

Do not scorn a weak cub. He may become a brutal tiger.

—Old Mongol proverb

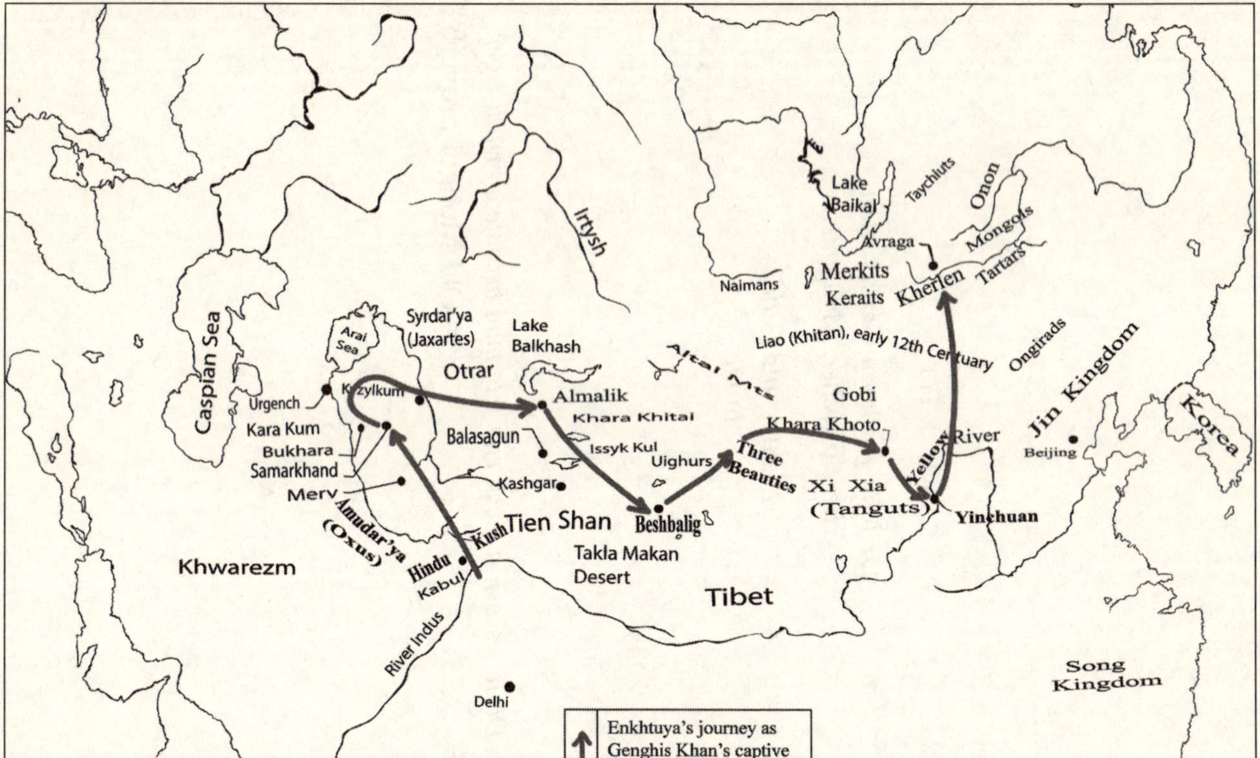
Caspian Sea
Arai Sea
Syrdar'ya (Jaxartes)
Lake Balkhash
Irtysh
Naimans
Lake Baikal
Taychiuts
Onon
Avraga
Mongols
Merkits
Keraits
Kherlen
Tartars
Liao (Khitan), early 12th Centuary
Ongirads
Jin Kingdom
Korea
Otrar
Urgench
Kyzylkum
Almalik
Khara Khitai
Kara Kum
Bukhara
Samarkhand
Merv
Balasagun
Issyk Kul
Uighurs
Altai Mts
Gobi
Khara Khoto
Three Beauties
Xi Xia (Tanguts)
Yellow River
Yinchuan
Beijing
Kashgar
Tien Shan
Beshbalig
Amudar'ya (Oxus)
Hindu Kush
Kabul
Takla Makan Desert
Tibet
Khwarezm
River Indus
Delhi
Song Kingdom
Enkhtuya's journey as Genghis Khan's captive

Cast of Main Characters

Temujin	young Genghis Khan
Enkhtuya	Sultana of Khwarezm, Princess of Ghaznin
Sultan Jalal-ud-din	Sultan of Khwarezm
Yesugei	Genghis Khan's father
Hoelun	Genghis Khan's mother
Targutai	Chief of Taychuits and Genghis Khan's sworn enemy
Chiledu	Hoelun's first husband
Börte	Genghis Khan's wife
Dei-Tsetsan	Börte's father
Shigi	Genghis Khan's adopted brother
Jamukha	Genghis Khan's blood-brother and later his enemy
Boorchu	Genghis Khan's friend
Prince Asha	Imperial Commander of Xi Xia
Gurbelchin	Wife of Prince Asha, daughter of the Onigirads' chief
Bolorma	Old, Mongolian maid to Enkhtuya
Khökh Tenger	Mongolian title for the Supreme Being

Clans allied to the Borjigins (Genghis Khan's clan)

(Ongirads, Keraits and Jamukha's clan initially)

Clans who were foes of the Borjigins (Genghis Khan's clan)

(Taychuits, Merkits, Naimans, Tartars and Jamukha's clan later.)

Prologue

River Indus exploded from the Hindu Kush Mountains furiously frothing and churning down the gorge that edged the quiet town of Malikpur. Its mighty roar had reverberated across the valley for years. Yet, this powerful voice would soon quail at the agonised shrieks from the little hamlet that would tear apart the tranquil skies of the vale.

Light glimmered on the eastern horizon as Wasim halted to try out his slingshot. Companion to the seven-year-old prince, son of Sultan Jalal-ud-din, Wasim wanted to be prepared to defend him, if necessary. With steady hands, the mountain lad pulled back the throngs and let go. The shot flew straight to the target which plopped to the ground; a black crow. Instantly, hundreds of black birds bolted up dotting the rosy dome overhead with inky smears. The clamour of fluttering wings filled Wasim's ears, deafening him momentarily. Consequently, he did not catch the sudden thunder of hooves splintering the new-born day.

A tremendous pounding reverberated the ground underfoot startling him. *Horsemen? Early morning? That always means trouble.* Fear clutched Wasim's heart and he began to run the few yards to the palace gates. But the horses were faster. They were coming from the direction of the Indus River, Wasim realised; not a few but hordes of horses were thudding up the sandy banks, crashing through the undergrowth spraying rocks and clods of earth along the track to the town. They were nearly on him as he swerved behind some uneven heaps of earthen pots piled before a locked potter's hovel and ducked down. He was just in time for the yelling horsemen flew past in a cloud of dust. In their wake, the pots teetered in the rushing wind. Wasim steadied the pots with both hands and then cautiously peeped through them. Shouts and screams of terror-stricken townspeople waking in panicky confusion rang in his ears.

Who are these men? What is happening? Wasim wondered. Through the dust, he could see smoky red smudges. *They are firing the houses…why?* Some horsemen were milling around the palace gates. When the boy observed them carefully, he broke out in cold sweat. Garbed in thick tunics with pantaloons stuffed into long leather boots, shaggy beards, long braids flying from furry caps, weather-beaten faces with flat, broad noses and narrow, slit eyes, they were no other than the fearful Mongols. Wasim recalled the prince's tales about how his father, the Sultan had fought these terrible nomadic legions but had been defeated. He had escaped their clutches by diving into the Indus River that plunged from the mountain ridges all the way to Malikpur. Desperately swimming across the vast expanse of swift waters had saved the Sultan because the Mongol warriors were afraid to breach treacherous currents. Just a month ago, the Sultana, his wife who was also Princess of Ghaznin, and his son had come down from Ghaznin to Malikpur since it was safer here.

But, now the Mongols had come to Malikpur.

Two of the Mongol soldiers had dismounted and clashed with the four guards at the palace gates, cutting them down. Their bodies sprawled before the gates, blood darkening the dirt. The Mongols waved short, broad swords, quite different from the curved, thin scimitars of the Sultan's soldiers. On their backs were slung heavy bows curved at both ends and quivers full of arrows. Blood-curdling whoops and bellows along with terrified squeals and screeches carried back to Wasim from the other end of Malikpur. He could see thatches already aflame. People were being dragged out of the burning houses and chopped down. As he watched, a small boy of about six years came running down the track followed by a mounted Mongol. As the rider drew abreast of the child, he stooped and simply sliced off the boy's head which tumbled to the ground. The torso took a few more steps before it collapsed. Wasim gripped his throat to choke back a scream.

Beyond the palace, all the houses built of stone or mud were on fire. Smoke rose in heavy, black clouds from the small town. Even the crops in the fields had been sparked off. Wasim's view was obscured by curtains of smoke. But, whenever they parted, he could hardly believe the horrible scenes they revealed. It was like a nightmare; a near-naked, screeching woman hauled through the dust by her ankles clutched in the fists of a hefty, bearded giant.

Even as Wasim looked in horror, a group of barbaric attackers pounced on her, literally tearing her apart like mad dogs in their ferocity to rape her; men, women, children turned into fiery torches spinning out of flaming houses; babies being snatched from the arms of screaming mothers, flung up in the air and being caught on wickedly gleaming spear points, their little bodies skewered like lumps of roasted meat. A few soldiers were grabbing people by their hair, two or three at a time, and nonchalantly hacking their heads off, saving time by not killing one at a time, as if they were slaughtering chickens. Wasim stuffed his knuckles into his mouth, eyes wide with terror.

Suddenly, he was distracted by angry shouts and the clanging of swords on the other side of the palace walls. *So, now the attackers were inside the palace and the Sultan's soldiers must have joined battle with them. Could the Sultan's soldiers save Malikpur?* However, Wasim couldn't help wondering, *why are the Mongols attacking Malikpur? This is a small town. Other than these few soldiers, it didn't even have an army.*

A thought struck him.

Have they come after the Sultan? But he has left...nearly fourteen days ago. Only the little prince and the Sultana are here.

Another scream made him turn towards the palace. What he saw stunned him. Two Mongols were pulling the Princess by her long, loose hair through the gates. She was resisting them while her old maid had grabbed her by the waist to stop the soldiers from dragging her out. The maid screamed abuses at the soldiers. She was telling them that this was the Sultana...a princess; that she was the Sultan's wife; that she cannot be treated vilely like any ordinary woman. They took no notice of her and kept heaving at the princess. For the first time, Wasim noted how the Sultana's round, flat face and narrow, tilted eyes somewhat resembled the faces of the Mongols. Then he pushed aside the irrelevant thought. He tried to think how he could save the Sultana.

All of a sudden, a whirlwind came through the gate. It was the little prince. He flung himself at the soldiers, biting and kicking them. Surprised, the men let go of the Princess. Instantly, the mother ran to her child, pried him off the soldiers and tried to hide him under her cloak. But it was a vain attempt. One of the mounted men bent down and grabbed a handful of the prince's long hair. Easily, he wrenched him, kicking and struggling, out of the Princess' arms. His companions guffawed at the squirming, dangling boy. Wasim felt like smashing a fist into their laughing faces. The riders began to toss the little prince from one to the other like a ball. The desperate mother screamed and tried to run to her son, but she was held back by two soldiers. Even as Wasim watched in horrified agony, the rider who looked like their leader shouted something. One of the mounted soldiers raised his sword. The little prince was tossed with perfect aim onto the point of his sword that pierced through the child like a knife through butter. The Princess collapsed in a faint in the maid's arms. Even so, the soldiers snatched her from the maid and flung her senseless body before the skittish hooves of their leader's horse. They uttered something, rapidly gesticulating towards the unconscious woman. The leader frowned looking down at her. Then he issued an order in a stern voice. Wasim saw the soldiers' faces turn glum. They pulled the Princess upright and yanked her to a ragged group of nervous captives sitting beside the track, roped together, most of them paralysed with terror. The old woman still supported her half-conscious mistress.

A surge of red-hot rage suffused Wasim, melting away his fear. He stood up behind the pots and took aim with a large pebble in his sling. Pulling back the throngs as much as they would go, he took a shot. The projectile went like an arrow and hit the Mongol leader on his forehead. Wasim had the pleasure of seeing his head jerk back. Blood oozed out of deep cut and dripped into the man's eyes as he roared in pain. The soldiers on foot turned and rushed at the pile of pots but Wasim did not care anymore. Head and shoulders clear of his hideout, he aimed at the nearest soldier. The man yelped as the stone smacked him between the eyes. At the same time, the other Mongol soldier rushed headlong at the boy. His sword gored Wasim's thin body, its point sticking out of his back. The world spun around darkly, and the ground rushed at a tremendous speed to meet the boy as Wasim whispered, 'Allah! Al-Rahman! Al-Rahim! Al-Aziz!'

1

Several rafts of tree trunks roughly lashed together washed up on the banks of the foaming Indus River. Loaded helter-skelter with the spoils of the Malikpur raid, the plunderers had somehow made it across the rapidly flowing waters. Behind them the bright, blue sky was marred with clouds of dense, dark smoke rising from the devastated town and surrounding cornfields. The rafts were unloaded, and a curious procession made its way to the Mongol camp half a kilometre away. Leading it were the horsemen, their bloody swords sheathed, bows and quivers slung back. Before them, they drove cows, buffaloes, sheep, goats and even a mare or two herded carefully from Malikpur. From some saddles hung bunches of trussed-up sqwacking hens and ducks. Most of the soldiers carried sacks and hastily-tied cloth bundles bulging with gold, silver, bejewelled ornaments and valuable artefacts. There were a few scimitars and daggers with ornate gem-studded hilts among them. The tail-end of this straggling column was brought up by the least valuable of their plunder; human captives. They were tied together at the waist by a long length of rope held by the last mounted soldier who tugged on it mercilessly. The exhausted, debilitated men and women struggled to keep on their feet stumbling and shuffling through the scrub. Right at the end of this line was a girl, nearly in a swoon, being supported by an old woman.

As this spectacle reached the camp, they were greeted by a chorus of cheers and whoops. While the livestock was driven off into corrals, most of the soldiers dismounted and began to unload the plunder. Their leader remained on his horse. After a terse command to his men, he trotted off towards the largest of the *gers*. Round tents of various sizes erected by stretching felt skins over circular wooden rafters and struts were the *gers* randomly spread across the camp. Only the largest one was on a raised rectangular mud platform. Each of the four corners of the platform was marked by a tall pole flying the Mongolian colours of a red flying falcon against a bright yellow sky. This *ger* was located slightly away from the others, its back against a sheer rock outcropping to protect its rear. The couple of steps to the *ger* platform were flanked by a pair of shafts: one had nine fluttery white yak tails and the other bore four black horse tails. The leader dismounted and signalled to a couple of soldiers holding the prisoners. Then he lifted the thick bearskin covering the doorway. Being a huge man, towering up to nearly seven feet, he had to stoop to enter the *ger*.

After the bright sunshine, it was gloomy inside. When the leader's eyes adjusted, they fell on a low, wide dais facing him. It was covered with more bear skins and sitting cross-legged on it, was a man. His brown cotton *deel* and baggy trousers nearly blended into the tan furs. His boots were hidden under the bent knees. A few silver strands threaded the black hair pulled back into a long braid falling down his back. He was not wearing the customary fur cap or any ornaments. Only the wide, leather belt clinching the *deel* gleamed with an assortment of knives hanging off it. Also dangling among them was a pouch for tobacco and pipes. Apparently unlined, the smooth skin stretched like burnished old gold over a strong bone structure with a flat nose but raised cheekbones. His thin lips were clamped on a pipe and the narrow eyes were nearly closed against the wisps of smoke rising from it. He was like a still, serene statue. An aura of calm girdled him not betraying in the least that this was the great Genghis Khan, Emperor of Mongolia, whose empire stretched from the Pacific Ocean to the threshold of Europe.

The leader of the Malikpur raid bowed deeply. 'My Lord,' he said, softly. Instantly, drowsy eyelids rose revealing a pair of alert, piercing eyes. They observed the man with his bent head, long braid sweeping the hard earth floor. Then a deep voice pronounced, 'Ah Shigi! You are back.'

'Yes, my Lord.'

Genghis Khan beckoned, 'Come closer.' Shigi lifted his head, pushed back his braid, walked to the dais and waited expectantly for his Emperor to ask him the vital question. He didn't have to wait long. 'Did you take the Sultan?'

'No, my Lord.' Shigi shook his head, eyes downwards. 'Unfortunately, he escaped. But he left his wife and son in Malikpur.'

For a moment, the Khan stared at Shigi's downcast face. Then he sighed. 'I told you he is a cunning fox. You thought you could spring a trap, but he is too smart. I knew he would slip out of your snare. What happened to your forehead?'

Shigi, Genghis Khan's adoptive brother, gingerly touched the stinging cut with a finger and said diffidently, 'Nothing, my Lord. A silly boy and a stone.'

'Was it the Sultan's son who wounded you?'

'No, my Lord.' He clicked his tongue dismissively. 'He is only a child.'

'Children grow up. What happened to him?' The Khan cocked his head.

'Dead, my Lord.'

'And the stone thrower?'

'Dead.'

'That was wise of you, Shigi,' nodded the Khan.

Emboldened, Shigi blurted out, 'My Lord, allow me to chase the wily Sultan into the plains and surely, I will capture him,' said Shigi.

Genghis Khan slowly shook his head.

'Please, my Lord.'

'No, Shigi, that is not prudent. I gave you one opportunity though I knew it would fail. I permitted you to cross the great river. The portents were not right. Didn't the unicorn warn us against crossing this river? The shaman had read the signs. We would not win if we crossed the river. Still, you insisted, and I could not refuse the pleas of a loyal brother. So, I let you go. And you come back without the Sultan and a wound with a stone to show for your efforts. No more, Shigi. No more foolishness.' The Khan's voice was mellow but firm.

'I beg you, my Lord. Give me one more chance,' Shigi pleaded.

'No, my brother. We cannot spend any more time on these plains. The warm and humid breezes that blow here carry many diseases. Our men are sick. Some are dying. They want to go back into the mountains. They want to go home. They don't like the heat and the dust of the plains. Chasing after the Sultan has been futile. Let him go. It is essential to assess when to fight and when to give up a fray. Your expedition to trap him has failed, Shigi...a complete waste of time.' Genghis Khan's tone brooked no opposition.

'Not so, my Lord,' Shigi ploughed on. 'The raid was not a complete failure. Malikpur is...used to be a wealthy town. The raid has yielded herds of cattle, poultry and much gold and silver. Malikpur has been burned to cinders but we could become richer if we moved further down the valley. This land of the Indus River seems replete with opulence but you…'

'Good,' the Khan said curtly, ignoring his brother's last sentences. 'At least the warriors are content with the booty from the raid.'

'And I have a gift for the Lord.' Shigi bowed ingratiatingly, realising he had gone too far in his pursuit of cupidity.

'For me?' A shadow of a smile flickered across the taciturn visage.

Encouraged, Shigi confided, 'Yes, my Lord. The Sultana…the Sultan's wife…' and he stopped to see the Khan's reaction.

'The Sultan's wife? A woman from these parts?' Genghis Khan grimaced. 'She must be a hatchet-faced female with eyes like large, dark pools…Shigi, don't you know I cannot even bear to look at these ugly women?'

'No, no, my Lord,' Shigi hastened to mollify his ruler. 'She has face like a full moon, beautiful eyes as tapered as a bird's wingfeather and her mouth…as delicious as a red cherry. You have to see her to believe me, Lord.' Shigi tried a small smile though it was considered impudent to smile if the Khan did not.

'Well, well. The Sultan seems to have a good taste in women,' commented Genghis Khan. 'So, where is my gift?'

'Right here, my Lord. Allow me…,' Shigi bowed. Facing the Emperor, he backed out of the *ger*.

When he returned, it was at the head of a small group. Behind him two soldiers held the arms of a young woman who was fighting every inch of their progress as they half-dragged and half-lifted her across the mud-packed floor of the *ger*. A couple more soldiers, their swords unsheathed brought up the rear. From outside the *ger* wailed a woman endlessly.

Genghis Khan removed his pipe and squinted at the struggling figure before him. She was dressed in the long, flowing tunic and pleated, wide-bottomed pyjamas favoured by women in the Islamic lands. Though muddied and blood-spattered, the Khan did not fail to note that the exquisite silk garments were intricately embroidered. Despite the long, dishevelled hair hiding her face, there was no doubt that she came from a noble, wealthy family. The flowing clothes concealed her curves yet hinted at a slenderness likened to a willow. She looked more like a girl than a woman.

'What is that caterwauling going on outdoors?' The Khan asked, frowning irritatedly.

'It is the girl's maid,' replied Shigi and growled at the soldiers. 'Take that woman away.'

One of the sword-wielding soldiers put his head out of the fur curtain and barked out Shigi's order. Inside, the soldier holding the captive gave a sudden, loud yelp. The Sultana had bitten his hand.

'Leave her,' commanded the Khan.

'My Lord, she...she could be dangerous,' warned Shigi.

'I can handle her,' said Genghis Khan. 'Unhold her.'

The soldiers let go of the woman who fell to the ground. However, she was up in a trice. Her head swivelled frantically in all directions seeking escape. The soldiers held their swords up to cut her down if she tried to attack.

But the woman scurried to one side of the *ger,* farthest from the dais and cowered there. Genghis Khan waved his hand at the men with one word, 'Go!' Shigi opened his mouth to protest, then thought the better of it and all five bowed and retreated out of the *ger.*

The Khan put the pipe back between his teeth and sucked at it. But his eyes remained on the woman, watchful and wary. When she saw that he was not coming after her, she relaxed a little. Genghis Khan made no move other than observe her. After a time, she sat back on the floor and lifting the long, thick tresses of dark-brown hair, gathered them behind her head. Excitement gleamed in the Khan's eyes as her profile was revealed. Small and round, her face glowed with a pale, peaches-and-cream skin. The nose perked up ever so little from a flat bridge that swept up to a flawless forehead. Curved lashes rested in a thick, dark fringe on cheeks dusted with rose. *She could easily be taken for a Mongol princess,* thought Genghis Khan.

He sucked in his breath sharply as she lifted the matted lashes. Oval-rimmed, tilting at the corners her eyes enclosed a pair of brilliant, blue pupils.

'A *semu...,*' breathed Genghis Khan and muttered to himself. 'Another one? Is it possible...two so similar?' Perplexed, he did not notice the look in those entrancing eyes. If looks could kill, he would be dead by now.

Eyes fixed on her, he slowly knocked the pipe out on the side of dais and kept it aside on the bearskin rug. As if in a trance, the Khan stood up and began to walk towards the girl who shrank further back against the felt wall. Terror had replaced loathing in her eyes. Blue eyes darted here and there looking for flight. She looked like a tiny rabbit about to be torn to pieces by a ravenous wolf. The Mongol ruler was a tall man with a broad chest and despite his sixty-odd years, muscled and fit as only a man who spends all his life on horseback can be. He went down on his haunches before the trembling girl and flicked a calloused finger across her cheek. She flinched making the Khan's lips twitch with amusement.

Then his eyes shifted to her white throat where a tiny pulse was beating rapidly. He was distracted by a talisman resting in its hollow. A black cord weighed down in the centre by a curious, dark object that looked like an inverted Y. The Khan held it with his thumb and forefinger, saying, 'What is this? It looks like...'

But before he could ascertain his assumptions, the girl snatched it out of his hand with a fierce whisper, 'That's none of your business.'

Genghis Khan swore and looked down at his hand. A long, angry scratch went across the back of his hand all the way from his middle finger to the wrist. It was already oozing redly. He growled, 'Bloody cat! I will teach you a lesson you will not forget.' She cringed at his scowling face, but his blood was boiling now. He wanted to hurt her as viciously as she had done. Anger lent him urgency as he grabbed the neckline of the thin, silk tunic and yanked it down. It tore sideways down the front, disclosing a small, alabaster globe topped by a rosy, puckered nipple. The girl tried to pull the torn edges up on the right side making the cloth slip from her left shoulder.

Involuntarily, the Khan's gaze shifted to the exposed left shoulder. He jerked back as if an arrow had thudded into his body. What he saw shocked him so much that he lost his balance and sat down heavily on the hard, mud floor. Against the pale skin of the girl's shoulder was a small, red circular spot with a fainter pattern like a sunburst around it. Aghast with horror, Genghis Khan's eyes were transfixed on the birthmark. Still sitting, he pushed himself away from the crouching figure, not for a moment taking his eyes off the mark. The girl knit her brows unable to understand what had frightened the man so much. She held the torn ends of her tunic together and slowly relaxed as the Mongol ruler moved even further from her.

Stiffly, Genghis Khan got to his feet as if age had finally begun to grip his limbs. He called out, 'Shigi!' But it was a whimper. He cleared his throat and raised his voice. 'Shigi!' The girl in the corner tensed again for the next unknown atrocity about to be unleashed on her.

His adoptive brother was waiting just outside the *ger* and came in running. Bowing low, he inquired. 'My Lord?'

The Khan gestured to the girl, 'Take her away.'

The Sultan's wife frantically crawled along the felt wall trying to put some distance between herself and Shigi, but the giant pounced on her like a vulture. He caught her by the arm and lifted her up, bodily.

'Gently, Shigi, gently,' murmured his ruler. Shigi glanced at him in surprise.

He tugged the girl towards the door whilst facing the Khan to exit the *ger*. The giant and the girl were passing before the Mongol ruler, when the she spat at the Emperor. A blob of spittle hit Genghis Khan on his cheek and dribbled down. Immediately, Shigi's blade was across her throat. 'Shall I kill her, my Lord? This woman has no fear. She must be a witch.'

The Khan wiped the liquid off his face with the back of his hand, saying, 'No, Shigi. She is a *Guunj*...a princess.' His voice seemed to droop with tiredness. 'Give her a *ger* for her own use and see that she has a woman to care for her.'

Confounded, Shigi stared at his leader. He could hardly believe his ears. *Why is the Lord so concerned about a captive…especially a female captive who spits on him?*

'Go! At once!' Genghis pointed to the door, regaining his former assurance and poise. Then, he turned away with a despondent gesture.

Shigi pulled the girl with him but she refused to go out so tamely. Hatred choking her throat, she screamed at the Khan, 'You are a savage…a bloodthirsty monster. God will rain hellfire on your head. You are the cursed vermin of the earth.'

Genghis Khan turned around. His eyes were inscrutable but grave. In an even tone, he said, 'I am a warrior of Mongolia, the land destined to rule the world. Khökh Tenger, the Eternal Blue Heaven, whom you call God, has Himself chosen me to lead my nation to that glorious future.'

As Shigi was finally able to jerk the girl beyond the fur curtain, Genghis Khan wondered what had prompted him to explain himself to this chit of a girl. He had never bothered to do so to anyone else before.

2

The year was 1162 CE. High summer had gifted Elysian evenings to the steppes of Mongolia. The sun kissed the peaks of Khenti Khan mountain ranges. The Mongols called it Burkhan Khaldun or the Sacred Mountain. An amber radiance from the diminishing sunlight lit up the entire valley. Scattered firs and maples, gentle hummocks and riverside foothills were wedged between the Khorkh and the Onon, two rivers that converged here. The old shaman sitting meditatively on a ridge half-way up the hills gazed down placidly at trees tinged by rays of the setting sun that reflected off their gleaming leaves and sparkling points of fir needles. Under them the crumbly, soft turf, interspersed by clumps of grasses, was aerated by hundreds of burrows wherein hid field mice and marmots. White anemones, lavender iris, orange Siberian lilies and yellow wild flowers dotted the pasture while dwarf bushes of violet rhododendron gently undulated in the breeze.

Gradually, the orange sphere dipped, and shadows of the trees lengthened across the valley. Contemplating on the benediction of Nature, the shaman calmly observed the evening grow into night. Overhead, the heavens darkened and stars were punched into the dark-blue velvet. The old man's breathing deepened as he soaked in the consonance around him. His inner being melded into the natural forces so that he became part of the cosmos. Only then would he be able to sense its missives and commune with the universe. When his trance broke after quite a few hours, he looked upwards. Exactly then, a brilliant trajectory shot across the heavenly vault—a shooting star. The old man whispered, 'He is come.' He glanced at the large, yellow full moon balancing on the peak of the Burkhan Khaldun. Sure enough, a form was etched on it. His eyes narrowed as he tried to decipher its outlines. Yes, the likeness looked like a flying falcon. Now the shaman had no doubts about his faultless reading of the signs.

He reflected, *if I begin now, I can reach the camp on the banks of the Onon before the night is over*. But first he paid his respects to the Supreme Power. The Mongols referred to him as Khökh Tenger or the Eternal Blue Heaven. The shaman brought together rocks and stones and piled them in a heap on the ledge. He looked around for a straight, strong branch from those strewn around. When he found one, he pushed it into the centre of the stone pile so that it stood erect and added more stones around its base. From the pocket of his long tunic or *deel*, he produced a wooden flask. Opening its mouth, the shaman sprinkled drops from it on the stone heap. A pungent aroma filled the night air. This was the *oovu* or shrine to Khökh Tenger. The old man went around the *oovu* three times muttering his thanks to the Benevolent Power for giving him the insights.

Then he set off down the mountains. *The great Khan has arrived. I must hurry to welcome him*, thought the old shaman as he nimbly leaped from rock to rock like a mountain goat.

About a dozen *gers* were clustered around a large roaring fire. Few of them glowed with oil lights for the women had begun their dawn duties starting by milking the mares. Around the campfire sat a few men. When they saw the old shaman approaching, one of them stood up. He bowed respectfully to the elder saying, 'You have come at the right time, O Wise Man. My son has just been born and we need you to read the signs that foretell his destiny.'

'I know about your son, Yesugei. Khökh Tenger, the Eternal Blue Heaven has already sent me the portents,' the old man replied.

Yesugei was the chief of the Borjigins, one of five original Mongol clans from the amorphous past between memory and legend. Many clans and tribes had spun off those five clans. While the other four clans had evolved and split up, the Borjigins had retained its identity for a hundred and fifty years now. Around 1140 CE, Kabul, the first Khan to rule over all Mongols had emerged from this clan. While the power of the Borjigins had considerably ebbed over the next twenty-two years, it was regarded even now as a royal house among the other clans.

Thus, Yesugei was not surprised that the old man knew his name. Besides, he was a shaman and shamans knew everything. The chief gestured towards his wife Hoelun's *ger* behind him. 'The women will bring him out soon.' Over the *ger* door hung a bow and arrows to protect its inmates from evil. Thin wails of a newborn babe came from within. No man, not even the old shaman was permitted to enter the *ger* at this time. Yesugei addressed the elderly man, 'In the meanwhile, come and share a bowl of *airag* with us.' The old man settled down beside the warm fire and accepted the wooden bowl of fermented mare's milk. He put his mouth to it and drank deeply, thinking contentedly, *finally the Khan has arrived to fulfil the destiny of Mongolia.*

Soon the baby wrapped in a soft, lamb's wool blanket was brought out of Hoelun's *ger*. He was placed in a wooden crib with bore-holes along its sides. Cords threaded through the holes would turn it into a baby carrier that can be strapped to the mother's back when she rode. Yesugei led the shaman to his baby son. The old man knelt on the grass and looked carefully at the babe. His lips moved as he read the signs that only he could perceive. His eyes fell on the baby's right fist which was tightly curled inwards as if the baby was holding something. The shaman gently pried the fist open and the onlookers gasped. A large blood clot lay in the tiny white palm. So filled it was with blood that the blob was nearly black. None of viewers could fail to grasp the significance of this unusual occurrence. Later, many of them swore that they had seen the clot pulsating like a live thing. The old man sprinkled some herbs around the cradle and tied an amulet to one of its holes.

Yesugei fidgeted impatiently as everyone waited for the shaman to declare the child's destiny. Finally, the rituals were over, and the old man stood up. 'This boy will grow to be a mighty warrior. He is the chosen one who will bring all Mongolia together. He will become the Khan, a great conqueror,' pronounced the old man, elated that his conjectures had been validated. Then he muttered prayers and anointed the babe with butter-oil. The baby's cradle went back into Hoelun's *ger* while the Yesugei led the shaman to the celebratory feasting that had already begun in the camp.

The next morning was the naming day. It was the father's duty to decide and confer a name on the babe. According to old Mongol traditions, a father was supposed to give his newborn the name of the man last captured by him in the latest war fought. In Yesugei's case, he had just returned from a battle with the Tartars and the chief of the tribe was in his custody. He walked over to the other side of the camp. There the captive, a large block of wood around his neck, was bound to a pole. Asked for his name, the man sullenly replied, 'Temujin.' So Yesugei bestowed his first born with a Tartar name, Temujin. He felt it was an auspicious name for *temu* means 'iron'. He later named two more of his children using the same word; a boy called Temuge and a girl called Temulun.

As the days went by and the baby became stronger, Yesugei was so entranced by his son that he would visit his wife's *ger* every day. He wanted Temujin to grow up quickly so that he could teach him all the skills of a true Mongol warrior. His wife Hoelun laughed at his impatience. Yesugei turned from the cradle to look at his wife and his heart overflowed with love for her. Tall and statuesque, she had a fine figure. Only a day after childbirth, she had gone back to her household duties of milking the mares, churning butter, feeding the sheep and livestock, cooking and caring for her family that consisted of Yesugei, two toddlers from his first wife who had died at childbirth and now the new baby. The fat of her pregnancy had melted away rapidly leaving her stomach as flat as before between the flaring hips. Only her breasts, heavy with milk, indicated that she had become a mother. To Yesugei, she looked as lovely as the attractive, sensual girl whom he had stolen from her first husband.

On an impulse, he asked, 'Do you remember the first time we met?'

Hoelun was braiding her long hair, stringing colourful beads, coral and silver ornaments into the fourteen braids that fanned out around her head. She smiled at her husband and nodded. The cosy interior of the *ger*, Yesugei's face and the cradle faded from her sight as she went back in time. Her first husband, Chiledu of the wealthy Merkits clan, had just married her and was returning home with his new bride to the forests of the north-west. He had been riding beside the small, two-wheeled, black cart pulled by a camel on which she was seated. Young Yesugei had been out hawking on the banks of the Onon. Just one glimpse of the beauty under the cart's cover and he had lost his heart to her. Moreover, the girl's clothes indicated that she was from the Ongirads clan who were traditionally linked to the Borjigins by marriage. Yesugei had galloped home to fetch his two brothers. They easily overtook the slow-moving horse and cart. Chiledu had fled around the flank of a hill, with the three Mongols in pursuit. But he was not ready to abandon his bride. Circling the hill, he had returned to save her. Knowing that escape was impossible for both of them, Hoelun had urged Chiledu, 'Leave me. Run and save your life. They look as if they want to kill you.'

Chiledu had slapped his horse into a gallop, chased by the brothers until they realised that they could not catch him. They had returned to the cart and picking up the reins of the camel, began to pull the cart behind them. It was then that Hoelun first laid her eyes on Yesugei. She had hardly known her new husband during the few hours that they had been married. Now, this tall, handsome warrior gazing down at her with such ardour was just irresistible. She fell deeply in love with Yesugei erasing from her mind the memory of Chiledu who had not impressed her even when she had first seen him during their wedding. From that moment on Hoelun happily accepted Yesugei as her new husband and protector. Joyously, she became his companion sharing his life of herding and wandering, raiding and being raided.

Hoelun's vision cleared as she came back to her present surroundings and found Yesugei looking at her tenderly. Her own eyes were moist with emotion as her husband said softly, 'This was ordained.'

Hoelun looked puzzled and asked, 'What?'

'This,' he replied, his eyes going to the sleep-soaked, rosy baby in the crib. 'You and I were destined to be parents of the ruler of Mongolia.'

'Are you not reading too much into the shaman's words?' asked Hoelun softly, more pragmatic of the two.

'No, Hoelun.' Yesugei shook his head. 'We will have more children after Temujin but it is for his birth that we will be honoured and respected through the years and long after.' He was quiet for a while and then added, 'I am convinced he will follow in the footsteps of his renowned grandfather and great-grandfather. Maybe he will overtake them, one day.'

Hoelun remained silent. She did not want to dampen her husband's fond aspirations for their son. She began to twist her braids with nimble fingers into a high coiffure at the crown of her head for married Mongol ladies never left their hair down. Only young, unmarried girls could have braids swishing against their cheeks. She shrugged on the red, thickly-embroidered, short, sleeveless coat pinched artfully at the waist. It fitted her snugly over the green, summer *deel* flowing to below her knees. The long sleeves of the *deel* were adorned with traditional Mongol patterns at their wide edges. Stuffing her baggy trousers into leather *gutals* or boots, she secured the laces firmly and stood up.

Yesugei had gone back to gazing at his son, his own face softly introspective. Hoelun sighed. *It was all very well for men to dream of the future. Women had to take care of the now.* Sheep baaing fretfully and hens clucking outdoors reminded her that the day's chores were waiting for her. Giving the father and son one more affectionate glance, she lifted the felt curtain at the opening of the *ger* and went out.

3

Men lined the wooden fence whooping and waving both arms in encouragement. The loudest among them was Yesugei. After all it was his son that they were cheering. Temujin was eleven months old and just able to lift himself on to his feet holding his mother's fingers when his father decided it was time he learned to ride. Despite Hoelun's trepidation, he put the child on horseback. Of course, he chose a gentle, old mare and tied his son to the saddle with a long sash. The baby was excited by this new game and chortled as his father led the mare around the corral. Many clansmen in the camp crowded around the fence, enthusiastically cheering the father and son. Hoelun watched from a distance, her hand covering her mouth and a worried frown creasing her brows. When he saw that the child was quite comfortable on the leather saddle, Yesugei broke into a run still holding the reins. The mare trotted gently along the corral fence, Temujin bobbing on her back. When he heard the frenzied exuberance of the spectators for his feat, the baby waved back to them with his pudgy hands. The men began to laugh at his antics and pointed the child out to one another, exclaiming, 'He is sure to be a great warrior. See how he rides.' Yesugei's broad chest swelled with pride for his son.

That is how Temujin began riding a horse even before he could walk. Not only by training him in the skills of a warrior, his father began in other ways to prepare him very early for his destiny.

Yesugei was now the chief of a clan that had fallen into insignificance despite its glorious past. But he had never forgotten the responsibility bequeathed to him by his ancestors and constantly aspired to retrieve the clan's rightful position amidst the prevailing anarchy of a divided Mongol nation. It was not easy for alliances between clans were made and broken every few days and factions of Mongols were constantly at war with each other. A sage summed up the indisciplined Mongol nation thus:

The crusty earth was turning and turning,
The entire nation was in turmoil.

Even during this chaotic period burdened by a poverty-stricken clan, Yesugei strived to weave patterns in this nomadic life by forming affiliations with other tribes which would prove significant in the later years. One of these was with a Turkish tribe, the Keraits, their neighbours to the west. Toghril, its leader, had come to power after killing several of his uncles to secure the throne. Around the 1160s he had been forced to flee when a relative tried to avenge the murders. It was then that Yesugei raised an army, fought for Toghril and helped him regain the leadership of his tribe. Since then, Yesugei and Toghril became 'sworn brothers'. This bond would prove to be a catalyst crucial in reinstating Mongol power in the future.

As soon as Temujin was old enough to understand, Yesugei began to tell him about his illustrious ancestry. He told him about his great-grandfather, Kabul who was the first khan to rule over all the Mongols around 1140 CE. He narrated to his son the story, 'Though united under his authority, the Mongol nation had been threatened by the politics of their regional neighbours. Their main rivals had been an upcoming kingdom to the south called the Jins. The Jin emperor had his eyes on two other rival kingdoms, namely the kingdoms of Xi Xia and Song. But to fight them, the Jins required securing their northern border peopled by the powerful Mongol nomads. So, the Jin emperor approached Kabul with a deal. To discuss the terms, he invited the Khan of the Mongols to journey to Zhong-du or Beijing.'

Little Temujin was astounded. 'All the way to Zhong-du? How did the Khan go?'

'On his fastest horse, of course,' answered Yesugei, pretending to pull on the reins of a galloping horse, 'Across the grasslands, crossing the swift-flowing Kherlun River, up the highlands and down the valleys.'

'Did he go alone?' The boy wanted to know, his eyes big as saucers.

'A few warriors from the Mongol clans accompanied him but it was a small group. After all, they were not going to make war with the Jins. They were going to make an alliance,' said Yesugei, warming up to the tale. 'When your great-grandfather entered the splendid hall in the palace of the Emperor of Jin, a hush fell on the gathering. They could not believe that a man could be so tall and mighty. Kabul Khan was like a giant.'

Temujin rubbed his arms with glee. 'Was he stronger than the Jin emperor?'

Yesugei played along. 'Oh yes, far, far stronger. But the Emperor welcomed Kabul Khan.'

'The emperor had no choice, did he?' The little boy reasoned. 'After all Kabul Khan was stronger.'

Yesugei shrugged, 'Maybe. The Emperor of the Jins sat on a high throne. Around him were seated his nobles dressed in silk and glittering ornaments. Kabul Khan had always shunned flamboyance. After all he was a Mongol warrior and so he went dressed as one. However, the Jin Emperor was gracious. He offered Kabul Khan a seat that was nearly as high as his. Between them was a table heaped with the choicest of dishes. Our ancestor was offered much good food and silver bowls of *airag*. Kabul Khan, who had been expecting a snub from the sophisticated, urbane Emperor was so delighted by the Jin hospitality that in a gesture of goodwill, he leaned across the table and pulled the Jin Emperor's thin, pointed beard.'

Temujin giggled at the picture in his mind; a giant in rough clothes tweaking the beard of a refined but snooty king. But he quickly suppressed his mirth as his father went on. 'Everyone in the room became absolutely silent. When Kabul Khan looked around, he found the entire Jin entourage staring at him. The Emperor wore a horrified expression. He realised that he had broken some rule of their social etiquette. He decided it was better for him to take his leave immediately though the terms of the alliance had not been discussed.'

'Why?' asked the little boy, frowning a bit.

'Maybe he had felt arrows of animosity being directed at him. Of course, the Emperor pressed on him many gifts. There were bales of silk, ornaments and bags of gold. But as soon as Kabul Khan and his warriors left the capital and were half way to the border between Mongolia and the Jin Empire, they were attacked apparently by mountain bandits. Though the robbers had their faces covered, when a few of them spoke, Kabul Khan identified the soft, round syllables of the Jin language. He knew at once that they were no bandits but Jin soldiers commanded to retrieve the gifts of the Emperor.'

'Oh no!' exclaimed the little boy in dismay. 'But that is treachery.'

'Exactly,' agreed his father. 'There was a fierce battle between the Jins and the Mongols but our men were few and the enemy outnumbered them. Kabul Khan was able to cross the border to Mongolia but was forced to leave behind all the gifts. Ever since then the Mongols have never forgotten or forgiven this dirty trick played by the Jins. They are completely untrustworthy.'

Temujin was quiet for a while staring into the red embers of the campfire. After a while, he looked up at his father and pronounced in a firm though childish treble, 'When I grow older, I will fight the Jins.'

Yesugei smiled at his son. He pulled him into his own pallet and rolled him in the blanket. Father and son slept embracing each other.

A few days later when the duo was returning after herding the clan's sheep from the pasture, Temujin brought up the topic of Jins again.

'Did nobody try to avenge the Jin insult to Kabul Khan?' he asked.

'His son, Ambakai attempted it.'

The child instantly asked, 'How?'

Yesugei regarded the far horizon where the rolling grasslands met the eggshell blue sky. A fierce, orange sun was beginning his descent. Black-and-white double-tailed swallows streaked across in perfect formation taking a last dive before turning to their nests. It was a perfect end to another perfect summer day yet his eyes seemed to see shadowy Mongol hosts from yesteryears thunder past in the hazy dust. When he spoke, it seemed his words came from another world.

'You see, the Jins are not nomads like us. We roam the steppes and go where we like. Freely, we partake in Nature's abundance. We pluck her fruit, eat her vegetables and hunt her meat. The land and its waters sustain us. We are hardy warriors and content in our freedom. The

Jins are mere farmers tied to their land. They are earth grubbers. Afraid of being overrun by our fearsome tribes, they have built walls around their cities to keep us out. They think we are wild and barbaric. Nonetheless they value our horses and don't mind trading them with us. We also encourage this barter because they have riches such as metals, silk, weapons and tea that are useful for us. Trading, even among foes is a not a bad idea for each of us can get what each wants.' Temujin nodded but he was waiting for an answer to his question.

Yesugei smiled at the child and went on. 'But the Jins have always been deceitful people and often cheated us in trade.'

'Just like they did with Kabul Khan,' interjected Temujin.

'Yes. So, in retaliation to their cheating, we have raided the Jin cities at times. Sometimes we have been successful and sometimes not. Besides, the Jins are not our only enemies. We have to also keep our eyes at the back of our heads for we have to constantly fight the vile Tartars, too.'

Temujin nodded, but asked impatiently, 'But what did Ambakai do?'

Yesugei smiled down at his son's face and continued the narrative. 'So Ambakai had already led a few raids against the Jins. Many Jins were killed in these and Ambakai's soldiers brought back a great deal of plunder from the Jin outposts. The Jins hated him now and were eager to get their hands on him. Unfortunately, during a skirmish with the Tartars, Ambakai was captured. Usually the Tartars would have asked us for a ransom and released him when we paid it. But Ambakai was a choice prisoner. They decided to get a higher price by selling him to the

Jins. The Jins were delighted to get their hands on the man who had raided them so often. Quickly they got rid of their enemy. Ambakai was crucified by the Jins nailed to the horrible 'wooden donkey'. Before dying in this grisly, painful manner Ambakai's last message filtered back to the Mongols:

Until the nails of your five fingers
Are ground down,
Until your ten fingers are worn away,
Strive to revenge me.

Kutula, your great-uncle, took up this rallying cry. Like Kabul Khan, he was known for his great strength. I have heard stories that his voice was like the growling thunder and his hands were like bear paws. He used to eat a whole sheep at every meal and could snap a man like an arrow into two. But he was unable to win against the Jin Empire. After he passed away to the Blue Heaven, the Mongol clans splintered into many pieces and Mongolia was no longer one nation.'

His father fell silent. Both the riders gazed up at the huge mastiff looming up in the distance. Once before, Yesugei had narrated to Temujin the story of the Mongols and how they had come upon this valley a very, very long time ago. Legends say that Mongols were people who had descended from the Wolf and the Doe and had originally come from the forests of Siberia. During their journey, they chanced upon this land where the mountains and forests of the north met the southern grasslands giving way further south to the gravelly wastes of the Gobi Desert; in this land drained by the three great rivers, the Onon to the east, the Kherlen to the south, the Tula to the west the Mongols had felt closest to the benign spirit that had led them here and would guide them to power and prosperity. Khenti Khan, the massive mountain dominating this heavenly land, was believed to be sacred. They revered it by calling it Burkhan Khaldun.

Father and son had now come close enough to the camp to see smoke wafting lazily from the *gers* below the gentle slope. The first of the sheep were already loping through the camp, straggling towards their pens. The rest would follow. Yesugei whipped his stallion's rump and it sprang ahead. As he passed Temujin, he screamed out a challenge. The boy laughed loudly and slapped his own horse. Both the riders raced down the grassy incline throwing up clods of soft earth. When they reached the gates of the corral, Temujin was leading by half a head. As they dismounted, he chortled at his father: 'I won! I won!'

'So you did, my son,' said Yesugei, mussing up Temujin's tightly braided hair.

As he had been taught, the boy unsaddled his *aduu,* as a horse is called by Mongols and vigorously rubbed the animal down. He combed its mane and gave it hay and water before turning towards their *ger*. He was ravenous and looked forward to the evening meal. On the way, his eyes again fell on the sacred mountain smoky in the evening mist. He whispered to himself, Ambakai's words, 'Strive to revenge me.'

4

The fiery sun had finally slipped behind the Hindu Kush. Streaked with scarlet and orange, the expanse of the sky was not broken by a single cloud while the hot earth below panted breathlessly. Water being sprayed on dusty, dry ground pricked with scorched brown grass hissed and steamed giving forth a damp petrichor. The Princess in the *ger* woke to its whiff drifting inside and twitched her nose appreciatively. Silently, she jeered, *these brute savages are afraid of our heat! It is not even high summer, and they are already watering the earth. What will they do when the hot winds blow?* Still not fully awake from the afternoon siesta, she heard the soft footsteps of her maid moving about in the cool, enclosed darkness. The gruesome happenings of the previous day came crowding into her mind and she did not want to open her eyes to face the world. *Maybe it is all a bad dream and I will soon wake up,* she told herself trying to erase the terrible, unbelievable spectres rising behind her closed eyelids. But they would not go away. She began to tremble reliving once again the fear and outrage of the terrible massacre. Eventually, the awful scene she never wanted to recall came back to torture her; her little son skewered on the sword. 'Oh God! Why?' she whispered, choking on the tears that squeezed from her closed eyelids wetting the thin pallet spread on a raised platform.

'My *Guunj*?' Instantly, the maid was by her side. She held the young girl to her ample breast letting the painful tears flow. 'Stop, my Princess, stop. You will make yourself sick.'

'How can I stop, Bolorma? My son! Oh, my son! My son lies dead in the dust somewhere. I could not even bury him...' She lifted her arms heavenwards. 'Oh God! He was only a baby. Why did you take him from me? Why are we suffering this affliction, Al-Rahman?' The old maid held her tightly as the girl was shaken repeatedly by a storm of unending tears. The old maid's face was wet, too.

Suddenly, a man's voice called out, *'Guunj?'* It came from the other side of the curtain covering the entry to the *ger.* The women became still and looked at one another with frightened faces. Bolorma put a finger on her lips and unclasping the girl's arms from her neck, went to the curtain. A whispered dialogue took place from both sides of the curtain.

Bolorma returned and said in a flat voice, 'The Khan has requested that you bathe, wear fresh clothes and join him for dinner when the moon rises.'

'No!' shouted the Princess, her face still ravaged with grief.

'My Princess, I think it is best we obey the Khan. Unless you meet him, how will you know what are his plans for you...for us?' The old maid spoke softly.

The Princess regarded the round, wrinkled face. The eyes, welling with kindness, were almost hidden under sagging lids. Bolorma had been companion to the Princess' mother. She had been the girl's caretaker since childhood and her well-being had been the old woman's foremost concern till now. The Princess looked around the spacious enclosure allotted to her. It was sparse compared to the opulent palace rooms she was used to; just a raised dais for the bed, a fireplace in the middle and some bear rugs spread on the mud-packed floor. Of course, the Mongols were barbaric but even by their standards this was a luxurious prison. *Really, what did this dreadful Khan have in mind for me?* Bolorma's wise words should not be put aside.

Slowly, she dipped her head in assent. The old woman got instantly busy. Dusk was a long affair in these regions but soon the moon would reign in the dark sky and there was little time to lose. As the Princess lay back watching her, the old maid managed to obtain wooden buckets of hot water. She took off the Princess' mud-stained robes revealing a slight form enhanced by small, high breasts and gently flaring hips. She was slim without the rounded contours of a mature woman. Her long legs and swan-like neck completed the impression of an exquisite, porcelain figurine. Gently, the old maid swabbed and cleaned the pale limbs murmuring, 'No scented water here,' and eliciting an irritated exclamation from the Princess.

Then Bolorma produced from a basket in the corner a red *deel*, grey baggy trousers and a wide white sash that made up the dress of a Mongol lady.

'Where did these come from?' asked the Princess, her brows furrowed.

'They are gifts from the Khan,' explained Bolorma.

'I refuse to accept gifts from my son's murderer. Where are my own clothes?' She was as imperious as only a Princess can be.

'My lady, we did not bring any of your other clothes from the palace,' said the old woman reminding the young girl of how unprincess-like her circumstances were. Gulping down sudden tears rising in her throat, she nodded silently.

Tenderly, Bolorma helped the Princess to wear the ensemble. The old woman commiserated with the sorrow of the young mother that heavily burdened her heart but their very survival was at stake at the moment. She adjusted the sash and began to comb out the long, tangled tresses. After braiding them into six long plaits with two framing the girl's round face on either side, Bolorma smiled and said, 'You look just like your mother...a true Mongol princess.' She had spoken in the tongue of the Mongols. The Princess stared at her. Though she was familiar with the speech of the Mongols, she and everyone around her had always conversed in a mixture of Turkish and Arabic, the language of her hometown, Ghaznin. Perceiving her astonishment, Bolorma enigmatically added, 'What is the use of denying your heritage? At a time like this, it is better to embrace it.'

As the Princess silently digested one more piece of advice, the maid placed before her a pair of embroidered slippers that the girl had been wearing earlier, now spotlessly clean. The Princess slipped them on and slowly exited the *ger* with Bolorma holding up the heavy curtain. Outside, the full moon was still playing hide and seek behind the pine and spruce forests that marched up the rocky heights. The placid gurgles of the Indus floated in the evening air redolent with the scent of damp earth as the two women went up the slight slope to the *ger* that was encircled by the others, dominating them with its size. The Princess realised that her *ger* had been erected a little away from the rest. *Why? To seclude me from the soldiers?* Bemused, she shook her head. *Why this concern for a goat that was to be slaughtered anyway?*

Soldiers guarded the entrance to the Khan's *ger* and were posted around its circumference, alert and armed to the teeth. They would spring to defend their ruler at the slightest sign of danger. The Princess expected that Bolorma and she would be stopped and asked their business but when they approached, the guards parted. With bowed heads, they stood on either side of a narrow path that opened up between them. The Princess held up her head and swept through the soldiers, though her heart was hammering fit to burst in her chest. Bolorma picked up the bearskin curtain and the Princess stepped in. The curtain whished behind her as her eyes fell on the dais. It was empty.

'How do you feel today?' said a deep voice from her left. The Princess swivelled towards the sound but could hardly see the tall, broad figure in the gloom. She did not deign to answer and stood on the threshold until Genghis Khan slowly ambled into the circle of light thrown up by the oil lamps flickering around the dais. He halted there and observed her for a long time. He was dressed as soberly as the day before, this time in a grey *deel* and trousers. The Khan's face was impassive but his coal-black eyes under the single-fold eyelids held hers steadily. After a few seconds, the Princess began to feel flustered for the cast of the Khan's scrutiny confused her. *It is not the lechery which I expected; it is not loathing; it is not anger but then what is it?* The Princess felt out of her depth alone with this man whose presence prevailed over the enclosed space and overwhelmed her. Somewhere in the dark depths of the Khan's eyes glimmered an understanding and was it…was it…regret? *Noooo…it can't be,* she told herself.

Finally, he beckoned the Princess gesturing towards the dais. It was then that she noticed that there were two low seats facing each other on the dais. Between them on the furs were several platters. Most of them were laden with large roasted portions of meat, seemingly complete haunches of animals with blood still congealed on them. They looked half-cooked and the Princess wrinkled her nose at the raw, earthy smell rising from them. Besides the meat there were wooden bowls full of mare's milk and *airag*. Genghis Khan stepped up and settled cross-legged into the seat on the right. With his hand, he silently motioned that she should take the left seat. Though, she felt a bitter liquid rising in her throat at the sight and scent of so much raw meat, she recalled her maid's prudent advice and came forward to take her place.

Once they were seated, Genghis Khan fingered the knives at his belt and picked out one. He carved a slice from the nearest haunch and offered it to her still holding it against the sharp edge. The Princess shook her head, so he took it to his own mouth and chewed on it. With both hands he picked up a bowl of milk and drank deeply from it. Wiping his lips with the sleeve of the *deel*, he said, 'What is your name?'

Taken by surprise, the girl blurted out, 'Enkhtuya.'

'Enkhtuya...Enkhtuya,' repeated the Khan, slowly as if trying out the name on his tongue. 'Light of Peace. Beautiful meaning but how does Sultan Jalal-ud-din's Sultana have a Mongol name?'

At once, she regretted divulging her name. But while Princess Enkhtuya was considering if she should reply to his question, the Khan followed it up by another. 'How does a girl from Ghaznin look like a Mongol and speak our tongue?'

Realising it would be futile to hide the truth, she said, sullenly, 'My mother was from Mongolia.'

'Oh was she, now?' He did not seem startled. 'And did you get your blue eyes from her?'

'Yes.' It was her turn to be astonished. *How did he know?*

'Of course, she must have been a *semu*...,' he murmured almost to himself. His hard eyes looked into her face as he commanded, 'Eat.'

Enkhtuya looked down at the platters. Everything on them was making her want to puke. Then she glimpsed a small bowl of grapes hidden between the meat dishes. She began to pluck the purple balls, one at a time and insert them delicately into her mouth, forcing herself to chew on the juicy fruit. In the meanwhile, the Khan sliced off hunks of meat and munched on them.

Wiping the remnants of *airag* from his mouth, he asked her, 'What was your mother's name?'

Enkhtuya was silent.

'I asked you a question and I expect an answer.' He growled making her flinch.

'Gu...Gurleen,' she stammered.

Now it was the Khan's turn to be reticent. For a few minutes, he stared into the flame of the nearest oil lamp. He was so absorbed that the Princess glanced at it wondering whether he could see something in the flame. But it was just an ordinary flickering lamp. Then with a deep sigh that seemed to rise from the depths of his heart, he turned to her. Pointing to the talisman at her neck he stated rather than asked, 'Your mother gave you that.' The girl instantly clutched the object in her fist as if to hide it. The Khan just shook his head and said, 'Eat.'

Enkhtuya picked two more grapes and popped them in her mouth.

'You eat like a wren,' remarked the Khan, unreasonably irritated. 'No wonder you look as thin and delicate as a wren. Eat the meat, Girl. Eat the meat.'

'I...I like fruit,' said Enkhtuya.

'Fruit? That is for birds and squirrels, not men. Men must eat meat,' he said.

'Not I.' The girl's tone was stubborn.

'You dare to disobey me?' The Khan roared, leaning across the space between them. His face was inches from hers, the deadpan expression wiped off. A dark scowl twisted his features. His lips drew back in a snarl exposing teeth sharpened to points.

Princess Enkhtuya blanched, tilting away from his ferocious face. With a quick movement, the Khan held the back of her head with his left hand and brought his right fist holding a knife with a sliver of bleeding meat to her lips. Enkhtuya closed both her eyes and mouth tightly expecting the blade to sink into her throat at any moment. Genghis Khan pushed his fist so hard against her mouth that it opened. He forced the meat in. 'Ah!' he pronounced triumphantly and let her go.

Instantly, she spit out the piece of meat, blood dripping from her lips. The Khan shouted at her defiance. He picked up the meat and was about to push it back when the girl jumped up. Pointing a finger at him, she screamed, 'You are not human. You are a monster. You are barbaric. You kill children and eat their bleeding flesh. I hate you! I hate you! I hate you!'

For a moment, Genghis Khan glared at the wild figure in front of him. Never had anybody dared to raise their voice in his presence. Then his expression changed and he began to laugh...uproariously. A couple of guards peeped in from behind the curtain wondering whether the commotion warranted their presence. But the Khan waved them away. Wiping tears of mirth from his eyes, he announced to the girl who looked at him with wary eyes, 'Yes. I am a Mongol and proud to be one. I am not a monster. The Mongols are fighting a war, here. Killing or being killed is a part of war. Tell me, did your Sultan's soldiers not kill the men who fought them? You think I am barbaric because I don't have the pretty manners of those people who fall at the feet of the Sultana.' He stopped to regard her gravely, 'You see, my life has been different from yours…so different that you cannot even imagine it. I have not lived in a palace, like you, where food is plenty. On the steppes where I have grown up, I have had to struggle to get my share of food. On the steppes, the law is to grab or go hungry. On the steppes, the law is to kill or be killed. Life was never easy for me. It was a hard life so it made me a hard man. However, I rule the world simply because I am what I am.' He shrugged eloquently…unrepentantly.

Something like pity tentatively tiptoed into Enkhtuya's heart but she pushed it away, resolutely. Her son's small body quivering in death rose before her eyes, once again. Pain, revulsion and hatred overwhelmed her. She turned and ran out of the *ger* into the moonlit night. Everything was pitch dark punctuated only by the campfires where the soldiers relaxed. For a moment, she lost her bearings. Letting instinct lead her, she found the track that Bolorma and she had walked down earlier. Nobody blocked her way as she sprinted blindly towards the ghostly, white form of her *ger*. While the Khan's scornful laughter still rang in her ears, a vague curiosity flickered in her about the life of this monster from the wilderness.

5

Little Temujin was so excited that he was in the corral before sunrise. He stood on a wooden block to place the saddle on his colt's back which was only a few inches above the head of the seven-year-old boy. His horse stamped his hoofs impatiently as Temujin adjusted the stirrups to the length of his legs. It was a beautiful summer's day; the sky was cerulean blue; a soft breeze gently bent the springy grass in patches forming waves in a green sea. A skylark warbled in the high filling the boy's heart with joy. 'A perfect day,' he whispered into the colt's ears. 'After so many days and so much begging, *Aav* has agreed to take me hunting today. I can't believe it...my first hunt. Tell me, *aduu,* will I kill a big buck today?' The colt's ears pricked up and it whinnied, softly blowing on the boy's plaited hair.

Outside the *ger,* Temujin sat on the ground to check on his bow and quiver of arrows. The re-curved, composite bow, if made to stand on its side, was taller than the boy, yet he handled it with ease. After all, he had helped his father put it together with wood, horn, sinew and glue from boiled animal tendons. It had taken them nearly a year to complete this bow. A splice of horn placed on the inside of the bow's wooden curve gave it resistance when compressed while animal sinews laid along the outer face gave it latent power. When forced out of its reverse curve and strung, it became a very powerful, unyielding bow. Temujin had practised day and night with it. He began by hitting static targets. When he mastered that, he shot off arrows while riding. He learned to release the bolt exactly when the horse's hoofs were off the ground in mid-gallop so that the arrow was not diverted from its path due to the horse's motion. He even practised shooting arrows behind his back by half-turning on horseback yet keeping both balance and accuracy. His latest shooting record was at 75 *alds*. An *ald* being the distance between the outstretched arms of a man or roughly 1.6 metres, it made the boy nearly as good a shooter as an average Mongol warrior. He had been preparing really hard for this day when he could go hunting with his father.

Yesugei came out of the *ger* and smiled when he saw the boy diligently twanging his bow. Taking a deep breath of the scented air, he growled, 'C'mon Temujin, the day is growing old. The bucks will go deep into the forests and we won't be able to catch any.' The boy scrambled to his feet. Strapping on the quiver and hefting the bow whose ends nearly scraped the grass, he loped behind his tall father. More nomads joined them. Some of them were warriors from other clans. They had decided to throw in their lot with the royal house of Borgijins and lived in the camp under Yesugei's leadership. Many of them were already mounted and waiting including Targutai of the Taychuits clan, the ambitious second-in-command of Chief Yesugei. Father and son got on their horses and led out the group, cantering over the steppes whooping enthusiastically at the prospect of a lively hunt.

They trotted along the River Onon on the lookout for herds of antelopes and gazelles. Soon enough, they spotted a large herd of grazing deer. Silently, the hunters halted and regrouped into a long queue. Temujin would always remember the scene; a maya-blue sky arching overhead with a lone falcon wheeling lazily in it, rolling verdant grasslands below with red flashes of spiky honeyweed and indigo gentians, on the western side gently sloping highlands facing dark, cool coppices of tall elms and maples, a few apricot trees between them laden with golden fruit and bright yellow flowering pea shrubs clustering in their shade. The placid ebony and speckled-brown deer rustling and munching through the tall grass amidst this natural consonance made for a tranquil tableau. The boy tried to burn the image of this idyllic panorama into his memory. After all, he would have to describe his first hunt in all its colours, scents and actions to his siblings and friends not lucky enough to accompany the hunters.

Slowly and soundlessly, the nomads began to circle the animals aiming to reach the slope of the hillock. Being on raised ground would help them guide their shafts better. The bright, rising sun had just topped the peak of the hill. This way, the fiery disc would be behind the hunters. If the animals picked up their scent and tried to identify their positions, the sunlight would blind them adding to their confusion. The men reached the slope and took up position behind a stack of boulders. Chief Yesugei was given the privilege of shooting the first arrow of the hunt. He notched a shaft on his great bow and pulled back the resistant string with three fingers. The distance to the nearest animal was about 300 metres. His bow twanged as the arrow was released flying in a gentle curve across the intervening space. Temujin squinted trying to follow its swift flight but all he saw was one of the biggest antelopes suddenly drop to the ground. It was a magnificent buck and Yesugei's bolt now quivered between his forelegs. It had pierced the heart in a clean shot killing instantly. The antelopes closer to the dead buck did scamper away a little but the rest of the herd kept grazing. However, it would take only a couple more shots for the herd to sense the danger and take to its heels. So, if the nomads wanted to use the full potential of the herd being in the open grasslands and pick out more quarry, it was essential to quickly kill as many as possible.

Temujin beamed at his father and began to fit an arrow to his bow but a shaft skimmed over his head and thudded into the nearest animal, a doe. Frowning, he twisted in his saddle to see who had committed the blunder, for the killing of does and heifers was banned by an unwritten covenant of the steppes. Targutai of the Taychuits grinned back at him. The clan's deputy wished to beat down the rights of the Chief's son. When Temujin next looked back at the herd, they were already aware of the jeopardy close by. The entire herd had begun to turn around heading for the cover of the forests to escape the deathly arrows. In the dark woods, the trees grew close enough to shield them from the hunters. It flashed on Temujin that he was about to lose his first chance of a kill.

Instantly, without a glance at his father for affirmation, he lashed his colt's rump sharply. The horse leaped forward and dashed down the slope. Faster than a speeding arrow, Temujin found himself in the midst of the chaotic melee. Clouds of dust rising from the churnings of hundreds of hooves filled his nose and blinded him. The panic-stricken deer were knocking into each other, some bucks wounding others with their branched antlers, the does trying to push nervous heifers towards the trees. Before Temujin could gather his wits, the herd had nearly rushed past him at a tremendous speed and his colt was prancing around the stragglers at its tail end. The main herd had already attained the safety of the forests. For Temujin, it was now or never. The boy hurriedly notched an arrow and took aim at a receding rump and let go with a shout. The arrow hit the target but only slowed the deer. Temujin kicked his horse to dash ahead of the limping animal and another of his arrows thumped into its chest. The young buck fell down dead.

In the blink of an eye, the entire herd had vanished leaving three still bodies on the flattened grass. The hunters came rushing down with Yesugei bellowing jubilantly. He thumped the grinning Temujin on his back, shouting, 'He is a true Mongol hunter. He is the Khan.' What could give more joy to a father than the triumph of his son! None of them noticed Targutai scowling darkly at the duo. While Yesugei and Temujin turned their horses homewards, the other nomads tied the carcasses to their saddles. Everybody headed back to camp hauling a supply of meat bumping behind them.

Half way to the camp, the air became chilly as a huge, dark-grey cloud covered the sun. One of the tumultuous summer storms was on its way. Suddenly, the bright daylight was erased by shadowy fingers rippling over the wildly waving grass. 'Take cover! Take cover!' called Yesugei as the nomads galloped hurriedly to a low pile of rocks and boulders rising from the pasture. They had just managed to wedge themselves under a rocky ledge when the roar of thunder and flashes of lightning filled the dark skies. Rain pelted down in frenzied sheets. The warriors hid their faces and turned their backs to heaven's assault. Booming thunder and cracks of light zigzagging across the clouds scared Temujin and he burrowed into his father's arms. Yesugei held him tightly, murmuring into his ears, 'Don't look at the thunderstorm. It is a display of the Khökh Tenger's fury. His angry voice is thunder and flashes of light show up his displeasure. We must not look at the sky when He is in a rage or He may strike us blind with his lightning bolts. Hide your face, Son.'

But as the tempest blew around them with all its theatrics, curiosity gradually overcame Temujin's fear.

He raised his head above his father's sheltering arm and peeped at the turbulence. Nothing happened to him. So, he slowly turned his head and gazed around. In fact, he found the furious drama that Nature was staging splendidly impressive and resplendent. He looked up at the sky but the Eternal Blue Heaven did not strike him down. As the storm slowly abated, it took away with it Temujin's fear…forever.

When they reached the camp, the sky was like a jewelled bowl. The clan came out to greet the hunters as they cantered in. After all, the carcasses the hunters had brought in would provide food for a couple weeks for all the camp families. That night the warriors sat around the blazing open fire. Two straight sticks on both sides of the log fire held a skewered whole buck, skinned and gutted, on a crude spit in the centre of the circle. Yesugei announced, 'By killing a buck on his very first hunt, Temujin has proved he is as valorous as any Mongol warrior. Temujin will eat with us, tonight.' Joining the circle of men, who were served the first and choicest portions of the meat, signified that Temujin, all of seven years, had formally attained manhood. The boy felt his heart would burst with pride at this honour. His brothers, half brothers and sisters looked at him with awe. Hoelun's smile was encouraging though a trifle sad. He would no longer be her little child who used to snuggle up to her in his sleep. He would now share the pallets with the warriors.

Yesugei made place for him beside his seat and the boy settled down. He tried to keep his face grave as the occasion demanded though he wanted to grin at the other children watching from a distance. When the huge joint of roasted deer meat was passed around, each man selected the sharpest knife from his wide leather belt that held an assortment of knives, big and small along with a pouch for tobacco and pipes. Blood squirted out as each of them cut a chunk of meat from the sirloin since it was still half-raw inside the crispy outer layer. The blood, they believed, would give them strength so it was sucked off before the tough meat was chewed.

Temujin carefully imitated his father and the other men as he chewed on bites torn off from his piece washing them down with bowls of mare's milk. After most of the huge joint was demolished, Yesugei leaned over the rest of the roast still turning on the spit and cut out a portion. He stretched his fist towards Temujin and slowly opened it. In the centre of his paw-like palm lay the dark heart of the buck. 'You deserve the best piece from the buck you killed.' He said as the boy looked up at his father's face and then at his palm, in wonder. Father and son were so absorbed in their exhilaration that they did not notice Targutai getting up and leaving the group. But some of the others especially the Taychuits noticed his exit. Obviously, the deputy was disgruntled by the Chief giving so much importance to his own son. A few nomads even followed him into the gloom.

That night as Temujin lay down beside his father, Yesugei pulled him close. Tucking the boy's head under his chin, he murmured, 'My son, you have a great responsibility. You must bring together the divided people of our land and build it again into the one unified nation as your great-grandfather, *the* Kabul Khan had done. It will not be easy and there will be many obstacles on the way. But remember that this is your destiny and you have been selected by the Khökh Tenger himself for this task.'

Temujin nodded sleepily. He did not understand everything his father said but he was conscious that his life will be different from that of others. Then his father moved. 'I have something for you,' he said.

Instantly, Temujin was wide awake. He sat up as innocently excited as only children can be about receiving gifts. He wanted to know immediately, 'What is it?'

Yesugei smiled and dug into his *deel*. Temujin stared at the object in his father's hand. It was a piece of bone with two branches. 'This is the wishbone of the buck you killed. It will bring you luck,' said Yesugei.

Enthralled by a piece of his very first kill, Temujin held it in his palm. He twisted it this way and that, examining it closely while Yesugei observed him indulgently. Finally, he carefully placed it in the pocket formed by his *deel* bunched up above the sash. It would remain there safely even when he rode. Yesugei rolled the child in the bearskin that formed both bedding as well as cover and gathered him to his warm body. Father and son slept as the stars looked down tenderly on them.

6

‘Tomorrow, get up early, Temujin. We are going to visit the Merkit clan,’ announced Yesugei. Hoelun, who was serving dinner of wild duck meat to her husband, the elder son and his siblings, paused. She frowned at Yesugei silently conveying, *but the Merkits are our enemy....* Temujin also lowered the bowl of mare’s milk he had been sipping and turned his eyes to his father.

Yesugei nodded to their unsaid comments. ‘That’s right,’ he said to his son. ‘The Merkits have been our foes ever since your mother became my wife. But we cannot let the situation continue. To build a nation, we have to first dissolve our mutual conflicts. Since they blame me for stealing Hoelun from them...’ He paused smiling at his wife, ‘...it is up to me to make amends.’ He paused to bite into a crispy wing. Temujin stared at his father thinking, *my father is relentless in the pursuit of his mission. It is this single-minded focus that makes a man a clan chief.*

Yesugei spit out the bone and looked at Temujin. The boy was disconcerted wondering if Yesugei had read his mind. ‘I need your help in this, Son,’ said his father and mentor. Temujin instantly nodded his head. He would do anything for his *Aav*. ‘I want you to choose a bride for yourself from the Merkits clan.’

There was a sharp intake of breath from Hoelun while Temujin stared at his father, confused. The rest of the family didn’t dare breathe for they were expecting fireworks to crackle between their parents. Silence was broken by Hoelun releasing her breath. Wordlessly, she continued to serve the meal. Only then did Temujin venture to ask, ‘Choose a bride?’

As Hoelun did not protest, Yesugei continued more confidently, 'Why not? You are past nine seasons and old enough to marry.'

'Will I have to stay with the bride's family, *Aav*?' Temujin's voice quavered a little.

'No, I don't think so,' said his father lessening some of the boy's unease. 'You are young and I assume so will your bride be. You can choose her. Her father and I can make a marriage agreement that both of you stay with your families until you are sixteen. Then the wedding can take place and we will bring your bride home.' Looking at his son's anxious face, Yesugei felt a pang of remorse. *He was too young to be used as pawn to erase enmity between our clans but I had stolen a bride from them. Only the offering of a son in return would cool their hatred.* 'Don't worry, Temujin. Merkit women make good wives. Besides, your mother and I are there for you.' His son dipped his head obediently.

Before Temujin left the *ger* to sleep with his father, he came up to his mother. Temujin adored his father but Hoelun was his pillar of strength. She placed a hand on her son's head that nearly reached her chest and said, 'Temujin, go with your *Aav*. He is planning for the future. I will welcome any girl you choose to be your bride and keep her under my wing.' Temujin put his arms around his mother hugging tightly this wise, strong woman. Her quiet assurance gave him the courage he was seeking and he went out to join his father.

Next morning, a group of nomads including Targutai, headed by Yesugei and Temujin galloped out of the camp. They followed the Onon for a few hours and then turned north towards the Khenti mountain range. It would take two days to reach the pastures in the northwest, the usual haunt of the Merkits. The sun had just slid under the peaks which were closer now when the horsemen came upon a group of *gers*. As Yesugei followed by the rest cantered in, a squat, broad man came running towards them. Yesugei dismounted and both men embraced. Dei-Tsetsen, Hoelun's cousin, slapped Yesugei on his back, greeting him loudly and happily. He was the Chief of the Ongirads clan and welcomed the nomads to spend the night in his camp.

Temujin was unsaddling his *aduu* to rub him down before corralling him, when he heard somebody call out, 'What's your name?'

He turned around. It was only a girl. She looked about his age though she was taller. 'Temujin,' he replied and turned back to unstrapping the stirrups. He didn't have time for girls.

'How old are you?' asked the sassy girl.

'Nine seasons,' mumbled Temujin, not turning his head.

'I am ten. One year older,' she sang out. On its heels came the next question, 'Will you stay at our camp?' *What a chatterbox*, thought Temujin, frowning. When he didn't answer, she said, 'So, you are our guest?'

She won't shut up until I tell her, thought the boy, annoyed with her needling. He turned to face her. Pulling himself up to his full height, he said haughtily, 'We are only staying the night.' And then, without knowing why, he added, 'I am on my way to the Merkits to choose a bride.'

The girl broke into giggles, saying, 'How silly!' Suddenly Temujin felt foolish. *Why did I have to blurt that out?* He wanted to slap himself. Still chuckling, the girl said, 'It is us, the Ongirads, who have the prettiest girls. Everyone chooses brides from our clan.'

With as much gravity as he could muster, Temujin turned his back on her and began to fiddle with the saddle straps, hoping the annoying girl would go away. But she was not finished. 'You could choose me as your bride,' she offered.

Astonished, Temujin twisted his head to stare at this shocking creature. She gave him a cheeky grin and began to run off. All of a sudden, a strange feeling came over the boy. He shouted at her retreating back, 'What's your name?'

She turned her head to give him a smile that lit up her entire face. 'Börte,' she shouted back, vanishing into a *ger*.

That night, after a dinner of horseflesh and *airag*, Yesugei came out to join Temujin who was lying on the hard ground and watching the stars glittering overhead. His father staggered a little drunkenly and slapped at the mosquitoes biting him. 'Are you reading your destiny?' He chaffed the boy as he rolled himself in his *deel* and lay down next to him.

Without a preamble, Temujin said, 'I met a girl today.'

'Hmm…,' intoned his father, sleepily.

'She said everybody chooses brides from the Ongirads clan,' he said, a little loudly to get his father's attention.

Yesugei blinked at his son, curiously. 'Well,' he ventured cautiously, 'that maybe so. They say that Ongirad females are beautiful. Look at your mother.'

'Why can't I have an Ongirad bride?' asked Temujin, sitting up.

Now Yesugei's eyes were wide open. 'I told you why,' he growled. 'We have to form an alliance with the Merkits. The best way is to marry into their clan.'

For some reason, Temujin was not afraid of his father tonight. 'Alright. I will choose a bride from the Merkits but I can practise how to do it, can't I?'

His father was silent, thinking, *where is this going?*

'I can practise the bride choosing tomorrow with the Ongirad girls, can't I?' Temujin persisted.

'Oh, alright. We will practise tomorrow,' agreed Yesugei, indulgently. 'I will speak to Dei-Tsetsen.' He mumbled yawning, as fatigue and draughts of *airag* overcame him. Soon he was snoring. Temujin pulled his *deel* around him and closed his eyes, content that he had got his way. All night, a small face with a smile as bright as the sun plagued his dreams.

Next morning, Yesugei smiled at his friend, Dei-Tsetsen who had arranged for all the marriageable females of his clan to be lined up for Temujin. Of nine or ten years old, each little girl's face was scrubbed pink. Their hair was neatly braided with bright corals or silver ornaments and each one wore her best *deel*, trousers and *gutals*, the leather shoes with up-turned toes. Temujin looked down the row and found the face he was looking for. The girl grinned at him and he quickly averted his eyes. *What a girl!*

Yesugei chuckled and said, 'Look at their legs and feet, Temujin. Women with strong legs make good wives. Also remember to choose the one with a flat, round face and the narrowest eyes. Large eyes invite the devil to enter the female and then she chatters and chatters making a man's head ache.'

So Temujin obediently walked the row of girls looking diligently at *gutal*-shod feet. There were just about seven to eight girls and very soon, he had reached the end of line and there were no more feet to observe. He stopped and glanced at the last girl who smiled at him. *But she is not the one,* remarked Temujin to himself. Now he began to walk back staring at each face. Other clansmen gathered around this interesting event laughing and joking among themselves but Temujin's face was grave. When he reached the girl, whose smile had filled his dreams last night, he halted. The men stopped speaking and watched him. Carefully, Temujin looked over the girl recalling his father's words. *Well, her legs looked strong. She had a round, fair, flat face and he liked her eyes; narrow and dark like the wings of the summer swallow.*

'I choose this girl to be my bride,' Temujin announced in a clear, loud voice.

Instantly, a hubbub broke out among the spectators. Through it all came Dei-Tsetsen's loud voice, 'That is Börte, my daughter.' He slapped the stunned Yesugei on his shoulder, saying, 'Your son chose my daughter. Hey! We are relatives.'

Yesugei frowned angrily at Temujin but his son stared back impassively. It was at that moment that the father realised that his son was as implacable as his great-grandfather Kabul Khan was reputed to be. If he wanted something, he would get it despite everything. Yesugei shrugged, *a leader needs to be like this,* he told himself and grinned back at Dei-Tsetsen, his friend.

That evening, the entire clan got together to celebrate the Ongirad chief's daughter's engagement to the Borjigin chief's son. There was a great deal of eating, drinking and ribaldry. The clanswomen placed one succulent dish after another before the two proud fathers who sat with their children beside them. Börte peeped from Dei-Tsetsen's knee and beamed at Temujin sitting on the other side of Yesugei. The boy could not resist the charm of her sunny smile and grinned back in turn. Dei-Tsetsan glanced at their young faces and remarked, 'Look at them, Yesugei. There is fire in their eyes and light on their faces. It was a good choice. Together, they will do well.' He did not know that he was foretelling a historical outcome though it would take time and persistence for his prediction to become reality.

After feasting all through the night, it was only by the next afternoon that Yesugei and his group were ready to leave. Temujin's future parents-in-law were rich and gave them many gifts. It had been agreed that Börte would live with her parents until Temujin crossed sixteen seasons. Then he would return to marry her and take his bride home.

As Temujin was adjusting the stirrups in the corral, Börte came to lean against the gate. Temujin smiled at her and was amazed to see her blush. Her beautiful smile flashed for an instant. Sadness lurked in her dark eyes as she whispered, 'Will you really come back for me?'

Temujin whispered back, 'I will really come back for you. I promise.' He dug his hand into his *deel* and approached her extending a closed fist.

Börte looked down at his fist asking, 'What is it?'

Temujin opened his fist. On his palm lay the branching wishbone of the first buck he had killed. As Börte lifted her eyes to him, he said solemnly, 'With this I seal my promise to you. This is my gift. Keep it till I return to you.'

With her forefinger and thumb, the young girl picked up this unusual token of Temujin's love. Her face glowing radiantly, she turned it round and round in front of her delighted eyes before closing her fingers over it.

Yesugei called out, 'Temujin.' Börte quickly thrust her keepsake inside her *deel,* dazzling Temujin with another sunny smile before sprinting across the camp.

It was a bemused boy who flung a leg over his *aduu* and cantered after his father's horse. The sunlight seemed warmer, the scent of the grass fresher and birdsongs sweeter as Temujin's heart soared joyfully heavenwards.

7

'Creeaak…creeaak,' went the wooden wheels of the wagon as it rolled over stones and gravel of the roughly-hewn mountain track. Clutching tightly to the sides, Princess Enkhtuya tried her best to prevent sliding, slipping and spinning all over wagon planks like a pumpkin. At the same time, she dug her chin into the high collar of her woollen *deel* blowing warm air into it to thaw her chilled limbs. The chains binding both her and Bolorma's legs to the wagon beams jingled and clanked with every turn of the wooden wheels. Despair cast a despondent air over the girl as the wagon moved further and further from the land of the Indus River where possibly her husband may be looking for her.

She recalled how just forty-eight hours back, she had woken up from deep sleep. She had been emotionally weary after the tensions of escaping her cruel captor and it had made her physically fatigued. As she tried to discern exactly what had woken her, a great deal of cacophony from outside the *ger* came to her. Groggily, she had sat up while Bolorma slipped out to bring hot water for her wash. Enkhtuya had climbed down from the high bed and walked on bare feet to the *ger* entrance. She had peeped from behind the thick fur curtain to watch flabbergasted at the entire camp in the throes of packing up. Bolorma had returned with a wooden pitcher of steaming water and told her, 'Get ready quickly, my *Guunj*! They are breaking camp and will be moving in about an hour.'

Stunned to know that she will be forced to leave the Land of the Indus River before the Sultan could attempt to rescue her, that is, if he believed her to be still alive, Enkhtuya had stammered, 'Wh…Where?'

'I don't know,' the old woman had muttered. 'Some are saying that we are going into the mountains.' And she became busy bundling up their meagre belongings into neat packages. Enkhtuya had been in tears as she washed, combed her hair and let the maid tie a broad sash to squeeze in her thick, grey *deel* and trousers. She eased the girl's feet into unfamiliar leather boots with upturned toes. 'These are Mongolian boots called *gutals*,' explained Bolorma. Enkhtuya scowled at her. It had been just two days since they had been captured by these nomads and the old woman was already sliding into the Mongolian practices quite comfortably. Enkhtuya resented her infidelity; after all Amin Malik and the Sultan had fed and housed Bolorma for many years despite her Mongolian blood. But a few hours of being with these crude, vicious animals and she was keen to don their customs.

Forlornly, Princess Enkhtuya now looked around her as the wagon bounced and rattled over the rough mountain track. Preceded by warriors on horseback with the Khan riding at their head, it was a long procession. She could see along the steep, narrow path as the wagons were winding up heaped with weapons and food, drawn by bulls and horses. Strange devices were also part of the procession; trundling trebuchets with their fire and smoke bombs, battering rams on wheels, scaling ladders, four-wheeled mobile shields, flame-throwing tubes, and the double and triple-bowed siege bows that could fire arrows to punch holes in baked-earth walls from a kilometre away. Genghis Khan's nomadic army was on the march taking along with it the formidable combination of siege weaponry that supported it. The tail end of this long cavalcade was brought up by a stumbling line of men and women; prisoners tied together. If one fell and did not get up, guards with whips would just cut the binding ropes from the body and shove it off the path to tumble down into the black, bottomless crevasse or gorge.

At least we are better off than them, thought Enkhtuya trying to catch her breath in the air low on oxygen, *though I don't know why we seem to deserve being treated better than them.* Bolorma's head, covered by a leather and fur cap, had fallen forward on her chest and low snores emitted from her. All around them were steep, snow-covered slopes. She glimpsed the glittering peaks high above them where the sun's rays touched them with bright fingers. Wheels dug through the mush of sleet and mud which was defined as a track in these high mountains. In just about two days and nights, they were already traversing the highest passes of the Hindu Kush. It was during one of the night camps that Bolorma had discovered where the army was headed. She had informed Enkhtuya that the Khan had decided to return home to Mongolia. The soldiers had been very elated and jabbered that they were going home after more than three years.

Enkhtuya's heart had plummeted with this news and she had scathingly retorted to her maid, 'You seem very pleased.'

Instead of looking chastised, Bolorma had said in Mongolian, 'I am old, my Princess. I came with your mother a long, long time ago to Amin Malik's land. But I was born on the highland steppes and now, I want to die there. Khökh Tenger must have heard my prayers. It can only be His will that I am returning to my own land.'

Enkhtuya had snapped at her, 'Shut up. Don't talk in that stupid language to me. It is bad enough that my ears are full of its guttural sounds all day and night.' The old woman only shrugged silently, musing to herself, *the child has none of her mother's wisdom*. A tableau from long years past flicked across her mind; Enkhtuya's mother trudging through the hot desert…sold as a slave despite being born into nobility. She had been a tenacious lady using all her sagacity to survive in whatever circumstances she had been flung.

Since she had ordered Bolorma to silence, Enkhtuya had only her own thoughts for company as the cartwheels creaked monotonously. She tried to shift her position to ease her aching limbs but every movement was painful. To distract her mind, she turned her thoughts to the days of her childhood. Her earliest consciousness was of hot sunlight beating down on her little head in her mother's arms. She remembered clasping her plump arms around her mother's neck and burying her face inside her mother's veil so that she could breathe without sand grains blowing in the blistering desert winds clogging her nose. It was a hazy picture; a sea of sand that had stretched for miles around them and her mother walking through it, her feet making soft swishing sounds. There had been other people too but she remembered them only as shadows. Her favourite memory that she could recall clearly was when she was older; playing with her mother among the fruit trees and fountains of Amin Malik's palace. Her graceful, stately mother in flowing robes would chase after her, while her sweet, tinkling laugh guided the little girl to her hiding place. Eventually, when her soft arms would go around Enkhtuya, it seemed she was in a garden of roses for their musky scent always formed an aura around her mother. Bound in her mother's arms, the little girl would look up into a pair of slanting, merrily dancing, brilliant blue eyes, so like her own, and giggle uncontrollably.

'…she must have been a *semu*…,'a voice murmured in her ears. Enkhtuya started and looked around frantically. The guards riding silently on either side of the wagon were looking straight ahead. Bolorma was still snoring.

Nobody had spoken and certainly not the owner of the voice. His voice was in her head. *Why had he called my mother 'a semu'? What does it mean? I must ask Bolorma…she would know…*thought Enkhtuya and a grimace crossed her face as she recalled her own reprimand to the maid some hours ago. Her thoughts slid off on another path towards the owner of the voice. *Where is he? What does he want to do with me? He hasn't called for me after that horrible day. Of course, I am thankful but still I wonder why? I can't stand this constant tension of being on guard. Being ravished is bad enough. But waiting for it not knowing when I will be attacked is worse. It is eating me up. Why is he not doing it? Is he waiting for me to lose my mind with fear? Is he expecting that if he gave me time I will submit to him? Never! Never will I give myself up to that evil, smelly devil! I will kill myself first.*

All at once Enkhtuya's impassioned speculations were ruptured by deep dejection as the wretchedness of the situation came home to her. *Do I really have a choice?* She was the captive of the most notorious tyrant in the world. How could she expect that he would allow her the luxury of consenting to her own assault? *Whom am I deluding?* Enkhtuya thought.

That evening, at least one of Princess Enkhtuya's questions was answered. As she was washing the journey's grime off with a little hot water from a bucket in the small *ger* put up for her and Bolorma, a message came in. The Khan had asked for her. *So, he is in the camp.* Though Enkhtuya was bone tired, she knew that the message was not a request. It was a command that better be obeyed. Bolorma managed to filch another bucket of hot water from the kitchen when nobody was looking. She took all the Princess's dusty clothes off and rubbed her all over with a warm swab cloth till the freezing numbness gave way to a warm tingling all over her body. Putting a soft tunic over her head, she made her sit on the empty, upturned bucket and combed out her long, silky hair. As she began to braid it carefully, Enkhtuya laughed grimly. 'Are you arraying me like the Khan's mistress?'

Taking time to reply, the old woman said quietly, 'You will be considered a princess only when you look and behave like one. In all circumstances retain your dignity. Don't you remember your mother? She was always the princess even when she was being auctioned as a slave.'

Enkhtuya silently contemplated the wisdom of Bolorma's words. Tears pricked the corners of her eyes as she promised her beloved dead mother, I *will not forget even once to be a princess like you were, Eej.* Though her mother and she would mostly converse in the language of Ghaznin, Enkhtuya always used to call her mother *Eej,* the way the Mongols address their mother.

This time when she entered the huge *ger,* the Emperor of Mongolia was seated calmly on the dais surrounded by oil lamps. The blue flames of a fire lighted in the central pit dissipated the icy night air inside the *ger*. Enkhtuya advanced cautiously, peering into the gloomy corners of the huge *ger* to detect whether there was anybody else inside. 'There is nobody else here.' Genghis Khan's sonorous voice informed her. The girl was close enough to see that his eyes were closed. She wondered, *how did he know what I was doing?* Instantly he replied to her unspoken query. 'I don't see only with my eyes. If I did that I would have not survived on the steppes. When peril lurks even in the breeze caressing your cheek, you must detect it with your senses.'

As she stared unbelievingly at the imperturbable face, she observed very fine wrinkles stretching across its flat surface, under the eyes and around the thin lips. His skin spread over the high cheekbones was like a well-preserved parchment retaining faint outlines of its folds. Slightly flecked with silver, the whiskers on his upper lip were brownish as was the small goatee below the lower lip. But his hair, as black as a raven's wing, had only a couple of silver lines. It was pulled back severely in a single plait down his back. He looked well in his prime and certainly not past it.

She became flustered to realise that his eyes were open and were appraising her with amusement. Enkhtuya coloured up for she had been staring at the man unabashedly. To her mortification, he chuckled, saying, 'Well, what did your scrutiny tell you? Am I good enough? How do I compare with your handsome Sultan?' Rattled, Enkhtuya looked at the mud floor. *So much for promising to behave with dignity*, she berated herself silently. Chuckling once more at her discomfiture, he remarked, 'I can see that your Sultan wins over me. However, at the moment, you have to make do with me. Your Sultan is far away. So, leave your dislike outside. Come and sit beside me.'

Beside him! Enkhtuya's heart leaped in terror and then steadied as she saw his hand pointing to a low stool on the dais. She had not seen it and gratefully lowered herself on it. The Khan clapped his hands sharply, twice. Instantly, the fur curtain was lifted and a low table heaped with wooden platters was brought in and placed between them. *Oh no!* groaned the girl, I *must prevent myself from puking, again.* But this time, she noticed the platters piled with roasted meat were placed before him. On her side there was basket of tiny pink peaches and a bowl full of dried almonds and raisins. Besides there was a platter with white ovals on it. They looked like...*yes,* like boiled eggs! Genghis Khan poured a plum-coloured liquid into an empty bowl and offered it to her, saying candidly, 'It is the wine my soldiers have brought from your palace. I expect this should suit your palate more than our *airag*.'

Enkhtuya flushed with sudden rage at his brazen words. 'My wine? You steal my wine and offer it to me! You have the audacity! How dare you!'

'Come, come Princess,' he responded, calmly. 'Who would drink your wine in that town of the dead? Ghosts? Isn't it better that we, rather you, enjoy it? Don't let anger sour your appetite. Be thankful that you have food to eat and wine to drink. It could be worse for you.' He spoke placidly but the threat rang clearly in his words.

Enkhtuya quietly picked up a peach and began to skin it. She knew her options were none and the bleakness of her position overwhelmed her. As she chewed on the fruit, he said, 'Is it juicy, these mountain peaches? A man broke a leg today fetching them from a tree growing on a rock face. I hope they are worth it.'

Enkhtuya managed to nod but could not resist a biting comment, 'So you want to dine and wine me until I am drunk and unconscious. After that, when I am unable to resist you anymore, you plan to take your pleasure with me.'

Suddenly, the unruffled façade of a composed mandarin cracked as Genghis Khan thundered, 'Stop it! We are Mongol warriors, not slimy cowards from Islamic kingdoms. We fight with our face to the enemy. We don't stab them in the back. Deceit is not a weapon of the nomads. Besides, if I wanted to assault you, I don't need to make you unconscious to do it. Don't be deceived by my age. I have more strength than you can ever hope to have.' The girl went pale but remained sitting at the table staring down at the peach in her still palm. Just like the summer storms of the steppes, his anger passed swiftly, and peace descended just as quickly. 'Eat, Woman, eat,' he commanded, his tone mild once again. 'I didn't expect you to be so foolish, Princess,' he added, tearing off a large slice of meat and chewing on it.

Enkhtuya felt it would be prudent to follow his instructions. So, she picked up an egg and bit delicately into it. It was not a poultry-laid egg. Possibly stolen from the nest of an unknown bird; whichever the fowl that had laid it, the egg was delicious. The girl decided she wanted to eat another one. For some time, the couple ate quietly satisfying their disparate appetites. When Enkhtuya could eat no more, she sat back and stole a glance at her companion. He seemed completely absorbed in his meat and *airag*. After a while, Enkhtuya plucked up strands of her courage to risk asking him what had been haunting her for days.

Clearing her voice, she demanded, 'Why did your men kill my son?'

Genghis Khan raised his thin brows and glanced up at her. His eyes seemed strange...a look in them that baffled Enkhtuya. *Was it...could it be...remorse...guilt?* Then it passed...passed so quickly that the girl wondered if she had imagined it. His lids fell and his jaws kept moving. Not getting a proper response, she repeated the query, 'You said that Mongols are brave warriors. Why do they kill unarmed children then? Was it brave to kill my son?'

'I believe seedlings that are in the danger of growing into poisonous plants must be uprooted and destroyed totally,' he remarked cryptically, still not looking at her. His attention did not shift from his meal as he sliced another piece of meat from the roast.

Enkhtuya stared at him appalled at his callous insensibility. 'He was only seven years old,' she whispered.

'Sultan Jalal-ud-din, the ruler of Khwarezm is quite unlike his insane father. He is the only Islamic ruler who defeated the Mongol army for the first time during our conquests of these Islamic lands. It happened only once but once is enough. So, I chased him across the kingdoms to the banks of the Indus River. I thought I had caught him, but he escaped me and my sword. He plunged into the mighty river as if he was protected by a charm and swam across. He is a brave man and a clever commander. Is it not logical that a father will nurture his son to be like him? It is reasonable to expect his son will grow to be as bold as him. Thus, it is better that while there is still time, the child should be…' the Khan swept his arm down making a cutting gesture.

Enkhtuya had no words to rebut this atrocious yet astute strategy. Only her blue eyes darkened with sorrow.

Slaking his thirst on bowls of *airag* made the Emperor expansive. So, he continued in a conciliatory tone. 'Princess, if Malikpur had handed over the Sultan to me, it would have been spared destruction and bloodshed. Defying the Khan is dangerous, and many countries know the consequences of such foolishness too well. Did they not hear of my reputation?'

In a choked voice, Enkhtuya said, 'But my son did not defy you.'

'Not now,' agreed the conqueror, 'But later he would have joined his father and then it would have been two strong opponents defying me. I can't have that. It sets a bad example for the other kingdoms. They must know that when Genghis Khan comes, he is like the Khökh Tenger's fury decimating everything in his path.'

'Your arrogance is preposterous. I hate you.' Enkhtuya's voice was full of suppressed venom.

'That you may, Princess,' said the Khan with a mocking smile. 'Now if I may, I will excuse myself from your delightful company. I think you should rest, too. We have a long journey tomorrow for I want to cross the mountains by nightfall.'

Instantly, Enkhtuya stood up, glad to be allowed to leave the presence of a man she loathed from the bottom of her heart. Without another word, she started crossing the floor when his sardonic voice stopped her, 'Princess, I advise you to leave the past behind and look to the future. Now, don't you think I deserve some thanks for my advice and this meal?'

She turned at the door and mumbled in a voice quivering with antipathy, 'Thank you, my Lord.' Genghis Khan inclined his head acknowledging her dubious gratitude, his face an inscrutable mask again.

8

A band of mounted nomads streaked across the undulating highlands through tall grasses bending at the breeze's caprices revealing brilliant flashes of vibrantly-hued flowers. Though the nights had begun to cool heralding the onset of winter, the days were still warm. A flight of wild ducks rose like an arrow into the azure sky. Any other time, Temujin would have taken excited shots at them but that day, his complete attention was on his father's stiff back atop his wildly galloping *aduu*. Temujin knew that his father was displeased yet he did not have an explanation for his choice of the bride. With what words could he describe the warmth that spread through him when Börte smiled? To gauge his father's displeasure, he gradually pushed his own horse to come alongside his father's and stole a sidelong glance at Yesugei's scowling face. *How angry was he?* For a few kilometres father and son rode side by side wordlessly. Eventually, Yesugei turned to Temujin and said, 'A man must choose his own woman.' Temujin's face broke into a slow, wide smile. His father grinned at him and yelled, 'Race you to the hummock,' pointing to a small bulge in the distance. The young boy clutched the horse's belly with his boots. With a few sharp lashes to its rump, his *aduu* lunged forward. Yesugei also thrust ahead, his laughter echoing in the wind.

By midday, they had come upon an old campsite where they could rest and eat a meal. When they alighted, Targutai pointed out to Yesugei another group of nomads who had also chosen the site for a noon meal. 'They look like the Tartars,' he warned.

Yesugei shrugged, 'So what? This is a common resting place and it is customary to be at peace in places like this. Let's quietly have the meal and go our way.'

They settled down at a distance but within sight of the other group. Opening the food baskets given by Dei-Tsetsan's family, they began to share the meal. Suddenly, Targutai uttered, 'Look!' All of them twisted their heads around. A server from the other group was approaching them. In his hands, he held a large bowl. Curiously, Yesugei and his men waited for him to come up.

The man held out the bowl to Yesugei, saying, 'Greetings from my master! He sends you the gift of mare's milk to wet your throat.'

Yesugei's eyes narrowed and went beyond the server to the leader of the other group who gave him a friendly nod. He held out his hands for the bowl, though Targutai hissed, 'It could be a trap, Chief.'

As the server turned back, Yesugei held the bowl to his lips and drank deeply. Targutai shook his head in disapproval while the other men and Temujin stared at Yesugei. He threw down the bowl and announced, 'Let us go. We must reach the camp before sundown.' Everyone stood up, untethered their horses and soon only clouds of dust on the horizon proclaimed their passage towards home.

The camp was within sight when Yesugei slowed his horse and turning to one side vomited violently. Temujin who was behind him slowed too. '*Aav,* are you alright?'

His father only waved his hand to show he was fine and began to canter towards the camp. Temujin followed him closely while the men behind them began to murmur. Without a word of warning, Yesugei keeled over. He lost balance and fell from the horse's back to the ground. As Temujin and the other horsemen milled around the prostrate man, Targutai exclaimed, 'Yesugei is dead! Our chief has been poisoned! I told....' His voice choked as a whip slashed across his face. He stared at the perpetuator; a nine-year-old furious Temujin. The man's eyes smouldered glinting rage and hatred at the boy. Then he turned away galloping back to the camp without helping his sick leader. The Taychuits went with him. The other men hesitated. Then they decided to follow a man rather than a boy and in one accord, turned their mounts to follow Targutai.

Temujin kneeled beside his father. His chest did not rise and fall with breath. He was frothing at the mouth and foamy liquid flowed from his slack lips. Temujin held his father's head on his lap while tears flowed down his cheeks. *How can you die? How can you leave me, Aav?* It was all that his numbed mind said over and over again. By the time Hoelun, his other brothers and sisters along with the shaman arrived, his father' body was already turning cold. They wrapped his body in a blanket and laid him in a cart drawn by horses. Then the family along with the shaman began to slowly march to the burial grounds. The shaman muttered prayers and sprinkled water before the cart. When he had finished the rituals of the dead, Begter, Temujin's elder half-brother untied the horses from the cart and lashed them to step away. The cart tilted, and their father's body slid to the ground to be readied for the pit they would dig. A loud shout came from the campsite. The family turned and were paralysed at the sight that met their eyes. Other than their *ger*, all the *gers* had been dismantled and the clan was moving off. Hoelun began to run towards the camp followed by her children.

Led by Targutai, the men of the Taychuit clan were driving off the sheep and the horses that belonged to

Yesugei's family. Hoelun rushed at the deputy's horse and pulling the reins, said, 'How dare you! Yesugei was your chief.' Targutai gave her kick that sent her flying into a loaded cart. Temujin began to notch an arrow to his bow aiming it at the vile man but he was grabbed from behind by the other men before he could shoot. One of them snatched his bow and flung it far away. Another Taychuit picked up a burning stick from the campfire and swung it at the only standing *ger*; theirs. The felt cover and wood struts were aflame in minutes. Hoelun and Temujin tried to run towards it to save their household goods, but strong arms held them back. Hoelun screamed at Targutai, 'You wretched man! You betrayed the man who was your leader! He brought your clan into our fold when you were starving. He gave you a position of significance. And you are stealing all his belongings from his son who is now your Chief. May you rot in hell! May your blood freeze in winter! May you and your clan starve to death!'

The man dismounted and strode to the screaming woman. Bringing his face close to Hoelun's and pointing to his chest, he snarled at her, 'I...I am the Chief now. The Taychuits now rule the Mongol clans not the Borgijins and certainly not your son. It is you who will starve now. It is your family that will freeze to death this winter.'

She spat on his face, yelling, 'My son will kill you for this.' Her other children even Begter, a stepson who was older than Temujin, clustered together nervously, not knowing what to do.

Targutai laughed and pointed to Temujin. 'Him? That runt?' The struggling boy was being held down by three men. Still, he was trying to bite at their hands. Targutai unsheathed his sword and held its sharp edge to the boy's throat. Temujin stared up at him fearlessly defiant.

'I will kill him before he can even raise his bow,' growled Targutai displaying rotten teeth in a humourless smile that resembled the grimace of a skull head.

Hoelun, held back by two more men, was not intimidated by Targutai's threats. Through gritted teeth, she screamed, 'Temujin is his father's son. He is a wolf cub. He will avenge his father's betrayal...our family's betrayal. What are you? Nothing but a slimy steppe fox. Get out Targutai, while you still can. Be assured that you won't go far. My son will come after you.'

Targutai's bloodshot eyes stared down at Temujin, whose fierce eyes were darting poisonous looks like sharp arrows at him. It seemed the bare blade was about to slice into his tender throat when Targutai eased the pressure. He grunted, 'I don't wage war on cubs. That is the law of the steppe and I obey it. I will wait for him to grow up and then I will fight him to death.' Scorn replaced the hatred on Temujin's face. *You have just made the worst mistake of your life,* he sneered silently at the traitorous man, *leaving a seed to grow into a tree is utter idiocy. You will learn that by and by.*

Targutai shoved his sword into his leather belt and strode to his horse. He mounted and ordered his men, 'Leave the runt and the woman. Let's go. We must catch up with the clans.' The nomads wheeled their horses and swept down to the Onon to join the procession of wagons and cattle on the other side. The clans so assiduously gathered by Yesugei and merged into the Borjigins had abandoned his widow and his family. They, including the Borjigins, preferred the security of the new leadership of Targutai of the Taychuits.

Hoelun had fallen to the ground, but when Temujin tried to help her up, she pushed his hand away. 'We are on our own now. Nobody can help us other than us. We are a family and only if we stay together will we survive.' The children gathered around their mother. With his death Yesugei's family was bereft of everything; home, herds, horses. Their entire world, their hopes for success in war, their insurance against catastrophe had suddenly vanished. His widow was left with no protector. However, she had the responsibility of caring for six children between the ages of three and nine, four of her own and two from his previous wife.

The family was destitute but Hoelun was a woman of spirit. With no herds, she became a hunter-gatherer, harking back to the days when the Mongols had first settled in the valley. With the help of the older children, she built a rude shelter beside a small lake, known as the Blue Lake at the foot of the Black Heart Mountain on the flanks of the great Burkhan Khaldun. Every day, with her younger children, she would dig with a sharpened juniper stick along the borders of the lake and the banks of the Onon for fruits and roots. The boys learned to make hooks and use nets to catch fish.

One day, Hoelun heard a thin wail of a baby among the maples that thickly edged the Blue Lake. She followed it to find an infant, weakly flailing its arms in the bracken. It was a male child. She picked the baby in her arms and looked around for its mother. Even after searching for an hour, she found nobody and assumed that the grey steppe wolves may have killed and dragged away the mother. She brought the baby back to her shelter. Dipping a corner of a clean cloth in warm milk made of root flour and water, she brought it to the baby's small mouth. Hungrily, he sucked at it and Hoelun smiled. She fed the child and wrapped him in warm blankets. When her sons came in from their hunting and saw the child, they were aghast. 'Leave it in the forest, *Eej*. We hardly have food for ourselves, how can we feed another mouth?'

Hoelun refused. 'If I had abandoned you when the clan abandoned me, what would have happened?'

Shamed into acquiescing, they accepted the child into their family. Undimmed by their impoverished straits, Hoelun's warmth and compassion drew the boy, whom she named Shigi, into her brood. As he began to toddle about, Shigi followed Temujin everywhere like a shadow. Affection was alien in the hard life that he was coping with, yet a fondness for his adopted brother grew in Temujin's heart.

Despite all the hardships, Hoelun never lost sight of Yesugei's aspirations for Temujin. In fact, his dream gave her strength and its realisation a goal to strive for. Yesugei's dream became Hoelun's dream. She constantly reminded Temujin of his mission. Mongols speak lyrically of how during those hard times Temujin's mother prepared him for the life he was destined for.

The sons who were fed on wild garlic
And on wild onions by the noble mother,
In time became rulers;
The sons who were fed on wild lily bulbs
By the high-minded noble mother
Became lawful and wise.

For these three or four crucial years, Temujin understood what it was to live without the secure network of family, companions and close friends. His mother, his siblings and he had no animals for meat, milk or felt for a *ger*. He felt trapped in this hand-to-mouth existence, yet his instincts of survival sharpened, and they were to serve him well all his life.

Living under a daily stress of survival, it was hardly surprising that a kind of rivalry rose between the two elder boys, Temujin and his half-brother, Begter. Both vied for Hoelun's attention and wanted to be the leader of their small family. One cool spring afternoon, Temujin, now around thirteen years, was able to snare a large minnow in his net. Joyfully, he and his younger brother, Kasar decided to scale and spit-roast the fish. They planned to take it triumphantly to their mother. That day's family meal would be provided by Temujin. *How proud Eej would be,* he thought, gleefully imagining the awe on the faces of his siblings when he brought them a whole fish for a meal. While the brothers were engaged in turning the fish on the spit, Begter came upon them.

'Oho! Roasting fish for yourselves?' He commented, his mouth watering at the aroma rising from the smoking fish.

Temujin frowned at the insinuation that they were going to gorge on the fish all by themselves. 'We are going to take the roasted fish to *Eej,*' he said briefly, continuing to turn the fish.

'I don't believe you,' shouted Begter and began to kick at the hot coals. The boys sprang up and a grappling match began. Begter was heavier and he threw Temujin so hard on the ground that the boy's head hit a hard root. For a moment, the world turned dark for him. By the time, he sat up rubbing at a large lump on his head, Begter had run off with the roasted fish.

When Temujin and Kasar reached their mother's shelter, she was serving the fish to the family. Begter gave them a sly smile as they took their places in the circle. That night Temujin approached Hoelun and told her about the incident. He expected her to commiserate with him and at least direct a scolding towards Begter. Instead Hoelun reproached him. She reminded him,

We have no friend but our shadows,
We have no whip but our horse's tail.

'This is not a time to fight with your brothers. It is a time to unite as a family. Don't come to me with such complaints. How does it matter who caught the minnow? What matters is that our family ate a full meal.'

But, the injustice of it all burned through Temujin's insides like acid. He knew that the only way to calm the storm inside him was to ensure his supremacy inside the family circle. He and only he must be the leader. All night, his eyes blazed up at the dark sky raging at the way Begter had cheated him of his rightful position in the family and displaced his mother's affections for him. I *must right the wrong,* he thought as his blood boiled.

Next morning, Begter sat on the slope of the Black Mountain minding the few geldings that the family had managed to barter for some woven wicker baskets. Temujin with the help of Kasar had stalked him all day. Now they stealthily came up behind him. Temujin put an arrow to his bow. Silently, he pulled back the string and let go. The arrow slammed into the boy's vulnerable back. Begter never had a chance.

No doubt there was a streak of ruthlessness in the boy who was destined to not only win but hold fast to the leadership of the Mongol clans. When his mother came to know of his crime, she berated her eldest son in scathing condemning words. 'You are no better than a wild boar or the snow leopard that slaughters life for the sake of slaughtering. You have killed with no purpose other to destroy your brother...your own blood. Are you an animal? Can you not understand that this is the time to stay united? How will our family be strong if we keep seeking revenge on each other for petty quarrels? You simply do not have the luxury of taking vengeance when only your shadow is your friend and certainly not on your own family. Each of us has only each other to stand beside us in the fight against this terrible world. We have to co-operate and be loyal to each other. Temujin, your strength lies in this family. Only they will watch your back when you are threatened. Keep them with you. Stop quarrelling with them.'

Temujin said nothing in response. His mother had always been his mainstay…the rudder that gave direction to his lifeboat. He accepted her lashings as his due. Her words engraved into his mind. He would remember them much later when he began to build and foster relationships based solely on loyalty.

9

Snow covered the entire valley freezing the Onon into a silver snake wriggling through the white landscape. Bare branches of trees were hung with glistening icicles that reflected the frail sunlight. There was no way to identify the hollows and dips, the hills and hummocks where summer had played her games a few months ago. Temujin tugged at the leather throngs around the necks of the two geldings his family had been able to procure. Begter's responsibility of keeping the animals alive had passed on to him, now. With a stout stick, he banged on the hard ice covering the river to make a water hole for his *aduu*. A halloo echoed above his head and when he looked up he saw three horsemen. *Tartars!* Even as Temujin turned to run with the geldings, they dived and skidded down the snowy slopes. Hindered by the geldings that he was dragging behind him and the deep snow sucking his legs in till his knees, the young boy could not run fast enough. The horse thieves snatched the throngs from his hands. When he tried to grab one of the mounted men, he received a hard kick that bowled him over into the snow. With whoops of triumph, the thieves galloped off, Temujin's geldings trailing after them.

Temujin was not hurt so much as he was sick at heart. He lay in the snow despairing and anguished. *How can I return home to give Eej this bad news? She will blame me for not being able to keep our only geldings safe.*

As his face chilled in the snow that melted with his breath and then froze again in the sub-zero air, he heard a cry just above his head. Thinking the thieves had returned, he tried to bury further into the snow, but a hand held his shoulder to pick him up. Temujin lifted his head and looked into the eyes of a boy nearly his own age.

'I am Jamukha,' he said. 'Who are you?'

'My name is Temujin,' replied the boy scrambling to his feet.

Jamukha mounted his horse and hauled Temujin up behind him. They cantered across the white expanse until a large flock of sheep came into sight. It was Jamukha's father's livestock. He was a wealthy man with many horses, sheep and a large family.

'A Mongol must always have a horse,' Jamukha remarked when they had reached his father's *ger*.

'We had horses, but the Tartars took them all. My family had some geldings but….' Temujin recounted the incident.

'Thieves! All of them,' declared Jamukha. 'But don't worry. I will give you some horses from my father's lot. You can take them to your family.' He offered Temujin a bowl of warm mare's milk.

Temujin, warming himself at the fire inside Jamukha's *ger*, stared at him in astonishment. After years of deprivation and being an outcast, here was somebody who was actually helping him. A warm feeling surged through him; gratitude for gaining a friend and his generous offer. He turned to Jamukha and blurted, 'Will you be my brother?'

The boy did not reply. Temujin was surprised to see him slide out his hunting knife. *Is he going to attack me?* He wondered, puzzled at his new friend's response. Jamukha laid the sharp edge of the knife across his own left palm and closed his fist. Then he jerked the knife downwards. When he opened his palm, blood oozed out of the deep cut. He picked up a bowl of milk and let a few drops of blood drip into it. Then he offered the bowl to Temujin whose eyes shone with emotion. He placed the bowl before him and took out his own knife. Slashing his own palm, he let his blood drop into the same milk. Then he picked up the bowl and after draining half of it, offered it to Jamukha. The boy took the bowl in two hands and drank the liquid to its dregs.

Looking at Temujin, he declared, 'Now we are *anda*... blood brothers and nobody can separate us.'

Placing his bloody palm against Jamukha's red palm, Temujin clasped it hard and said, '*Anda!*' Looking deep into Jamukha's eyes, he said, 'When I become the Khan, I will make you my Second-in-Command.'

Jamukha stared at this boy in rags, without even a horse to his name, making such a preposterous statement and burst into guffaws. But when he saw the gravity on his friend's face, he stopped laughing and nodded his head. Then the boys wiped their hands with a rag and went out to Jamukha's father's corral. There, Jamukha picked out two pale-tan geldings and put their leather ropes in Temujin's hands, 'For you,' he said laconically.

Temujin went back to his family with this amazing tale of friendship. Over time, Jamukha helped Temujin's family in every way he could. Temujin reciprocated Jamukha's loyalty with equal fervour for after many years he had found a friend.

Temujin never doubted that he would one day become the Khan of all Mongolia. *Didn't Aav tell me that I had been chosen for this purpose by the great Khökh Tenger?* Hoelun constantly fanned Temujin's aspirations, too. She was convinced that only by realising the divine will predicted by the shaman at her son's birth can their family regain the wealth and power that they had lost. She never let him forget that he was intended for a great destiny. 'You have been chosen by Khökh Tenger to be a conqueror like no other. It is a divine decree that you will one day rule Mongolia,' she would whisper to him when he shivered in their *ger* while freezing winter winds blew through the tears in the walls.

When his stomach rumbled, and he looked askance at the little food that was his portion, she would say, 'Only for a few days, Temujin. Bear these hardships. They will make you so strong that no misfortune will touch you ever. You will learn to survive in the vilest conditions. Always call on Khökh Tenger when you see no way before you and He will open a path for you.'

Temujin would recall the stories related by Yesugei when he was a child. He knew it was his duty to finish what his great-grandfather, Kabul Khan had begun; one, unified Mongolia.

One very cold night, the family woke up to the thudding of hoofs and loud shouts as horses pushed through the snow towards their *ger*. Hoelun ran out and in the light of the flaming torches held by the horsemen, she recognised the ferocious face of Targutai. She rushed back inside and shook Temujin awake. 'Go! Go from here. Run into the mountains. It is the Taychuits and they are seeking you.'

Temujin stumbled out into the dark, freezing night and began to struggle up the slippery slopes. There were no trees or undergrowth to shelter him as there would have been in summer. The Taychuits knew this and so they had come after him in this cold season. Still, he went higher and higher up the Black Mountain to put a distance between himself and his pursuers. Finally, he found a small cave and tried to fit himself inside it.

All night he stayed there, shivering in the freezing temperature while the Taychuits searched for him on the slopes. He trembled when he heard their grunts close by and melded into his rocky hideout. By dawn, he could not hear them anymore. He was stiff with cold and weak with hunger. Slowly, he came out of the cave and listened for the sounds of horsemen. When he was sure they had left, he began to descend taking a circuitous route to reach his mother's home. But just as he slid to the bottom of the other side of the mountain, he heard a shout. Before he could get to his feet and run, he was surrounded by the Taychuits.

'How long can the cub hide?' rang out Targutai's hateful voice. Everyone laughed as he was scooped up easily by one of the horsemen. Bound and seated behind the man on a bucking horse, Temujin became a prisoner of the vicious Taychuits.

The next morning found the fourteen-year-old captive with a *cangue* round his neck. This was a collar made of a pair of thick wooden planks each with a half-circle to fit around Temujin's neck and bolted together. It was not so heavy as uncomfortable. Sorkan-shira, an elderly Taychuit, and his family were given charge of the boy with explicit instructions to feed him well, so that he grew quickly. Targutai was still adhering to the law of the land. He would fight and kill Temujin only when he had grown into a man. All day long, tied by a long rope to a pole dug into the frost-hardened ground, Temujin was forced to work at household jobs supervised by Sorkan-shira's wives. One day, he would be made to hack meat; another day he would be ankle deep in a disgusting mixture of horse-dung with dried hay to knead it for dung cakes for the cooking fires; some days he would be cutting logs from a tree trunk. But each day, the old Sorkan-shira would bring him hot stews or roast meat three times a day. The *cangue* prevented Temujin's hands from reaching his mouth, so the old man would feed him. Sometimes, the boy would refuse to eat knowing about his fate on growing taller and bigger but Sorkan-shira would persuade him with soft words.

Every other day, Targutai would arrive to bait him, 'So where is the wolf cub's teeth now? Does he snarl?'

When he did not find Temujin's height increasing fast enough, he would shout at the old man, 'Why is he not growing taller? Are you giving him the extra food I send or do your children swallow it all?'

The old man would shake his head, but Targutai would kick him into the dust and stomp off. Only Temujin, the silent spectator, saw the glint of hatred in the old man's rheumy eyes as he scowled at Targutai's retreating back. Not just this. Escape was always topmost in the boy's mind and he was alert to everything going on in the camp trying to find his means to flee. Since Temujin began to observe the clansmen, he realised that they were not satisfied with Targutai's leadership. He sought for the reasons and intuitively deduced it was due to Targutai's arrogance who claimed the rights of being chief of the clan based simply on his birth. His belief was not unusual; birthright was paramount among all Mongol clans. Only the son of a clan chief could succeed his father. Yet, there were chiefs like his father who also earned that right by dedicating their lives to the well-being of the clan. In Targutai's case, as the clan chief he felt he had the first right to everything of the clan irrespective of the needs of the other clanspeople. This made the people resentful and eventually they could revolt against him. It consoled Temujin suffering imprisonment to see his odious opponent hated so much but it also made him reflect on how one could be a better leader. He realised that to attain a man's loyalty, a leader must acknowledge his meritorious deeds. Besides, a good leader should never forget to reward a good turn or a loyal act.

All this learning was very useful, but it wouldn't help to release him from his doeful situation. By then after days of caring for the boy, Sorkan-shira, his wives and children had begun to feel an affection for the boy. One full moon night, the clan was celebrating Red Circle Day by feasting and drinking around the campfire. Sorkan-shira left his son, a young man, in charge of the prisoner. But the young guard could not resist the lure of *airag* that all the nomads were getting drunk on. He decided to join the fringes of the feast. Untying Temujin's rope from the pole, he held it in his hand so that he would know if Temujin tried to flee. Sorkan-shira's son got himself some bowls of *airag*. After a few hours of drinking, he lolled half asleep near Temujin who sat on the ground watching him. The boy looked around and saw that the others were also drunk or sleeping off their drunkenness in the *gers*. This was his chance. Temujin jerked the rope out of the man's hands, clouted him on the head with the *cangue* and ran across the grasslands. He heard the fallen man cry out, 'The prisoner has escaped.'

Temujin knew that soon they would take up the chase. On his feet, he would not be able to outrun horsemen with the weight of the *cangue* around his neck. Still Temujin ran as fast as he could along the snow-bound banks of the Onon until the thudding of the hooves began closing in. The white blanket of snow was the worst place to hide in. Even a speck on it would show up for kilometres. Desperate, Temujin dashed into the river, broke the ice and dived into the glacial waters. His wooden *cangue* helped him float just under the surface of the slow-moving waters keeping only his nose above the water level. He thought he was well-hidden until a shadow fell over him. Temujin opened his eyes to see a face above him; it was Sorkan-shira's wrinkled visage. As astonished as the boy, the old man whispered, 'No wonder they say fire burns in your eyes and light shines in your face! No wonder they are jealous of you!' Putting a finger to his lips, he whispered, 'You just lie here and I won't say a word.' Rising to his feet, he began to shout, 'He must be on the slopes. Let's go to that side.'

Thus Sorkan-shira diverted the search away from Temujin's hiding place. The young boy never forgot his debt to the old man and his family. After long hours of hunting for their captive, the Taychuits returned to their camp empty-handed. Temujin, half-frozen, his woollen clothes sodden, the *cangue* still around his neck, emerged from the Onon only by dusk. With chattering teeth and unable to stop himself from shaking uncontrollably, he found a deep cave to shelter during the night. He tried to light a fire, but the twigs were moist, and nothing would set ablaze. Temujin was convinced he would die in the frigid night. All his senses were at the edge of an abyss. All he could see before him was a deep pit. Its velvety darkness invited him to embrace it and give up this unending struggle. Kneeling on the ground in a shivering heap, he clasped his hands together. Bowing his head, he uttered, 'Oh Lord! Oh Khökh Tenger! Light my way…lead me. Show me how to reach my destination.'

He was so absorbed in his prayers that he did not see or hear the animal step gracefully up to the cave entrance. It was a large, grey wolf. Cold moonlight glittered on its thick winter fur turning it to silver spikes. Its nostrils quivered, and red lights glowed in its eyes as it observed the boy half-kneeling, half-lying on the frosty floor. It stood staring at Temujin for infinite moments before slinking away.

Fatigued, aching and chilled to the bone, Temujin slept deeply till dawn crept into the gloomy cave. His eyes flicked open. Gazing at the long, sunny fingers reaching out to touch him, a wonderful feeling of lightness and joy overwhelmed him. The boy sat up and then looked down at himself, amazed. The *cangue* lay broken into several pieces on the floor beside him. He looked around…*had somebody come in during the night? Who? Was it Khökh Tenger? It could only be He who could have worked this miracle.* Temujin's hands plucked the clothes sticking to his stiff body and found that they had dried somewhat during the night. He got to his feet and found new strength surging through his body. The pale sky was lightening with sunlight as he turned his feet homewards. It took him a few days of travelling by night and hiding by day to reach his mother's *ger*.

The idea of taking sweet revenge on Targutai did play on his mind once he was safe and at home, but he thrust it away resolutely. Revenge would be worth it only if it could give the family back security and an opportunity to build what had been lost. 'For that,' Hoelun reminded him, 'you will need something more than mere bravery or a warrior's skills. You will need the social and political skills of a true leader. You will need to build in yourself the ingenuity to attract followers.' Temujin had already begun thinking how that could be done.

10

The snowy peaks of the Hindu Kush were behind them. Thundering along the verdant forest paths of the foothills was the contingent of Mongol warriors mounted on the powerful stallions that they had looted from the conquered Islamic kingdoms. Genghis Khan galloped ahead of the armed cavalry accompanied by his commanders. The heavy siege weapons; bows, battering rams and wagons of armaments and food had been left behind looping slowly down the lower ridges of the mountain range. Since the Mongol army was now in regions controlled by its own iron fist, it was not seeking to join battle or lay siege. Thus, it could afford to travel light and fast. The warriors carried their bows, quivers of arrows and swords which were enough to quell any daring rebels.

Enkhtuya bounced uncomfortably on a horse behind the giant Shigi. She closed her eyes and tried to balance, fearing she would slip off the saddle at the next jolt. As it was she was keeling over with nausea in the cloud of fetid odours that reeked from the man. *Don't they ever bathe?* She wished she could have ridden on her own horse. She looked over her shoulder at Bolorma, similarly seated behind another horseman but the old woman seemed quite relaxed. In fact, she was sleeping. Shigi had informed the Princess during lunch break that they would reach Samarkand by nightfall. Enkhtuya had heard so much about the golden city of Samarkand that she was waiting eagerly for a glimpse of it. Soon they were passing serais, mosques and sprawling villas. Enkhtuya guessed that they were on the outskirts of Samarkand. What struck her was the deserted look that most of the buildings wore. She could see no people. *How strange! Where has everyone gone?*

Further down the road, they passed a caravan consisting of several camels and horses laden with goods. The animals and men had moved off the road to give way to the military cavalcade. Bent down in deep *kurnishes,* the camel drivers and a few richly dressed merchants stood on both sides while they passed between them.Enkhtuya was relieved to see that the area was not completely uninhabited, though these looked more like travellers not residents. She wondered aloud why they were paying respects to a Mongol Emperor, an outsider.

Shigi explained, 'These men are traders whose business takes them on journeys from Khwarezm through Khara Khitai. They cross the mighty Gobi Desert and take their goods to faraway kingdoms like that of the Jins in the Far East to barter silks, copper bowls, and jewellery for furs, amber and sheepskins.'

'I know! I know!' interrupted Enkhtuya, impatiently.

Shigi clamped his jaws. He disapproved of women who spoke unnecessarily, especially if they interrupted him. However, he continued, 'Earlier, their trading routes were riddled with raids by dacoits and unruly nomads. The merchants could not fight them, and they did not have enough guards to protect them against these threats. So many of them lost their goods and several merchants died in the attempt to bring in business from far-off lands. But ever since the Great Khan has come, the roads have become safe.'

'I don't understand.' Enkhtuya shook her head. 'How does your Khan's coming make the roads safe?'

'Our Lord has a wonderful way to keep in touch with his commanders and armed forces even when they are *alds* and *alds* away. He has set up a fast messenger service with riders on ponies. They ride all over the vast lands that we have conquered and administer from Khwarezm to the Jin kingdom. That way he is in constant contact with all his forces wherever they may be battling. Now, these fast riders need to change horses regularly. To provide fresh horses and rest houses to them relay camps have been set up for them all along the routes. Since these camps are well guarded they keep dacoits and lawlessness at bay. They also provide resting places for travellers. Now all travellers, merchants and caravans pass safely through the secure passages provided by the system that we have set up according to our Lord's plans.'

'Oh! A messenger service!'

'Yes. Our messengers can cover about 1200 *alds* in one day,' said Shigi, proudly.

'No wonder the merchants were bowing so deeply to your Khan,' mused Enkhtuya.

'No doubt about it. They are immensely grateful to our Emperor. I have heard that our armies have now reached a river called Volga on the western side of the Caspian Sea. At the moment, they are engaged in fighting the red-faced Russians. Soon we will have people from the land of the Volga and even Russians travelling to the Jin Empire. What a day that would be when our Lord will be worshipped across the whole world!' Shigi's eyes were shining as he visualised the future of the Mongolian Empire.

'Hummph!' derided Enkhtuya, 'It is not that easy to conquer the whole world.... Imagine! Your Lord was so afraid that he could not cross even the Indus River and you expect him to conquer the world? The whole world!' Her tone cut Shigi to the quick. He opened his mouth to reprimand her but closed it when he recalled that the

Khan had given her the status of a *Guunj*. Not for the first time, he wondered why his leader was so lured by the Sultan's wife. Granted, she was attractive but the way he was showering gifts on her was unreasonable. Still, he was nobody to doubt the Emperor's reasons; they must be justified if the Lord has decided so. Nevertheless, his mouth tightened, and he decided not to say another word to this silly, arrogant girl.

Enkhtuya had already forgotten Shigi as the minarets and domes of Samarkand etched a silhouette on the horizon. She smiled in anticipation. Soon she could see in the distance that the Mongol cavalry riding several horsemen abreast had narrowed to three rows as they filed through the main street of Samarkand. In anticipation of marvels, her eyes took in both sides of the street. But in moments Enkhtuya's smiles dried up. Bewildered, she wondered, *where are the teeming bazaars that sell golden birds and pigeon-egg pearls? Where are the stately mansions? Where are the gorgeous palaces I had heard about? For that matter, where are the citizens of wealthy Samarkand?* All she saw were burned-out shells of buildings, hollow walls, gaping holes, caved-in floors and piles of rubble. Then she squinted at something moving on the heaps of debris...*what was it?* She made out a human figure scrabbling amongst the broken bricks, metal and tiles. Then her eyes picked out dozens of men, women and children in tattered rags grubbing in the piles of rubbish. They looked like rats digging for morsels in a giant, stinking heap of rotten leftovers. Sick to the heart, Enkhtuya turned her face away.

The truth was that only a few of the proud palaces, mosques and mansions of the grand city of Samarkand remained standing after Genghis Khan's juggernaut had rolled into it around 1221 CE. When its ruler, Shah Mohammad had escaped, the merchant princes and clerics of the city had sued for peace. Yet, when the Mongol commanders and troopers entered the city, they took their choice of treasures, wealth and women from the city. With no eye of appreciation for the works of artistry, during their occupation of the many grand palaces, the Mongol soldiers had carelessly destroyed much of the beautiful fretwork, intricately worked mosaics and slender minarets just to intimidate the citizens into subjugation. Genghis Khan had spared the city. However, it has been said that its population of 350,000 had been reduced by three-fourths due to the havoc that his forces brought in their wake.

The cavalry was now approaching the massive gates leading out of the city. They had entered Samarkand and had cut across the urban localities. Enkhtuya was surprised enough to blurt out, 'Are we not staying the night in Samarkand?'

Shigi did not reply to her query. Instead, he pedantically declaimed, 'Well, the city and the surrounding areas are being administered by a Khitan commander. He is called A-Hai and is a very capable man. He has used resources such as the skills of the Chinese, Khitans and Tanguts who joined our forces to manage the farmlands around the city. They know how to produce food that we need for our men stationed in a city who do not have access to the yields of the countryside. He has put Chinese artisans to work at rebuilding the city. You see, that is what happens when we take strong, skilful men from the kingdoms we conquer and put them to work like A-Hai is doing,' explained Shigi.

'Very clever, this A-Hai!' retorted Enkhtuya, drily. 'But my question is why are we leaving the city?'

'Oh! A-Hai had proposed to put us up at the main palace of the Sultan,' said Shigi.

'Oh good! Finally, a night under a proper roof,' sighed the girl.

He went on with a spiteful gleam in his narrow eyes, 'But, he knows that the Khan prefers a tent under the open skies. So, he has arranged for tents to be put up on the banks of the Amudar'ya River. We will have to ride some kilometres out of the city to reach the camp.' He liked the way the girl's face fell as all expectations of spending a comfortable night vanished. *Such an irritating girl…how dare she criticise our Lord!*

Genghis Khan had just concluded a meeting with his generals and the governor of Samarkand. They were giving him the latest reports on the progress of the Mongol troops beyond the Caspian Sea. The governor assured him that all the news that had been brought by the pony messengers was favourable. His generals were pushing on through the Caucasus Mountains towards the Bulgars.

'There is still much to be done in the city,' Genghis Khan remarked, as A-Hai bowed to him.

'The Chinese architects have promised that everything will be rebuilt by the year end. If not, they will be flogged. But the fields are yielding already, my Lord. In the morning light, you can see for yourself around the camp. The wheat in the fields is green,' A-Hai smiled.

'Alright, I will take a tour before I leave,' agreed the ruler.

'I shall myself take you around, my Lord,' promised the Khitai, backing out of the large, round tent simulating a Mongolian *ger*.

When he was alone, the Khan sat back in an ornate chair, one of the several that were scattered around the enclosure along with a low table inlaid with gems and mosaic and a similarly engraved massive, four-poster bed. There were rich carpets on the floor and metal filigree lamps all around. He looked around the tent and grimaced. 'I am just a simple nomad,' he murmured to himself. He preferred plain clothes and unpretentious, minimal furnishings. His senses were revolted with the cloying, rich luxury of his surroundings. They suffocated him, but he would have to bear them for the night. 'Better that I sleep on the ground. Soft beds keep me awake,' he told himself, clapping his hands loudly.

Instantly, a long queue of slaves, captives taken from regions under the Mongol rule, entered the tent bearing aloft several dishes. Under the supervision of the Khan's steward, the men silently spread the platters and bowls on the table and left the tent.

'Has the *Guunj* been informed?' Genghis Khan asked.

'She is here, my Lord' said the steward.

As if on cue, Princess Enkhtuya stood framed in the doorway. Her teal-blue *deel* lit up the interior of the tent. An embroidered, short coat tightly encased her tiny waist and flared over hips displaying her seductive curves. Her hair had been teased into several long braids interwoven with bright coral beads as well as gleaming silver ornaments and piled on top of her head in an elegantly high coiffure. Her feet were shod in a pair of shiny red engraved Mongolian leather *gutals* with upturned toes and thick soles. The girl looked poised and confident; a far cry from the dirty, ragged, terror-stricken victim of a few weeks ago.

Even Genghis Khan could not help splintering his cold mien with half a smile and a cocked brow, remarking, 'Well, well. What do we have here? A perfect Mongol lady! Today, *Guunj* looks every inch the princess that she is.'

A quick burst of pleasure passed through Enkhtuya but she quashed it instantly. She reminded herself, *this man is a murderer, a ravager, maybe even a rapist.*

But his words gave her courage. She lifted her chin and demanded, 'Why do you want me?'

'Now, don't spoil the refined, graceful picture you make by behaving like a spoilt child. Come and sit here. You can see the meal on the table. Can we eat in harmony instead of arguing?' Today even the Khan's rebuke sounded reasonable.

Reluctantly, Enkhtuya approached her side of the table. For the first time, she noticed the opulent furnishings and carpets in the tent. Her eyes widened, *this is different from his crude and spartan living space of before.* A thought struck her bringing a silent sneer to her face, *his goons must have looted all this from one of Samarkand's merchant princes and now he is using his plunder to entice me to his will.*

'Sit down,' the Khan ordered sternly, as if he had discerned her contempt.

Suddenly, the girl felt immensely fatigued. Her shoulders drooped, and the corners of her luscious lips turned down. She pulled out the chair, brooding, *how long will he play this game? I am so tired of being the mouse to this wildcat…I can't keep this up much longer….*

Her eyes fell on the plate before her. *Plates? Since when had this Mongol rustic begun to use plates? He is certainly making an effort to impress me…*and she subdued a derisive yet nervous giggle gurgling up her throat. Then she realised that only her place had a plate. The Khan was carving slices of meat out of a large joint put before him whether of a deer or a boar, the girl could not make out…the slices dripped black blood from the point of his knife. Placed before him were bowls of creamy mare's milk and *airag*. His focus was on his knife and he did not glance at her.

Her stomach gave a deceitful rumble forcing Enkhtuya to look down at what was edible to her taste. Pleasantly surprised, her eyes slid from a bowl of figs to another filled with golden pears to yet another overflowing with blood-red cherries. There was a bunch of fat bananas too and lo behold! A couple of poultry legs fried crisp and brown. And there were even those small bird eggs. And wine! It was a feast, and her appetite was quite sharp after travelling all day on horseback. Without wasting words, she dug into it. For nearly half an hour, the duo gave its full attention to the food. Finally, licking the delicious spicy oil off her fingers, Enkhtuya began to observe the domineering man opposite her. His jaws moved slowly and rhythmically as he cut still another piece off the haunch. She tried to gauge his mood, *was he satiated enough to grant me something I desire badly?* She so wanted a mare that she could ride by herself, instead of sitting behind the smelly Shigi.

'Ummhh…,' she began and then said it all in a rush, 'Can I have my own horse tomorrow?' She held her breath.

Pausing the motion of his knife, he looked at her speculatively, wordlessly. The Princess stared back defiantly. After a few moments of the eye-to-eye match, Enkhtuya's eyes dropped. To stop her hands from trembling, she picked up a pear and tried to gouge a piece out of it with her fingernails. Genghis Khan moved. Like magic, a small knife was held out to her…by the hilt not the blade! As her puzzled gaze went to the knife and then up to his face, he nodded towards the pear in her hand. *Oh! He is offering me a knife to slice the pear!* Enkhtuya slowly took the knife, began to pare the fruit, putting thin slices into her mouth, completely mystified by the Khan's gesture.

She kept peeping at the deadpan face from under her lashes as she chewed on the pear wedges she cut out with the small, sharp knife. Her eyes strayed to his belt and she scanned the several scabbards hanging from it. Obviously, he kept a collection of knives for use. She was stunned at his supreme assurance. By giving her the knife, he had displayed that he was not afraid of her. He was convinced that she was completely in his power. She recalled his claim that he had the strength to overcome her, if needed. I *wonder…wonder if I can turn his presumption to my benefit,* Enkhtuya reflected as she kept the knife down gently next to her plate and slowly slid it under the rim.

Frightened that his sharp eyes would detect her duplicity, she knocked about her mind seeking something to distract him from the knife. Enkhtuya blurted out the first thing that came to her mind, 'Do you never feel any regret or sorrow for the thousands of innocent people that you and your warriors kill?' *There! That should be enough to make him argue violently enough to forget about the knife.* She patted herself mentally.

However, he did not rise to the bait. He kept masticating the meat between his jaws washing it down with mouthfuls of milk. Eventually, he raised the bowl of *airag* and drained it, wiping his mouth with the sleeve of his woollen *deel.* His stomach let loose a series of contented burps. Enkhtuya shuddered delicately and averted her eyes. She could hardly bear to be in the same room as this gross Mongol, but her brain was ticking overtime devising how she could steal the knife.

Genghis Khan leaned back in the chair and fingered the pipes inside the pouch at his belt. After selecting one, he began to pack it with tobacco. He lit it from one of the nearby lamps and took a long drag. The wide mouth of the pipe glowed red as smoke from his nostrils filled the room with the pungent aroma of the weed. He squinted at the girl. 'Didn't we go over all this the last time?' He drawled lazily but Enkhtuya was startled. *Had he guessed at her game?* With wide, blue eyes, she stared at him silently as he puffed a couple of times on his pipe. I *have to carry this off. It is my only chance,* she reminded herself.

Clearing her throat to give herself courage, she dived in. 'Your war is with the rulers. What harm have the people done to you? Why does the Mongol army kill common people, pillage their homes and rape their women? You are their Emperor. You can stop them. Only a monster with no heart allows that.'

Genghis Khan's eye slits narrowed even more to observe her, as watchful as a hawk. Enkhtuya felt a leap of panic. *Have I gone too far?* But when he spoke, his voice did not betray any emotion. 'As I said the other day, men, women and children will be killed during a war. Humans are the most dispensable fraction of a country's wealth. In fact, they hold hardly any value for my soldiers. If rulers want to protect their people, they must submit to me. I have spared the cities that have been prudent enough to open their gates to me. Look at Samarkand.'

'Yes, Samarkand,' repeated Enkhtuya, bitterly. 'I have heard that only a quarter of its entire peoples have survived the Great Khan's coming.'

'You see,' he explained slowly as if speaking to a recalcitrant child, 'I have to satisfy the demands of my warriors, too. A conquering army will always loot and rape. Plunder and women are its rewards. . .its earnings. That is the reason they follow me. . .give me their fealty.'

Enkhtuya glowered at him. The Khan ignored her, his eyes following the smoke wavering in the still air rising to the roof of the tent. The girl's hand went towards her plate and her fingers closed on the sharp blade of the knife.

Still observing the smoke, he reflected, 'Loyalty must always be compensated. I have always honoured my commitments and promises, even those that I made in the childhood. I learnt early in life that men do not follow you because your birthright makes you their leader. You become a leader only when you fulfil the promises made to them, win their faith and convince them that you are taking them to a better future. Khökh Tenger chose me to rule the Mongol Empire but it has been up to me to bring my people together and work towards fulfilling that destiny.'

His sight clouded as if he could see beyond the walls of the tent to a time yet to come. The girl recalled the deep *kurnishes* by the merchants on the road. *Yes, they were grateful to him for the safe passage his conquests have allowed.*

Enkhtuya's hand moved swiftly and covertly. The knife was safely in the pocket of her tunic under the *deel*. She breathed out her relief and tried to divert him, 'But what about compassion or kindness? Apparently, Mongols have none of that.'

Again, his eyes raked her face and she was frightened that he knew her secret. However, Genghis Khan deigned to respond to her. 'I have been taught from a very young age to erase all pity or kindness for enemies and those disloyal to me. At times, I have discovered disloyalty even among my friends and family. I have not spared them and dealt strictly with any traitors. Or for that matter those who may pose a threat to my future plans. Sorrow, regrets, sympathy are alien to me,' he declared, drily.

Yes, thought Enkhtuya, rancour rising in her breast, *he did not spare even my baby son.* A sudden terror seized her.

What if he came to know of my deceitful act? What will he do if he knows I have been disloyal despite all his care?

Without a warning, the man rose and with a quick movement, belying the effects of the bowls of *airag* he had quaffed, came around to her side. The girl stared up at him, her eyes darkly violet with fear. His hand came towards her and she stiffened thinking, *this is it!* His fingers, calloused with lacerations of reins and bowstrings, touched her soft cheek and traced a line from the corner of her eyes to her jawline. The Princess closed her eyes, while her fingers closed on the knife in her pocket. The skin at her throat prickled expecting a rough hand to close on it. But his touch, feather-light, soft and surprisingly tender, stopped at her lips. And then she could no longer feel his fingers. Her skin tingled all along the path they had traced. Enkhtuya lifted her lashes, cerulean iris looking into the dark depths of Genghis Khan's narrow eye-slits wherein a peculiar passion lurked.

He straightened abruptly. 'It is late, and you should go to bed, *Guunj*.' His voice sounded different; a little ragged as if he had run a long distance. Gratefully, Enkhtuya rose and began to walk to the door, one hand holding the knife in her pocket.

'*Guunj!*' She stopped in dismay and swivelled around. 'You will have your own *aduu* tomorrow,' he said. Relieved, she nodded her thanks. He did not see it for he had already turned away. Allowing a horse to a captive who could use it to attain freedom seemed a routine decision for him. Enkhtuya was perplexed by his equanimity. Then she shrugged, *he was still a barbarian*. Quickly, Enkhtuya ducked through the door and made her escape.

11

Two seasons had passed since Temujin had returned from the Taychuits. It was spring once more and he was no longer a boy. Lean and rippling with muscles, he could feel vigour pulsing through his sinews. A hard life lived outdoors amidst daily threats had its own merits. The strapping youth leaned back against the sweet-smelling tender shoots pricking the dark earth. Idly chewing on green leaves of the pungent wild garlic root, he gazed down at the bay-geldings grazing on the slopes. Below them were herds of fat sheep dotting the meadows. His brothers and sisters ran among them to keep them in one tight group. Full-throated, the song of a skylark winging away across the clear skies made him look up lazily. White feathery clouds scudded the translucent, sky-blue sphere reflecting in the crystal waters of the Blue Lake like a flock of fat geese. The sap was rising in all living things. In the forests the maple trees had sprung tender new leaves. White anemones, orange lilies and blue gentians dotted the spongy grasslands. Lambs frolicked around the ewes. How could Temujin remain unaffected? Börte's round face, merry eyes and her wide, sparkling smile haunted his dreams at night and his thoughts during the day. His family was in a better situation now with Jamukha's clan helping them. Now they had herds of sheep and nine horses; it could hardly be called wealth but was enough to keep them comfortable. Besides, all his siblings were old enough to focus on building the strength and security of the family.

Early that morning, Shigi had gone marmoset hunting with the best horse while Temujin was watching over the other eight. His spirits were high; the warm spring with all its tangy pheromones was back and he could expect a marmoset roast for his dinner today. After a long time, life seemed good. Thus, half-asleep in the mellow sunshine, Temujin did not notice the thieves creeping towards his horses until they cantered in. By the time he picked up his bow and notched an arrow, the horse-robbers had flung ropes around his eight geldings and had galloped off with them beyond the range of his arrows. Temujin was furious at his own carelessness. He was unable to follow them as the only mount left had been taken by his brother.

He had to wait for agonising hours before Shigi rode back. When his adopted brother heard about the raid, he at once, offered to chase the thieves but Temujin would not let him. After all, it was he who was supposed to guard the geldings. Besides, he was the eldest. So, he flung a leg over the saddle and whipped the horse into a headlong run across the meadows in the direction that the raiders had gone. He tracked them for two days, staying nights in hollows ringed by rocks, mostly awake and on guard against bears or other wild animals. He would eat the green, sour blackberries growing wild when his stomach rumbled but he constantly went down on all fours searching the soft soil for signs that the thieves had left behind carelessly. They would guide him to their route.

On the fourth day, he came upon a single tent and a large herd of horses. He remained hidden behind a boulder and observed them wondering whether they belonged to the raiders. But he soon realised that there was just one herdsman grazing them. He was a young man about his own age who was energetically riding around the herd keeping them together; an alert sentinel. Temujin left his hiding place and began to walk towards him. Seeing a man walk out of the trees, the herdsman stilled his horse waiting for him. When both were within earshot, the man called out, 'I am Boorchu. Who are you?'

'I am Temujin,' was the reply. 'And I am looking for horse thieves who have stolen eight of my bay geldings.'

'Oh. That is bad,' said Boorchu.

'Have you seen anyone like them passing this way?' asked Temujin.

Boorchu scratched his head, thinking. Then he said slowly, 'Well, yesterday some men did pass by with a large herd of horses. I think there were a few bay geldings among them.' He saw Temujin eagerly looking at him, and shrugged, 'They could be yours. But we have to see them to be sure.'

Temujin had already turned away to mount his horse but he stopped. 'We?' He asked puzzled.

'Yes. I hate horse thieves, too. Today they stole your geldings, tomorrow they will steal mine. We must teach them a lesson,' said Boorchu, earnestly.

'Yes, of course,' agreed Temujin as Boorchu called out to his father in the tent. The old man came out to see both the riders already at a distance.

By midday, the two youths came across the thieves. Once they had identified Temujin's geldings, they struck like lightning. Thundering down the slope they were among the herd before the men knew what was happening. The horses scattered at their sudden approach, making it easy to reach the centre of the herd where the geldings had been strategically placed. Sharp knives in hands, Boorchu and Temujin cut through the throngs tying them. Each one holding four horses, they veered off around the forested hillocks while the men shouted at each other trying to get together for a counterattack. The youths' horses flew across the grasslands, hooves scarcely touched the ground despite tugging four geldings behind them. Temujin and Boorchu easily escaped the thieves and reached Boorchu's father's tent by sun down.

Once they were seated inside, his geldings safely corralled and guarded, Temujin broached what was upper-most in his mind. 'Boorchu, four of the geldings are yours.'

Boorchu stared at him.

'My friend, you deserve a share of what we have rescued from the thieves. Without your help, it would have been impossible for me to get them back. Tell me, how many do you want?' Temujin insisted.

Boorchu's father gave Temujin an appraising look. *What deep-rooted ideas of fair play and justice!* 'Which clan are you from, young man? Who is your father?' he asked aloud.

'I am the son of Yesugei, the chief of Borjigins,' replied Temujin.

'Oho! Yesugei! I know of him...grandson of Kabul Khan,' exclaimed Boorchu's father thinking to himself, *this Temujin will go a long way...maybe become a Khan like his forefathers*.

But Boorchu shook his head. Putting an arm around Temujin's shoulders, he said, 'No, no, my friend. I went with you because I wanted to get back what belonged to you. And I detest horse thieves who want to grow rich stealing from other people. My father is rich, and I am his only son. I have all that I need. All the geldings are yours and will remain yours.'

Boorchu's father also nodded in agreement. 'May your friendship with Boorchu prosper. In this hard life, we need loyal friends who will be with us without expectation of any rewards. Temujin and Boorchu, your wealth will be your love for each other,' advised the wise, old man.

After spending the night with the father and son, Temujin went on his way with his eight geldings. As he hugged Boorchu, promising to return one day, he vowed to himself that he will always keep Boorchu by his side even when he became a Khan.

His family cheered Temujin's feat. After all, the eight geldings made up a considerable part of their belongings.

As languid spring melted into a summer blazing with colour and heat, a thought gnawed at Temujin's mind. Seven seasons had gone by since Yesugei's promise to the Ongirad Chief that they would take Temujin's bride home. He was past sixteen now and it was time for him to fulfil his own promise to Börte.

Hoelun noticed his restlessness and asked him, one evening, 'Why do you fidget so? Are ants crawling up your *deel*, Son?'

'I made a promise, *Eej*,' he muttered.

'Then fulfil it,' she responded, instantly.

Temujin looked up at her. 'You did not ask to whom I made this promise.'

Hoelun smiled at him. 'Son, it is your promise that matters, not the person it was made to. If you give your word to anyone, it is your duty to keep it. So be careful when you make a promise but never break it once made.'

Temujin nodded, his mother's words searing into his heart.

Next morning, he saddled his *aduu*, calling out to his mother, 'I am going to get my bride, *Eej*.'

By the time Hoelun and the rest of the astonished family came out of the *ger*, the bushy tail of Temujin's horse was just about to vanish between the trees edging the Blue Lake.

Dei-Tsetsan and his family were pleasantly surprised to see Temujin trot into their camp by evening. Börte's father had heard what had happened to Yesugei and the tragic events that had followed. He had assumed the worst and had already begun to look for another groom for his daughter. But when Börte came to know of it, she had shaken her head. Dei-Tsetsan had never been disobeyed by any of the women in his clan and certainly not his daughter. He had frowned at this defiance but his efforts to search a suitable boy for her had slowed down. Still, he was worried for Börte was seventeen and at a very marriageable age. So, the relief on his face when Temujin arrived was palpable.

He welcomed the tall, broad, handsome youth into his *ger* and plied him with bowls of sweet mare's milk. Temujin came straight to the point. 'I come here to keep my father's promise. I come here to wed your daughter, O Chief of the Ongirads.'

Dei-Tsetsan smiled and said, 'Let me ask my daughter. She has been refusing to marry all this time.' He clapped his hands.

A shadow fell across the *ger*. Temujin looked up and could not look away. *Who is this vision?* Slender as a young juniper yet voluptuously curved, she was a wood nymph. The summer *deel* hardly disguised the full bosom and wide hips that promised inherent passion in every line. His eyes travelled to her face; a perfect oval of glowing fairness, eyes glimmering with embers of some subdued fire edged by dark eyelashes curling upwards, a nose hardly discernible between high cheekbones that were twin spots of colour. But it was her red, luscious lips that made Temujin suck in his breath. A kind of tremor rose from below his stomach. He had never felt it before; this curious churning of his insides. *What is it?*

Dei-Tsetsan observed both the young man and his daughter with contentment. But the formalities had to be gone through. So, in a grave tone, he asked, 'Well, Daughter! Your betrothed has come after seven years to fulfil his father's promise.'

Temujin's brow creased into a frown to see a sudden trembling of her lips. *Oh no! She is going to refuse…*thought he. Then he realised to his mortification that the damsel was desperately trying not to smile.

'Do you agree to wed him?' Her father asked in a booming voice.

With the eyes of the men on her, one anxious and the other indulgent, the Mongol lass tilted her head once and then in a flurry of long braids flying and a tinkling of bells, turned on her heels and fled.

'Ho, ho, ho, ho!' laughed her father, delighted. The groom heaved a sigh of relief.

The shaman indicated that the very evening was a propitious time for the couple to bow to the Eternal Blue Heaven. Temujin ate and rested the day in the midst of Ongirad's hospitable clansmen.

When the sun was nearing the horizon, he came to stand before Dei-Tsetsan's *ger* accompanied by a few of Hoelun's distant relatives who posed as his family. The bride, now bedecked in a red *deel,* a short coat embroidered with silk and gold thread and new leather *gutals* stood before the *ger* entrance with her family. Her hair was curled and rolled into a chignon displaying a long, white neck and shell-like ears. Her thick eyelashes hid her eyes fanning out on her milky skin as was becoming of a shy bride. Temujin found it difficult to keep his eyes off this striking beauty who was soon to be his wife. He could not believe that this poised, lovely lady facing him was the laughing girl of his childhood. She distracted him so much that he constantly lost focus of the shaman's poetic litany as he reeled off both Temujin's and Börte's ancestral genealogies. It would prove not just their noble lineage but also establish the fact that they were from different clans. Finally, the old shaman invoked the blessing of Khökh Tenger on the wedding and it was done.

Temujin was welcomed into his father-in-law's *ger* with his bride with bear hugs and best wishes from the relatives and guests. Dei-Tsetsan offered his son-in-law a new set of *deel* and trousers along with a bow and a quiver of arrows.

This ceremony was followed by the *pièce de résistance* of the occasion—a feast consisting of several varieties of meats, such as venison, wild boar, duck and wild geese accompanied by fresh summer vegetables and juicy fruits followed by bowls of mare's milk and *airag*. The haunch of an antelope roasted mostly rare was passed around. The meat was so raw that it was difficult for the guests to even slice pieces off with their knives. Many used their sharp, strong teeth to bite off pieces and chewed on them stubbornly. This particularly tough piece of meat was commonly served at weddings to signify that the conjugal union being celebrated was so strong that nothing could tear it apart. It was no different at Temujin's and Börte's wedding and the guests who were the members of the entire Ongirad clan laughed and cracked nuptial jokes as they tried to tear apart the antelope meat. Even as the platters emptied, the *airag* flowed profusely going well into the night nearly till dawn.

Börte had long retired to the nuptial *ger* allotted to the newly-wedded couple but Temujin was held back by the young men who would not finish drinking to his health. By the time, he staggered onto the blankets spread on the ground, he was dead drunk. At sunrise, he was woken by a bowl of milk held in the hands of a smiling Börte. Despite a splitting headache, Temujin realised that they had to start riding back soon if he wanted to get his bride home by nightfall. He decided to dunk his aching head in the watering trough at the cattle corral and began to scramble up. Börte held him down by his shoulder. She was kneeling by him and when he looked up at her, she parted the neckline of her *deel*. Hanging around her neck by a red string was the wishbone that he had given her seven long years ago. 'This keepsake has always imparted to me a deep faith that you will return. I knew a day would come when you would return to claim me,' she said softly. Temujin's heart could hardly contain the love that spilled over for this beautiful girl whose loyalty and trust in him was unshaken despite all the uncertainties.

Before the couple began their journey, Dei-Tsetsan called them into his *ger*. Inside was a large basket that held Börte's trousseau. Her father was a rich man and had given the couple many gifts. Nevertheless, something still needed to be done. He called Temujin to one corner of the tent. 'This is Börte's dowry,' he announced. From another basket, he held up with both arms a magnificent sable gown; jet black as the night when the storm is over, as sleek as still oil, soft and gleaming as baby's hair. It had long sleeves to cover the hands in the cold weather and a hem reaching mid-calf. When he placed it in Temujin's hands, the young man's arms sagged with its weight. *It must have taken a great deal of time and effort to hunt scores of elusive sables to make this gown*, thought

Temujin. Placing it carefully back in the basket, he thanked his father-in-law.

Finally, the couple set off with many a banter. As Temujin uttered the ritualistic words expressing his wish to stay back at his bride's home, her family drove the newly-married couple off with mock abuses. Animal dung was thrown at them, equivalent of nomadic confetti while Temujin kicked his *aduu* and whipped Börte's into a gallop. At midday, the couple halted by an icy brook to lunch on the packed meal given to them by the Ongirad women. They ate quickly, their appetite sharpened by the hard ride.

Once they were back on their mounts and cantering through the trees, Börte remarked softly, 'You have not touched me even once. Don't you like me?'

Temujin gave her a bashful smile and said, 'You are as exquisite as the delicate edelweiss. If I touch you, my rough hands will split you apart. I am afraid to hurt you.' Börte laughed. To Temujin it sounded like the tinkling of the Onon waters when pieces of broken ice float in them.

When they began to skirt the Blue Lake a sickle moon hung above the Black Mountain. Three stars just above the moon held up one of its horns. Börte stood still for a moment looking at the moon. Temujin also halted a few *alds* away uncertain about what had distracted his bride. As he watched her, she uttered, in a slow monotone, 'Obstacles are many in our path but...but we will overcome them, eventually. It will take time, but the conqueror will certainly rise. Victory will finally be ours.'

She turned to him, a white face and dark hollows with glowing luminous centres for eyes. Hairs at the back of Temujin's neck crackled in alarm. He could not reconcile the surreal sight before him with the pretty girl he had married just yesterday. *Who is this woman who tells the future? Is she a shaman?* He was thoroughly confused. Börte's *aduu* moved forward and the moonlight fell full on her face. It was the same lovely face that had allured him since yesterday. As she trotted up to him, he forced a small laugh and remarked, 'What? Are you reading the moonlight?'

Börte matched his laugh with her tinkling one, saying, 'Sometimes, I can read nature's signs. Sometimes, words come to my lips and I let them fall.' She shrugged. 'Let's go home.' Bemused, the young husband led the way up to his family's camp.

Temujin's sisters had seen them coming up the slope from the Blue Lake to the coppice where their *gers* were clustered. They rushed to tell Hoelun. So, the matriarch, with her children gathered around her, was waiting to receive her son and his bride when they trotted up to the small camp. She welcomed them into her *ger* with Temujin's sisters exclaiming over their new sister-in-law's fair complexion, rosy lips and elegant clothes. His brothers chaffed Temujin for his new status of a married man not realising that this was the impetus that would hurtle him faster towards his pre-ordained destination.

Inside the tent, Hoelun seated the new couple and offered them bowls of milk sweetened with herbs. In the light of the crackling fire dancing in the central pit of the *ger,* Börte observed her mother-in-law; her graceful dignity despite her sorrows, the comeliness of her visage and the wisdom in her fine eyes. She went to the basket and returned with the gorgeous sable gown in her hands. Offering it to Hoelun, she said, 'It is a gift for you.'

Hoelun smiled; a slow, sweet smile of understanding. Accepting the gown from Börte's arms, she caressed it with loving hands, saying softly, 'It is the most valuable gift I have ever received.' She appraised the deep sensibility in her daughter-in-law's dark, grateful eyes and told herself, I *am sure we will get on well…the two of us.*

12

Börte found her young husband sitting at the entrance to their *ger* and staring at the herds of gazelle grazing in the tall, summer grass in the cool of the dawn. She wondered if their sleepless night of hot passion had tired him out. Her heart overflowed with love for this strong yet infinitely gentle husband of hers. *How lucky I have been that he is not as domineering as most Mongol men are!* She laid a gentle hand on his shoulder. Temujin roused himself from the depths of his thoughts and looked up into the dear face of not just his wife but his best friend. Reading the silent query on her face, he sighed, 'It is time.'

Börte did not need any explanation, their spirits were so much in tune. Instantly, she acknowledged, 'Yes. It is time, Temujin. You must begin the work for which Khökh Tenger has marked you out.'

'I am now a married man and the head of my family. I must call for all my clansmen who have scattered due to the deceit of the Taychuits and gather them around me. *Aav* always said that being a Borjigin, it is my ancestral duty to bring unity to all the Mongol clans,' Temujin reflected.

'I agree,' said Börte. 'Send word to the Ongirads to join you. My *Aav* will ensure their loyalty to you.'

Temujin stood up and stretched. *Yes. It is time,* he told himself. 'Shigi,' he called. His devoted brother, hardly a youth, came running. 'Take a message to Boorchu. Tell him to come here with his men.' As Shigi went scuttling to carry out his mentor's command, Temujin said, 'I will meet with Jamukha, myself.'

That night, as the family sat around the fire tearing into the roasted gazelle that Hoelun and her daughters had cooked, Temujin's three brothers, his surviving half-brother and Shigi compared notes. Boorchu had already come with his men, sworn fealty to Temujin and left. Dei-Tsetsan had sent a message that left no doubts about the Ongirad clan's support.

'Boorchu will be a general in my forces,' declared Temujin, 'Jamukha is now the head of his clan. His support, his clan and his forces are with us,' he added.

'So that is done,' said his half-brother Belgutai, satisfied. 'Two sworn brothers and the Ongirads are with us.'

'But it is not enough,' mused Temujin.

'What about Toghril of the Keraits?' suggested Hoelun. 'He had sworn friendship to your father.'

'Hmmm...,' Temujin considered.

Nevertheless, the very next day, he saddled his fastest *aduu,* and with Shigi by his side, Temujin was off to look for the man with the real clout in all Mongolia. He found Toghril in his palace on the banks of the Tuul River. As the young men dismounted before the unusual structure, Temujin was staggered by its sheer grandeur. Having seen only tents all his life, never had he seen such a dwelling. Several brick floors built one above the other towered above them. Only by tilting their necks off their shoulders could the brothers glimpse the roof covered with gleaming tiles. Three brick drains emerged from the building carrying the filth and waste from the palace.

'Never...never could I imagine something like this,' breathed Temujin in awe.

'Yes, brother. Neither have I,' echoed Shigi.

'When I am Khan, I will build a palace like this. Nay, I will build a city,' Temujin declared snapping his fingers. 'Now, let's go in. We have work to do.'

They entered through a doorway to be stopped by a pair of armed soldiers. 'What is your business?' asked one.

'I am Temujin, the son of Yesugei, your chief's sworn brother. I want to meet Chief Toghril.'

They had to wait for some time but were eventually granted audience with Toghril. He was an old man now but had lost none of his arrogance. After all, the Kerait leader commanded twenty thousand warriors and held sway from central Mongolia to the Chinese border of the Gobi Desert.

To the man sitting on a silk cushion surrounded by his commanders, Temujin and Shigi bowed humbly. Then Temujin said, 'O powerful Chief! I am Temujin, son of your friend and brother, Yesugei. It had been both your and my father's dream to gather together all the clans of Mongolia to form one nation. I come to seek your support in fulfilling that dream.' Very cleverly, he spoke as if it was also Toghril's desire to build a nation. But it did not cut any ice with the sly fox.

'Yesugei? Who is that?' growled Toghril.

Temujin was prepared for this refutation. Like a magician, he spun out the shining black sable gown from a basket. He had been prudent enough to bring along with him Börte's dowry. As he flung it on Toghril's lap, the spectators around him gasped in amazement. The chief's wrinkled face lit up as his fingers caressed the soft, rich fur. Temujin waited patiently, until the avaricious Kerait chief raised his eyes gleaming with greed and said, 'In return for the sable jacket, I will unite your scattered people.'

Thus, Temujin won over a slippery but powerful ally to his cause.

More and more people of the Borjigin clan who had separated from Hoelun and the family after Yesugei's death began to follow the twenty-two-year-old Temujin's leadership. Some men even came from the Taychuit clan. So, it was a large group that now moved to the headwaters of the Kherlen River to graze their herds on the western steppe land with easy access to the mountains in the north, straddling the route to the Burkhan Khaldun. The grass was green and plentiful here for the numerous livestock now owned by the consolidated clans.

News of Temujin's rise had reached the ears of the forest-dwelling Merkits. Ever since Yesugei had stolen Hoelun from Chiledu, he had been smarting to avenge his humiliation. The Merkits felt this was a good time to attack before Temujin became too strong. Just after dawn, horsemen holding burning torches rushed into the camp on the banks of the Kherlun River. As the *gers* emptied in panic and the people fled into the thick forests of the mountains for safety, Chiledu combed through the camp. At one point, he came across Hoelun who screamed, 'Chiledu? You?'

'Yes, it is I, Chiledu,' her old, first husband, crazed with revenge, yelled at her.

'But I am not seeking you, Woman, old and wrinkled that you are. I want Temujin. Where is he?'

'You will never get Temujin,' gloated Hoelun. 'He is not here. You won't find him.'

Chiledu lashed at her with his whip. Leaving a welt across her face, he wheeled his horse around, shouting to his men, 'Come on. He is not here. Set fire to the *gers* and let's go after Temujin.' And the Merkits dashed off leaving behind cinders of ransacked, burned *gers* flying desolately in the wind.

Temujin and Börte had gone to the slopes below Burkhan Khaldun. In the predawn coolness they had lain together on the soft, grassy carpet. In the afterglow of their lovemaking, Börte revealed that she was with child. Temujin felt a deep tenderness spread through him like sweet treacle. Cupping her radiant face in both palms, he looked down at her. His dark eyes were bright with tears of joy. They spilled down his cheeks and Börte laughed in contentment. 'Why are you crying, my powerful chief? I am only having a baby like so many other women.'

'No, my sweet. You are having our child, the fruit of our love,' said Temujin, smiling and wiping his cheeks.

All of a sudden, a whoop floated up in the rush of wind through the junipers. The lovers turned to look behind them. Coming up the slope was a whirlwind of horsemen waving swords and bows. Both scrambled up and Temujin shouted, 'Run! It is the Merkits!'

Quickly mounting their horses, they galloped up the slope chased by their pursuers. As soon as the couple was within range, an arrow flew over their heads. Temujin put an arrow to his bow, turned around in his saddle and exactly when his *aduu* was midstride in the air, he drew the string back and let go. His arrow found its mark in the neck of one of the Merkits' horses and the man tumbled as it collapsed under him. Another arrow wheezed past Börte's face to embed itself in Temujin's thigh. Börte screamed, 'Temujin!' Still pulling furiously at the reins, he slumped in his saddle.

Both horses pulled up short as they reached the edge of the cliff from where the scrubland fell away into a kind of valley. Börte took a quick decision. She whipped the flank of Temujin's *aduu* and shouted, 'Take him home!' Then she unclamped her heels from her horse's belly bringing it to standstill. She waited on top of the cliff to distract the wildly hooting Merkits climbing up the slope. Temujin's horse half-slid and half-walked down the incline of gravel and grass into the valley. It galloped with the injured man into the safety of a forest of junipers and firs that climbed upwards into Burkhan Khaldun. Temujin had fainted and did not see the Merkits carry off a struggling and shrieking Börte. He did not know that the triumphant Chiledu handed her over to his brother to use as his chattel.

Temujin's *aduu* slowed down as all noise of the chase died away. It was tired and halted beside a mountain brook to wet its dry throat. The unconscious man slid off its back and lay on the ground while his *aduu* munched fresh grass nearby and occasionally whinnied at his supine master. Temujin regained consciousness only when dusk was falling and swallows were returning to their nests. Loss of blood had weakened him, but he gritted his jaws and pulled out the arrow. He dragged himself to the brook to wash the wound. When he felt a little stronger, he crawled in the undergrowth looking for certain herbs to tie a poultice around the gash in his thigh. After munching a few apricots fallen under the trees, he slept the night away despite his sorrow for Börte, whose sacrifice was now quite clear to him.

For two days and nights, Temujin lay in the bushes shivering with fever and the pain of the wound. On the third day, he felt better. That night, he got on his knees, closed his eyes and prayed to Khökh Tenger to give him strength and guidance. He did not see the huge wolf, its thick fur gleaming with silvery tips, pass through the trees nor that it stopped to gaze with smouldering red eyes at the kneeling figure.

When the grey dawn came, Temujin felt a new vitality ripple through his limbs. The pain was gone and the scab on his wound was itchy. He looked up at the misty peaks of Burkhan Khaldun and gratitude overcame him. Folklore quotes his reverent humility towards the sacred mountain thus:

Thanks to Burkhan Khaldun
I escaped with my life, a louse's life
Fearing for my life, my only life,
I climbed the Khaldun
On one horse, following elk tracks;
A shelter of broken twigs
I made my home.
Thanks to Khaldun Burkhan
My life, a grasshopper's life
Was indeed shielded!

Temujin vowed that he would always honour the mountain as his place of deliverance by remembering it in his daily prayers. He faced the rising sun, draped his belt around his neck, removed his hat, beat his chest and made the ritual nine-fold obeisance to the sun, kneeling to anoint the ground with animal fat and *airag*. He promised humbly, 'The seed of my seed shall observe this.'

He truly believed that he had survived because the sacred mountain had embraced him with protection. How or why such a man as he, a 'louse' as he himself states, was given this privilege was a mystery to him. In the days to come, along with the arrogance of being the one chosen to unite, lead and conquer, it was the strength of this belief that would justify to him to use every means to achieve Heaven's purpose. As an ordinary man, he was overwhelmingly humbled by the divine purpose of his existence. He was convinced that he was only a medium through which Khökh Tenger was achieving His desire. Probably it is this anomaly that fashioned a unique vortex of destructiveness and ingenuity, of ruthlessness and generosity that eventually became the hallmark of the enigmatic personality that the world came to know.

As Temujin began his long trek home, he was intensely aware of how insignificant he really was in the grand scheme of the universe designed by Khökh Tenger or the Eternal Blue Heaven. He muttered, 'I am nobody. I am only a humble cog in this huge universe forged by Khökh Tenger. Who am I to question the right or wrong of his decision? It is Heaven who has decided that I am to be entrusted with building a nation of the Mongols and ensuring its safety, its prosperity. Since Divinity Himself is by my side, I will work hard, and my efforts will surely bear fruit. I will lead, rule and conquer using all the means at my disposal to achieve Heaven's purpose.'

Feeling uplifted and inspired by the clarity of his divine assignment and the right to carry it through, it was a determined Temujin who returned to his camp that night. His soul-searing experience on the sacred mountain also added a tinge of ruthlessness and arrogance into his hitherto simple, generous and unprejudiced nature. For him, it initiated the belief that the welfare of the Mongols and building their nation must be above all other considerations, personal or otherwise.

13

Kazakhstan spread before them. Skirting Lake Balkhash, the long contour of the nomadic cavalcade snaked along the River Ili that began in the Tian Shan Mountain and drained into the lake. Ahead of her, Princess Enkhtuya could see the standards of the Mongol cavalry festooned with banners bearing the blood-red flying falcon on the yellow background. Genghis Khan must be at their head with his generals. She looked over her shoulder to see the serpentine curves of the procession behind consisting of the slower wagons, heavy weapons and trebuchets.

Today, Bolorma had chosen to bounce along in a wagon but Enkhtuya finally had her own mount. The Khan had kept his promise and a skittish mare had been brought to her *ger* that morning before they broke camp. Of course, compared to the sedate rides in a palace garden, the Mongol army moved at a much smarter pace and it had taken Enkhtuya considerable time to keep up with them and get used to the gait of her mare's long stride. Now, she began to appreciate the Mongol attire that she had been forced to don. Not only did it keep out the cold, the sash tightly wound around her stomach helped to support the internal organs on this hard ride over stony paths. And the *gutals* with their upturned toes held her feet firmly in the stirrups. Best part was that she was riding her own horse. Better anytime than perching precariously behind the smelly Shigi. She looked sideways at the giant who was trotting alongside apparently as her escort, guard, or whatever. His face brought to her mind the amazing conversation they had had during the lunch halt.

They had been on the green banks of the Ili River. Slaves were running between sitting groups of soldiers serving them steaming roasts and bowls of milk. As Enkhtuya picked delicately at some fried fowl brought to her by Bolorma, she observed the chatting, laughing men and thought, 'It looks like a jolly picnic until one notices the piles of weapons lying around.' Her eyes picked up Shigi sitting alone on a grassy mound, some distance away from the rest of the chattering soldiers. He was bent over his saddle bags. Other than the Khan, he was the only other man to whom she had spoken during their long journey.

Somehow, she felt uncomfortable with the other men who rode around her. She could not forget the scenes of Malikpur's pillage by these very men…and the brutal murder of her son. Recalling it churned up her insides painfully with a fusion of agony, revulsion and savage hatred. Besides, she had often caught glances coming her way that were quite grim. It seemed to her that most of the men detested her. Though it did not show in words or acts, their contempt for her presence was subtly eloquent. *It should be the other way around,* Enkhtuya would muse, acidly.

Though she disliked his foul stench, Enkhtuya did not get the same vibes from Shigi. In fact, she quite favoured a certain scholarly air about him. She sensed an innate gentleness in the huge man. Thus, seeing him engaged in some solitary pursuit during lunch, piqued her curiosity and lent her boldness to approach him with silent steps. Coming up behind him, she looked over his shoulder and observed that he was scratching strange symbols onto a sheet of white, Chinese paper. In his hand was a quill and a bowl of dark, thick ink stood beside him. *Was he writing something?* Enkhtuya wondered. It looked like she was right for there were several sheets covered with smudgy writing lying on the grass. Her brows knit as she tried to decipher the symbols. Enkhtuya had learnt to read and write Persian in Malik Amin's palace but this was different. She was unable read Shigi's scribbles on the paper. Besides, as far as she recalled her mother's tales of Mongol life, the nomadic people had no written language.

'Are you writing something?' Enkhtuya had queried. Shigi jumped at her voice and the bowl of ink nearly overturned.

Balancing the bowl carefully, he had looked up into a pair of frank, blue eyes that perfectly reflected sky overhead. He had growled at her, 'Must you creep up behind people's back and startle them? Everything is a game to you, isn't it?'

Unrepentant, for she knew his bark was worse than his bite, Enkhtuya had settled down near him and said, 'I am sorry I startled you. But are you writing? Or is it a secret and your Khan has directed you not to tell.'

'Yes, I am writing and no, it is not a secret,' replied Shigi, a little sulkily, thinking, *here she is...the spoiled brat to spoil my work, now.*

'But I can't read any of your writing,' complained Enkhtuya.

'Do you know the Uighur tongue?' asked Shigi.

'Uighur?' Enkhtuya shook her head. 'No, I don't. Who or what is Uighur?' she wanted to know.

'Uighurs are a nomadic tribe that came from the Altai mountains. Very intelligent and cultured, they were the first people to submit to our Lord. The Khan has bestowed many Uighurs with the power to administer the lands we have conquered. It was my Lord who told me to learn the Uighur language and script,' explained Shigi.

'So, what are you writing? Is it about the Uighur people?' Enkhtuya's interest was whetted by the fact that Genghis Khan, who was known to be illiterate, had wanted his brother, Shigi to learn to read and write the script of another tribe.

'No,' replied Shigi. 'I am writing the history of the Mongols.'

'What?' exclaimed Enkhtuya, 'Why?'

'So that our unborn generations will come to know how Mongolia became a powerful empire. They will learn about our great ancestors, about the formidable Genghis Khan and about the monumental events that have made our nation the best in the world.' Shigi pronounced solemnly.

'Hmmm...interesting...,' remarked Enkhtuya. 'And are you writing this history on the orders of your great Khan?'

'Of course,' replied Shigi, his tone conveying his disdain for the Princess' silly, ignorant question. *Does anything happen without our Lord's command?*

However, she took no notice of his scornful tone. Instead, the girl had said, 'And it would portray the mighty Genghis Khan in all his glory, won't it? And what about all the killings in his name, of innocent children and women and men? Will you write of their torment too?' She looked at Shigi's scowling visage with blue, guileless eyes.

Shigi had bristled at this criticism of his idol. 'You are a woman. What would you know of the grandeur of history? Go and finish your lunch. Don't ask about things you know nothing about.' And he had thrust the papers into his saddle bag and begun to pack up the quills and ink.

Knowing that he would not divulge anymore and realising that the army was getting ready to move, the Princess had walked slowly towards her mare. Her head swirled with contradictory images of the tyrant that she was discovering almost daily. The world knew of Genghis Khan's atrocities but nobody knew about the fierce loyalty he commanded of his people; that other than Mongols there were many people from other nations who believed in his vision and followed him; that he had freed from the threat of lawlessness entire lands all the way from the shores of the Pacific Ocean to the beaches of the Caspian Sea so that merchants and travellers could move safely and now this...unlettered himself, he encouraged others to learning and aspired to leave behind him recorded history for his forbearers.

Enkhtuya heaved up and down with the stride of the horse, musing, *how many more faces does the tyrant have?* So lost she was in her thoughts that she didn't notice that the cause of her bemusement was riding right beside her. When she raised her head and found his cool, dark eyes on her face, she caught her breath. Shigi and the other soldiers had dropped back and only both their horses cantered along the banks of the sedate Ili. 'Do you like it, *Guunj*? Being on your own *aduu*?' he asked softly, his eyes suddenly shadowed in concern.

'Yes, my Lord. Thank you,' replied Enkhtuya hardly noticing in her agitation, that she had addressed him by the title that she despised when others used it.

He nodded. 'Good.'

They rode along in silence for a while. Princess Enkhtuya's gaze passed over the green meadows and mulberry trees lining the path, but she saw none of it. Her heart was thudding in her chest. On the other side, her hand went surreptitiously to the tunic pocket and felt the sharp edge of the little knife. She forced herself to relax. *After all, here in the open countryside, in full view of his men, he could not possibly attempt to attack me,* she assured herself. *Besides,* she reminded herself, *if I am polite to him, I may be able to wrangle more concessions from him like this mare. Then…then…maybe, one day…I will be able to escape to freedom….*

Strategising it all in her mind, she started guiltily when he spoke. 'So, no questions today?' When Enkhtuya silently shook her head, he added, 'Then let me ask you some.' Instantly, the girl's heart began to flip-flop.

'You told me that your mother taught you the Mongol tongue. But how do you speak it so well living in Ghaznin?'

'Well, actually my mother was from the tribe of Ongirads but she had married a Tangut from Xi Xia. She was keen that I must not forget our roots. So, she would often converse with me in the language of her land.'

'Yes. Yes. You told me she was an Ongirad. That explains it. But what was her real name? Gurleen cannot be her name. It is not a Mongol name.'

Irked by his questions, she thought, *why is he after my past life? What difference does it make what my mother's name was when all he is after is my honour?*

Enkhtuya sighed, explaining, 'I came to Amin Malik's palace in Ghaznin with my mother when I was a babe. She was the Malik's concubine. She had been given her own rooms in his harem and I grew up there. Everyone in the palace called her Gurleen. Whether it was her real name or not, I don't know.'

Suddenly, the tall, elegant form of her mother rose before the girl's eyes. A deep longing throbbed through her, but Genghis Khan was coming up with the next question. 'How did your mother reach Ghaznin from Xi Xia?'

She blinked back tears, answering, 'She was taken there by a slave trader and sold to Amin Malik, the ruler of Ghaznin.'

'Hmmm…I see. So, your father was a Tangut from Xi Xia?'

'I suppose so. I don't know,' Enkhtuya said in a sullen voice.

'Don't know?' Disbelief lined his expostulation. The girl remained silent. He repeated the question, 'Do you mean to say you don't know who sired you?'

Misty and unformed, a silhouette from her childhood tales floated into Enkhtuya's mind; a man astride a steed flying to the moon. *Did the horse have wings? I used to ask Eej. But how can I tell the tyrant that my father was a man from the moon?* So, she curved her mouth around a firm, 'No.'

'Where is your mother now?'

'She is dead.' The girl's voice was soft. Like always whenever she uttered those dreadful words, tears would choke her. But if she was expecting any empathy from Genghis Khan, it was a futile hope.

'Hmmm…,' he replied, not the least perturbed. 'But your mother shifted her loyalty from her husband to the ruler of Ghaznin. Happily, she entered the Malik's harem.' He wagged a finger. 'No. No. I do not like those who change their loyalty like the wind…blowing one way then another.'

Bitten to the quick by his derisive tone, she retorted, 'How did you know that she was happy to enter the harem?'

'Why else did she do it?'

Gritting her teeth, the girl replied, 'She had to survive. If she had not submitted to Amin Malik, both she and I would have been put to death when he had bought her.'

But the Khan was not to be diverted. 'In my opinion, loyalty and commitment to one's word is the greatest virtue in a man or a woman. I have always valued fidelity.'

The princess lifted her head and pronounced, 'And I believe compassion is the greatest of all virtues. But compassion…' She gave a bitter laugh. 'What would a heartless killer like you know about such things?'

Genghis stared for a long time at the leaves of the mulberry trees gently waving in the cool breeze. Clouds of dust marked the advance contingents of his troops. Then he spit it out, like an apricot kernel, 'Compassion?'

The Princess flinched at the sneer in his tone, but she nodded. *Was she to be punished for saying that?*

'Well,' continued the sixty-four-year-old conqueror of the world, 'There was a time when I tried compassion. Börte had warned me that at a time only one sun can rise on the horizon of the Mongol Empire. But I ignored her in my pride. I was foolish enough to think that my love for my blood-brother was supreme. It would surmount all rivalry between us. And so, I was punished…' He shook his head at the memory. '…Oh! How I was punished for my naivety and my compassion! It is a lesson that I have always remembered and have never forgotten to apply to my life thereafter.' His hand cut the air sharply. 'No compassion. No mercy. No regrets.'

Enkhtuya forgot to be afraid in her eagerness to find out what was the memory that had aroused such raw pain in the great Khan's voice. 'Who…who was this blood-brother…who betrayed you?'

Genghis Khan sighed deeply. 'Jamukha.'

14

Temujin rested in his mother's *ger* for a few days until his wound was healed completely. But he was restless. 'I must get Börte back, *Eej*.'

'Of course, you must,' agreed Hoelun, 'but you cannot do it alone. The Merkits are too rugged and well-protected. Go to Toghril for this is the time to test his loyalty.'

'And there is Jamukha, too,' added Temujin.

The very next day, the young leader was galloping across the highlands to the palace of Toghril. This time, no guards stopped him. Even Toghril's commanders listened indulgently to Temujin's tale of the deceitful Merkits. Toghril considered him through narrowed eyes as Temujin held his breath. Finally, the old man pronounced:

In return for the sable coat
Even to the complete destruction of the Merkits
I shall rescue for you your Lady Börte.

Temujin breathed a sigh of relief. The powerful leader of the Keraits had not forgotten the magnificent gift. Toghril offered him two divisions of warriors; each division consisting of about ten thousand men.

Jamukha, now the leader of his clan, also came to Temujin's aid with two more divisions. At one time, he had also suffered at the hands of the Merkits and welcomed an excuse to deal them a blow. As for the real cause of the fight, he teased Temujin saying, 'Don't tell anyone that Jamukha is seeking to fight the Merkits to rescue a lady. People will laugh at me.'

When Temujin protested indignantly, 'She is not *any* lady. Börte is my wife.'

'And your soul,' added Jamukha, thumping his back and laughing loudly at his friend's discomfiture.

A week later, the combined armies of Toghril, Jamukha and Temujin worked their way north over the mountains towards Lake Baikal, approaching the tributary of the Selanga River called the Khilok. The Merkits were camped on its other bank. The army crossed by night, each man building a float of reeds and swimming across with his *aduu*. The entire operation was too huge to retain the element of a surprise attack.

Huntsmen ranging the Khilok's opposite bank saw what was happening and galloped off to warn the Merkits. The entire clan fled, scattering in panic all the way down to the Selanga and along its banks. The attackers galloped behind them in hot pursuit. Temujin rode at their head calling out for Börte. The lady in question, being a prized hostage, was concealed in a cart driven by Chiledu's brother who whipped his horses repeatedly. As the cart pulled away ahead of the fleeing Merkits, there seemed a possibility that he may still escape Temujin and his allies taking Börte with him. By then she was heavily pregnant.

But Chiledu's brother had not reckoned with the lady's determination. In the swaying cart that could overturn any moment, Börte balanced on the hitching beams behind the man. Curling her fingers around the hilt of a knife bouncing on the back of her kidnapper's belt, she held it firmly. The man was too engrossed in keeping the cart upright while whipping the horses to speed up to notice the knife being slid out of his belt. She slammed the knife into his vulnerable back once, twice, thrice until he slumped over the panicky horses. At the last moment, Börte jumped off the cart, before it tumbled into the river with its poor horses entwined.

Temujin who had been chasing the cart saw her standing alone sketched against the background of a desperate mob of fleeing Merkits. He reined in his horse and jumped down. Within seconds the lovers were in each other's arms. Jamukha observed the romantic picture that the tightly embracing lovers made encircled by a halo of silver moonlight with a river babbling melodiously at their feet. It formed a brief spot of tranquillity in the midst of fear and turmoil. He smiled at his friend's youthful passion.

Having found Börte was enough for Temujin. He shouted to his companions, 'I have found what I wanted. Let's go.' He placed his wife carefully on the saddle and flung his own leg across. The others were wheeling around as Temujin rode off into the night with his precious possession. The chase was called off, but it taught the Merkits a lesson they would never forget.

The news of Temujin's audacious raid spread far and wide. It came to be known as a famous victory. The Merkits were scattered, many of their women taken as concubines and servants, Chiledu's brother was killed; Börte was saved. It served to establish Temujin as a great Mongol leader, as great as Jamukha was. The only shadow over the triumph was that Börte's pregnancy was suspected to be caused by the Merkits. Hoelun pursed her mouth with disapproval when her daughter-in-law entered the camp.

'She carries my son,' said Temujin, looking into his mother's eyes.

Hoelun did not refute him but she knew that the child's right as Temujin's heir would be challenged later due to the cloud on his paternity. But wisely, she did not express her doubts.

Jamukha and Temujin became inseparable friends. For the next eighteen months, the two families lived as one.

The young men did everything together. They exchanged sashes, gave each other horses, feasted together, drank from the same cup and slept beside the other.

Börte watched this powerful friendship with distrustful eyes. Jamukha was like a sharp knife casting asunder her beloved Temujin from her. Also, her sixth sense was intuitively sharp, and it forecast that trouble was about to brew. One night, after long hours spent drinking with his friend, when Temujin came to her *ger*, she revealed to him her misgivings in no uncertain words. 'Jamukha will not let you rise.'

'Why not? We are blood brothers,' argued her husband. 'You are just jealous of the time I spend with him.'

'No Temujin. Jamukha is ambitious. He wants to rule the Mongols. It is you who has been ordained to be the ruler of Mongolia, not he. You have been born with a destiny to fulfil. Don't forget that two suns cannot shine at the same time, on the same day, above the same horizon.'

Temujin did not agree but he did not disagree either.

Jamukha, sensing Börte's dislike, told his friend, 'If my wife had spent so much time in another man's *ger*, I would have never accepted her. Instead, I would have slashed her throat.' Temujin did not like the insinuation but he forgave his so-called brother out of love. He decided to keep silent.

The very next day, one of his soldiers came to him. 'Your warriors want to speak with you,' he said.

When Temujin went to them, the commander of his men placed a sword sheathed in an engraved scabbard in his hands and said, 'Here is a handsome sword that I took from the Merkits. It is a gift for you.'

The young leader acknowledged the gift. He asked the other soldiers, 'What did you want with me?'

'It is about the plunder from the Merkits,' they explained. 'Jamukha has taken most of it. What is left over belongs to us. Tell us how to distribute it.'

Temujin considered for a moment and then declared, 'I will take a tenth of what is left over of the plunder. Divide the rest equally amongst all of you. Also, don't forget the families of the men who were killed in battle. They deserve something, too.' Smiling at his commander, Temujin put the magnificent sword back into his hands, saying, 'You took this sword with a lot of effort. You deserve the gift, not I.'

The astounded man bowed and backed away towards the murmuring men. Till now no Mongol leader had given away so much loot to his men and certainly none to the families of the dead. But Temujin could not ignore the call from his soul to endorse the sacrifice of those who had supported him nay even died for him.

Jamukha's brother had observed it all and reported to him, 'Temujin is trying to buy the loyalty of his men by giving them large shares of the plunder. When our men know of it, they will demand the same from you. He is trying to make trouble between you and your men.'

But Jamukha did not pay attention to this warning. He believed Temujin was too dependent on his support to plot against him. Besides, he wanted to keep Temujin under his wing to prevent him from becoming too notable a leader.

Jamukha kept assuring Temujin that he would always be with him; that he would always look after his sworn brother.

One day Temujin gently told him, 'I am used to being on my own.'

To this his friend replied, 'You will never be able to survive on your own. You need my backing.' Jamukha then added, 'I will make you my second-in command.' Temujin smiled and shook his head but Börte's words whirled in his head, *Jamukha will not let you rise.*

Jamukha's brother who had heard the conversation took the clan chief aside and berated him. 'If you make Temujin your second-in-command, what will happen to me? You promised me that post.'

Jamukha was not perturbed. He retorted, 'Temujin is my blood brother.'

'And I am your own brother,' his brother shouted. 'That man has already given away his share of the plunder to his men. Soon he will give away your share too. This will make the warriors love him more than you. They will be loyal to him, not you. They will follow him, not you,' he warned.

When both friends' family groups began moving to the summer pastures along the Onon, Jamukha suddenly proposed that each of their families make a different camp. Temujin was puzzled by this suggestion. *Does Jamukha want us to separate?*

That night, in their *ger*, he asked Hoelun's advice, but it was Börte who burst out, 'Everyone knows that Jamukha tires of things quickly. He must be tired of us.'

From that day onwards, Temujin's suspicions grew into conviction. *If we part now, we cannot be companions. If we cannot be companions, we can only be rivals. If we are rivals, then one of us must dominate and I cannot be a follower.*

After thinking deeply through the day, when evening came, Temujin led his group away from the camp. They travelled all night to put as much distance as possible between Jamukha's camp and his people. When dawn came to the grasslands, Temujin's men saw strange occurrences. Three brothers who were leading members of a minor clan, and their families, caught up with Temujin. Then another five families appeared. Then more men and more families; Tarkuts, Bayuts, Manguts, Arulats and many more. All of them had opted to follow Temujin rather than Jamukha. These were not the greatest of the nomad families for Jamukha had the loyalty of the established leaders, but they formed a sizeable number. These men had decided to put in their lot with Temujin simply because the young leader offered them something that Jamukha could not; a fierce commitment towards all who were loyal to him and relied on him, a kind of hope that meritorious deeds could elevate those who were not of noble birth and otherwise had no possibility of any upward growth.

Among the Mongol clans rumours began to spread like forest fires that Temujin is the one chosen by Heaven. He is the divine leader. The grapevine strengthened hope among the hopeless and it was their powerful longing that led to the prophecy....

Heaven and Earth have agreed: Temujin shall be the Lord of the people.

15

People began to flock in large numbers to Temujin. They had chosen of their own violation to serve him. To prove their fealty, they swore an oath; they would pursue their new leader's enemies, bring him the finest women and the best horses, and would hunt for him.

'If in war we disobey,' they declared in unison, 'throw down our vile heads upon the ground! If in peace we disobey, throw us out into the wilderness!'

The process of uniting the Mongol clans took several years. Temujin began to take the first baby steps towards building nationhood, but it took seventeen years to actually transform him from a clan leader to the founder of the nation. On the steppes, everything is fluid. Tradition dictated that leaders could not fool around with bonds of family, clan and sworn brotherhood. But traditional dictates were sometimes blown away with the wind if there was a powerful reason to do so. The bottom line was power and survival. In Temujin's leadership, the clans found that significant reason. He revealed himself as a ruler with the surest instincts, steadiest ambitions and most firmly grounded character. His strength was in his firm belief and deep faith in Heaven's guidance. To the nomads his leadership indicated Heaven's directions.

Thus, it was in 1189 CE that the clans controlled by Temujin declared him their Khan. Preceding the title, he was given a unique name—'Genghis' that meant fierce, hard, tough. Temujin decided that he would formally acquire this title at a ceremony held at no other place than at Blue Lake in the foothills of the Black Heart Mountain.

The place was close to Temujin's heart for it was here that his family had etched out a living after being abandoned by everyone at the behest of the Taychuits.

The Blue Lake was a gorgeous place surrounded by hills. Some metres above the peaty lake was an open platform of grass. On it was set up a white marquee flanked on one side by a pole flying nine white yak tails, the emblem of power. On the other side was another post flying Temujin's fighting emblem; four black horse-tails. At a distance, a kind of *ovoo* was built out of a pile of boulders draped with a length of blue silk. A flagpole rose from the centre of the *ovoo* bearing a silk pennant that flapped in the breeze. It displayed a red flying falcon on a bright yellow background. Temujin had chosen the falcon, sometimes referred to as a mythical or divine bird as his crest. The rising sun made a halo edging the hills mantled with thick forests of pines, firs and junipers. Its gentle heat raised a hazy drifting mist from the lake. A cuckoo called distantly, and a skylark warbled from the blue curved roof overhead. It was a perfect day for the crowning of an Emperor.

Positioned around the grassy ledge and overflowing down the slope were vast legions of warriors, their spears glinting in the mellow sunlight. Despite their numbers, there was a hush in the air. It was a solemn occasion for it was a day for the prophecy to come true. From the *ger*, emerged Temujin; tall, broad-chested, wearing the new, yellow *deel* and trousers his mother had stitched for him. His head was bare and braided hair fell on either side of a face that glowed with an inner radiance. The spectators envisioned him as the progeny of the rising sun; golden and illuminating like the orb. Around his neck was a silk scarf woven by Börte, now mother to three sons and one daughter.

Temujin approached the *ovoo.* He beat his chest and bowed to the rising sun nine times. With a bowl of *airag*, he went around the *ovoo* pouring the liquid in a circle around it and anointing the ground. He knelt on the ground facing the sun and prayed silently to Khökh Tenger to grant him strength and wisdom. Then he stood erect and facing the warriors, unsheathed his sword. Holding the gleaming blade above his head, he announced, 'From this day on, I become Genghis Khan, Ruler of all Mongolia.'

The men, who had been quiet while the rituals were under way, broke into cheers and bellowed with one accord hailing him three times as, 'Our Lord, Genghis Khan!' Temujin, now Genghis Khan for the world and posterity, sat on a raised, wooden platform. Four men at each corner raised it to their shoulders. Thus, seated like a Khan, the twenty-seven-year-old leader was taken through the crowds who bowed and vowed their fealty to their new Khan.

However, not everybody was happy with this episode of Mongol history. Jamukha was not going to allow Genghis Khan's dominance to prevail without challenge. Foreseeing friction with the new Khan, he made his first move. It took time to prepare a battle against the forces of Genghis Khan that were growing every day. For nearly a year Jamukha had to take care of his clan's herds, ensure loyalties and mobilise an army. Finally, when he was ready, Jamukha used the murder of a relative as an excuse to attack Genghis with a force of some 20,000–25,000 warriors.

It was summer, and Genghis' consolidated clans were roaming in search of green pastures when herdsmen from a minor clan rode up. 'Jamukha is coming! His army is on the march to fight you,' they warned. 'Prepare yourself!'

Genghis had hardly any time to rally his own forces. In a hurry he managed to send the families along with the herds into the safety of the mountains. His men quickly erected a defensive wall with boulders. Behind it they dug themselves in, bows ready to pick out the first rows of the rival's soldiers.

When Jamukha's army came into view, its sheer numbers seemed to stop Genghis' heart. He knew his men would also feel the same. Genghis went up and down the line of men reminding his warriors that they were fighting not just for themselves but also for their families. They nodded grimly at him as it sunk in that today the battle was not for plunder but for the lives of their dear ones. As the enemy forces approached, Genghis gave the order to notch arrows to bows but wait until he commanded them to be released.

When the first row of horsemen was within range, Genghis shouted, 'Let go!' A shower of arrows arched through the air and most of them found their targets in human bodies or in the horses that collapsed under their riders. 'Fix arrows!' he shouted immediately and as the next row came on, he ordered, 'Go!' The first mounts and riders were well decimated by these tactics but soon, too soon, the armed cavalry had overrun Genghis' defences. Now it became every man for himself as arm-to-arm combat ensued. Swords clanged fiercely, spears were thrust in and daggers stabbed as men grunted, gasped and screamed with pain. Neighing horses and war cries resounded all around the clashing soldiers while the grass turned slippery with blood.

Genghis gritted his teeth. He slashed here, beheaded there, dancing on the balls of his feet to avoid sure death by inches. But despite their bravery, Genghis' forces were outnumbered. Nevertheless, they refused to retreat and fought on ferociously. In a few hours the ground was littered with bodies, many of them Genghis' men but surrounded by the bodies of the enemy that they had taken with themselves into the arms of Death. All of a sudden, Genghis found himself surrounded by three of Jamukha's soldiers. He swung his sword in a furious arc pushing them back, but a blow dealt from behind laid him low. As darkness swallowed him he heard triumphant cries above his head.

When he regained consciousness, he realised he had been dragged before Jamukha. As he raised himself to his knees, the victorious Chief grinned at him. 'So, Blood Brother, did I not tell you that you cannot survive without me? You cannot live on your own.'

'Yes, I can. I have been doing exactly that until you decided to plunge the dagger into my back, Brother,' growled Genghis.

'Well, now you are my captive,' said the unrepentant Jamukha. 'What do you propose I should do with you?'

'Let me go,' Genghis replied instantly.

'Why? Why should I let a man who abandoned me go free?' Jamukha cocked a brow.

'Because we are sworn blood brothers,' retorted Genghis.

'No longer. A disloyal man is no brother of mine,' snarled Jamukha. He growled to his soldiers, 'Take him away.' Genghis struggled until a hilt of a sword slammed into his head and he fell unconscious.

When he came to, he found himself tied to a long line of captives, each tied to the other at the waist by a long rope. They were goods belonging to Arab slave traders. On horseback, the Arabs whipped the prisoners as they struggled to keep erect. Genghis Khan only focused on putting down one foot after the other. The sorry string of men trudged through the hot sands of the Gobi Desert.

One of the Arab horsemen held the free end of the rope. He tugged at it cruelly not letting up the pace. Genghis had seen the fate of those who could not remain on their feet to shuffle through the burning sands. They were cut from the rope and left to die in the desert. So, he concentrated his mind and body in keeping upright though his limbs ached terribly. Only when they halted for the night were the slaves allowed to sit or lie down. Genghis would curl up on the freezing sands trying to ignore his bleeding, bare soles. The man who had been crowned Khan only a few months ago had been sold as a slave to Arab traders by his sworn blood brother, Jamukha. He would recall Börte's warnings about Jamukha. I *have been naïve but not anymore,* he vowed to himself.

After an interminable journey and crossing the muddy Yellow River, the Arabs reached the kingdom of Xi Xia, the land of the Tanguts. Yesugei had mentioned the Tanguts when he had spoken of the endeavours of his ancestor, Kabul Khan to his son but he had never known any. Nor had Genghis. Therefore, he was completely stupefied by the huge buildings, splendid palaces and teeming bazaars as the traders pulled the slaves through the gigantic gates of the capital city of Yinchuan. Half the day, they had waited outside the gates with the other visitors as their Arab masters bargained with the guards. Only after a satisfactory bribe had been handed over, were the traders allowed to enter with their human merchandise. To his disappointment, Genghis was not allowed to enjoy this treat to his senses for the traders immediately separated him from the rest of the slaves. One of the Arabs dragged him off by the rope still around his waist and marched him away.

Genghis was taken into the compound of a garrison that had many soldiers milling around. There he was pushed into a room by the trader. Inside sat a man, richly garbed. His gown was worked in gold and silver threads that glittered as he moved. He was past his prime, but his chest struck out like a proud peacock's. However, the small, puffy, cold eyes in a lean patrician face glinted with spite. The trader bowed down cravenly to the man who looked down from his height and pronounced, 'Well?'

'Sire!' he stammered, 'I bring to you a wild Mongol who is known for his destructive nature. He is a dangerous animal, so I thought that it was best that the King's Imperial Commander decide what to do with him.'

The King's Imperial Commander, given the title of *Gambu* by the Tanguts, looked Genghis up and down. After days of travelling through the steppes, deserts and rivers, his clothes were hanging in rags and his long hair was matted into unruly strings. Barefoot and eyes feverish with hunger and fatigue, the captive certainly looked like a creature from the wilderness.

The *Gambu* pondered over the problem. 'Hmmm… alright.' Apparently, he had hit upon a solution. 'Leave him here. I know what to do with him.'

The Arab tied the rope with Genghis at its end to the door handle and slyly muttered, '…our reward, Sire?'

'Your reward? I will have you whipped for even daring to open your mouth. Get yourself off before I call the soldiers.' The Arab scuttled off as fast as he could.

'Guard!' shouted the *Gambu*. When the man came in and bowed, he was instructed to call the Keeper of Prisons. Genghis understood only a few words of the conversation that passed rapidly between the two men. The language of the Tangut resembled the Mongol tongue but only somewhat. The Keeper took Genghis away. He was pulled by the rope around his waist for a long distance through the streets of the Tangut city. People who were roaming around them stopped whatever they were doing to stare at Genghis. He also stared back at them for he had never seen people clothed in such luxurious silks and furs with ornaments glittering on them. Eventually, the Keeper reached a flat rock wall and began to climb a steep staircase cut into one side of it, dragging Genghis behind him. When the streets were quite a long way below them, the Keeper unlocked a great wooden door. He stood back to let Genghis go forward and then gave him a mighty shove. As Genghis tumbled onto the floor, the door slammed behind him. He heard the key turn in the lock.

When he looked around, he realised he was in a large cave cut into the rock wall. While two sides were solid rock, the locked wooden door was on the third side. But the fourth side was fenced by iron bars from the roof to the floor. However, natural light poured in through the barred side lighting up the cave's dark interiors and making it airy. He noticed a large bolt with a heavy lock on one side of the bars and concluded that the iron fence could be swung open if required. As he stood behind this cage-like barrier, Genghis looked down the sheer cliff face to a walled-in area. Two sentries walked up and down inside the wall. Beyond it was an enclosed yard with a strong iron gate. Swinging above the walled area and parallel to the bars of his cage was a bridge on bamboo slats. The bridge swayed at a distance of two *alds* from the cage and could be accessed by rickety bamboo stairs on either side. Genghis craned his neck and managed to see a corner of the bazaar through which he had walked a few moments ago. Not only was he incarcerated in an inaccessible prison, he felt as though he had been caged in like a ferocious animal.

He felt even more of an animal when the guards walked up the swinging bridge at night. From there, they tried to fling a few hunks of meat through the bars at him. Some pieces fell inside the cage, but the rest tumbled down to the bottom of the rocky wall for the aim of the guards was not perfect. Genghis chewed eagerly on the morsels of tough, stale meat for he had not eaten anything since morning. In one corner of the cave, he found a mouldy earthen pot of water to quench his thirst. All through the night, he sat in one corner thinking despondently why Fate had dealt him such a blow. It was only towards dawn that he kneeled on the rough floor, bowed his head, closed his eyes and called on Khökh Tenger to deliver him.

16

Trotting along the Ili, the cavalcade entered the town of Almalik. Princess Enkhtuya was tired to the bone. As her eyes roved over the verdant banks spread with tiny wildflowers, shaded by the spread of mulberry trees and a ground thickly covered by tight bunches of the red-and-purple fruit fallen from the trees, her spirits lifted. *This seems like a large town. Maybe we will be housed under a proper roof this time and not in tents,* she hoped. On this long trek across unknown lands, she had expected they would pass through Ghaznin, her childhood home. Presently juggling between moments of abject terror, periods of anguish for her murdered son and clever plans to squeeze out some concessions from the terrible Khan, Enkhtuya had longed for the balm of seeing once more the minarets and domes of the grand city she had grown up in before vanishing into an uncertain future. But that was not to be. For some whimsical reason, Genghis Khan had decided to take a direct route through Kazakhstan and the Altai mountains to his homeland.

As her mare pranced beside Shigi's stallion, Enkhtuya looked around with interested eyes at another new place. What struck her almost instantly were several gardens planted with straight rows of trees whose thin branches seemed to rise from the ground.

'What are those trees?' She turned to her well-informed companion.

He looked to where her finger was pointing. 'Those are *alma* trees. Everyone grows them here.'

'*Alma*?' queried Enkhtuya.

'Yes. Red and green balls of fruit. They have a thin skin and crunchy flesh but are sweet and juicy. In fact, the town Almalik gets its name from this fruit,' explained Shigi.

'Hmmm...' Enkhtuya turned over the information in her mind. I *must try to get a taste of this wondrous fruit,* thought she. And then she forgot all about the fruit as a woman hotly pursued by a man wielding a stick ran by their horses. She craned her head to follow their passage and found that the woman had literally thrown herself before the Emperor's horse. 'Oh, no!' she cried out involuntarily, certain that the woman would be crushed to death.

Shigi began to push ahead through the cavalrymen to reach the venue of the commotion. Enkhtuya eagerly manoeuvred her own mare through the space Shigi created in his wake. Soon, both were part of the circle of spectators behind the Khan as high drama unfolded. The Princess could make nothing of the rapid and voluble ricochet of words being exchanged. She whispered to Shigi, 'What is it all about?'

Without taking his eyes off the players, he whispered back, 'The woman is complaining that the man always beats her even though she cooks, washes and cares for him. She is saying that she is his first wife but as she couldn't beget him an offspring, he got himself a second wife. Now both the man and the second wife ill-treat and abuse her. She is pleading for justice from the Khan.'

Blue eyes wide, Enkhtuya could not help whispering back, 'But the woman belongs to the man. He can treat her any way he likes.'

Shigi shook his head. 'Our Lord does not believe that.' He placed a finger on his lips as Genghis Khan began to speak.

Enkhtuya listened carefully but could not understand a single word as the Emperor spoke in the dialect of his subjects. She could only stare as two soldiers dismounted and led the husband away. The man's face had crumpled into a mask of panicky tears. The woman, she saw, was bowing in the dust, her head on the ground perilously close to the powerful hoofs of the Khan's steed.

As the Emperor turned his *aduu* away and the procession continued, Enkhtuya demanded impatiently of Shigi what the Khan had decreed.

'As expected…' shrugged Shigi, secretly enjoying Enkhtuya's annoyed face at his cryptic reply.

'Come on, Shigi,' retorted Enkhtuya. 'Don't tease me.'

'Well, the Khan ordered twenty lashes to the man for ill-treating his faithful wife. He also ruled that the woman could divorce him if he continued to beat her and the man would have to return her dowry if she so decides.' Shigi explained the details of the judgement.

Enkhtuya's eyes were as round as saucers. 'But in my country, it is the woman who would have been lashed,' she blurted.

'That is the reason the Mongols are superior to all people. That is the reason it is the right of our Lord to rule all lands. Only then will true justice reach all people.'

For a change, the Princess did not spit out an acidic riposte. Stunned, she was still integrating this astonishingly upside-down social norm of the Khan's empire.

The inn that was commandeered for the night's stay of the Khan, his generals and the Princess boasted of a hamam. Enkhtuya was overjoyed and that evening, she gratefully lowered herself into the steaming, hot water of the hamam. Bolorma scrubbed away the fatigue with herbal leaves as the girl groaned with pleasure, *'Ahh… how long since I have actually bathed…*With her entire body loose and relaxed, her mind tripped back to the incident of the day.

'Bolorma, when you used to live in Mongolia, were women allowed to divorce their husbands?'

'When I lived in…?' Bolorma's eyes looked into the distance.

'Yes, yes,' prompted Enkhtuya, impatiently.

'No…I don't think women could divorce their husbands. But women in my land had certainly more authority than the women of Ghaznin. Men would listen to the advice of their mothers and wives.' She nodded wisely.

'But, today the Khan has permitted a woman to divorce her husband if she wants to. Strange!'

'Hmmm…,' she considered, 'I have heard from some of the men in the kitchen that the Khan is different from the earlier Mongol rulers. He has new ideas about many things other than the status of women. To him a man's loyalty is his true measure; he allows advancement on merit rather than as a birthright. I have heard that he has been training women to fight wars; he believes men and women should enjoy equal position in society and family.'

Observing the girl gaping at her speechlessly, a smile wrapped itself around the old woman's wrinkles. Her kind eyes twinkled. 'Strange but true!'

That evening, as expected, an invitation came for the *Guunj* from Genghis Khan. Dressed in a new, red *deel* and brocaded coat, her limbs snug and soothed by a long, hot soak, the Princess was no longer a bundle of nerves when she entered the Khan's room. Of course, the little knife in her tunic pocket pressing against her thigh also gave her confidence, but she was less combative in her demeanour.

On the far side, glowed a crackling fire and the small wooden room was warm. Other than a few carpets on the floor, the furniture was sparse. Heavy silk curtains enclosed probably a window on one wall. Spread before the fireplace were two deep seats with silk cushions and a wide, low table already piled with platters and bowls. Genghis Khan was sitting on one seat, but its cushion was flung on the rich, wool carpet. His back was to the door and yet he called out, 'Come in, *Guunj!*'

Refusing to be baited into expressing surprise at his keen consciousness, Princess Enkhtuya glided into the room on silent feet. For the sake of comfort, she was wearing her Persian slippers and not the *gutals.* At a gesture from the Khan, she lowered herself onto the seat opposite his. He did not raise his eyes to her but continued to stare into the fire. She sat quietly observing him. His profile was etched in the orange glow; a broad forehead with the hair pulled back, thin arching brows, dark eyes, now pensive but usually searing in intensity, skin translucent over sharp cheekbones, thin lips hidden under a thick, drooping moustache and the tiny goatee under. *His nose is not as flat as it had earlier seemed to me. There is a sharp ridge to it,* reflected the girl.

'Well?' His sharp eyes were on her face, no longer thoughtful. Silently, she shook her head. To her surprise, her heart did not thud as he contemplated her. 'Was your visit to the hamam pleasurable?'

Colour rose up the girl's cheeks. *Am I not allowed some privacy?* But she nodded.

'Hmmm...I thought it would be. I like hamams too. They bring tranquillity to my mind,' he remarked.

Her bewilderment wrung a comment out of her. 'Oh!' she exclaimed.

Her companion chuckled. 'I know...the very idea that a Mongol may want to bathe is an antithesis of the uncivilised savages you believe us to be. I apologise sincerely for splintering your fond picture of me.'

The irony in his tone made Enkhtuya bristle. 'I never ever said that.'

'But you thought that.' He was remorseless. Then he went on in a softer tone. 'There is a lot you don't know about me, *Guunj*. But it is better not to assume things, isn't it?'

The Princess did not reply.

'Did you know that I am a disciple of the Holy Immortal Changchun?' He enquired, one brow raised sardonically.

Nonplussed, Enkhtuya stared at him for even in Ghaznin, they had heard of the renowned Jin Adept Changchun of the Sect of Complete Perfection, a spin off from Daoism.

The Khan nodded. 'You see, I always wanted to know about the meaning of life. Then I realised that everywhere men were seeking the same thing. Wherever I went, I saw people had raised pagodas, tombs, mosques, temples and monuments dedicated to their belief of what they imagined the Truth to be. Even so they continued searching for the route to that Truth. When I asked the Master about this endless search, he had declared, "Most men only know the greatness of Heaven. They do not understand the greatness of Dao". He explained how our life essence becomes unbalanced due to our hunger for sensuality and emotional attachments. To regain that balance, he advised me to practise quietism, asceticism and meditation.'

Enkhtuya could not take her eyes off the face glowing with some kind of inner light. She whispered, 'Did you do that?'

The Khan sighed. 'I tried. For a time, I gave up luscious foods, abstained from desire, curbed my appetites. But I could not sustain it. Still, I keep trying…' Contemplating the fiery flames with unseeing eyes, he continued, his voice as light as floating mist. 'Yes. I try…one edict that I ensure is strictly obeyed in my Empire is to grant equal respect to the followers of all religions. Let each man choose the path he wishes to take to reach the Truth…to attain his Heaven.'

Her mind frothing with beliefs and disbeliefs, Enkhtuya shifted her gaze into the fire. *What is this creature? Is he an erratic tyrant or a savage mystic? Is he a stone sphinx pitted with fissures of impenetrable secrets?* Flummoxed to the core, the flames hissing in the fireplace seared into her soul.

'Guunj!' His voice had regained its normal heaviness. 'I apologise. I have kept you from your dinner which must be cold by now. As it is you peck at the food. Come, come, Girl. Eat heartily. You will need your strength tomorrow for we traverse the desert.' And he held out a red, round fruit to her. 'Try an *alma* of Almalik. They are famous, you know.'

His voice brought Enkhtuya back from a long way off. Bemused, she looked at the rosy fruit in his outstretched hand. Then she laughed, 'Oh! It is an apple!' She looked up into a pair of warm, beaming eyes crinkling at the corners.

17

Kneeling on the rough stone floor, the creature could hardly be called human. The hanging bamboo bridge was dangerously curved in the middle with the weight of the men, women and children thronging it. They were visitors who had come to view the wild animal that walked on two feet but was not a man. It was a freak from a foreign land. Somebody threw a pebble that struck its cheek opening a cut. As blood dripped, the visitors laughed and pointed, 'Look! Look! It bleeds.' The creature closed its eyes. People still waiting on the bamboo stairs wanted to have their turn to sight the monstrosity, too. They vigorously shook the bridge which swayed to and fro making the spectators on it scream in delicious fear. When night fell, the viewers would go home. Then it would be the turn of the guards to throw some meat into the cell and poke the creature with sticks to ensure that it ate.

This was the way each day and night had passed by for months now. Genghis had become a shadow of his former self; more like a bag of bones. His clothes hung in tatters, long hair had rolled with dirt into dreadlocks, beard fanned out across his chest. Lack of sufficient healthy food as well as sunshine had covered his skin with scaly shingles. Open wounds crawling with maggots marked his limbs. He certainly did not look human. A Khan reduced to an entertaining spectacle to feed the cruel appetite of common people was a calamity that would have taken a toll on anyone else's sanity. But not so with Genghis Khan. He was made of stronger mettle. He sat through the torture day and night with his eyes closed not only to shut out the sadistic sights and sounds but also to focus on his mental strength.

One night, he had been burning with fever. Shivering in one corner of his cell, he ignored the food flung at him. For some time, the guards shouted at him and tried to reach him with their pointed poles, but he only stared at them without stirring. Then they returned with a long key that one of the guards leaned across from the bridge to fit into the lock on the barred door. Suddenly, Genghis realised that if the door was unlocked, it could spell freedom for him. He could try rushing the guards if they came in and jump the twenty feet from his cell to the ground. Slowly, he sat up ignoring his aching limbs. He held his breath waiting for the door to swing open. But the other guard said something and after a whispered conversation, the first guard removed the key from the lock. As they walked away, Genghis let out his breath. *So close yet so far!*

Only during the wee hours of the night, just before the sky lightened, could Genghis rest. There were no visitors then and the guards would finally sleep. He would then bow his head and pray to Khökh Tenger to give him strength till he would be released. For he was convinced that the Eternal Blue Heaven would free him. It was just a matter of time.

One morning, Genghis woke up to dark skies and pelting rain. It had been pouring heavily since before dawn. Genghis went up to the bars and extending cupped palms let the cool, clear water fill them. Then he brought his palms to his mouth and drank deeply. He washed his face, hands, legs clean with the water. When he looked around, he realised his cell was awash with puddles of water that the rain had splattered through the bars. As Genghis crouched in the only dry corner of his cell, he was thankful for the downpour. Visitors would be discouraged to come to view him and he could relax. The guards also stayed inside their shelter. All day it rained and by evening Genghis had begun to shiver in the dampness. He curled himself as tightly as he could for he could expect no succour from his keepers. To avoid getting wet his guards did not even throw him any food that evening. All night, Genghis lay shaking with cold and hunger. When the gray daylight entered his cell, he realised the rain had not let up. *Another wet, hungry day,* he told himself, filling his gnawing stomach with handfuls of rainwater. He washed the earthen pot and filled it with fresh water. Genghis consoled himself, *at least the spectators won't be here.*

But he was wrong.

Towards midday, his gaze fell on the bridge. It was swinging wildly as it did when somebody stepped onto it from the stairs. Tensely, Genghis stared at the shaking span as a figure hove into sight. It was gowned and veiled, so Genghis could not even make out if it was a man or a woman. He sat cowering in his corner, eyes closed expecting a fresh outrage. And he was not disappointed. A projectile slammed against his chest and fell to the ground. Slowly, he opened his eyes seeking the object on the ground. Then he saw it; a black cord snaked along the stone floor. Attached to it was a pendant; a black stick branching in two opposite directions. Genghis could hardly believe his eyes. Slowly, he picked it up. *Is it… can it be…the…the…wishbone…my wishbone? But…didn't Börte…have…it as keepsake on her neck?*

He looked up.

A pair of eyes glittered from behind the veil and a hand beckoned. Astonished, Genghis went up to the bars and looked closely at the figure. It looked like a woman but was too heavily covered for him to be sure. A husky voice whispered, 'I have been sent by my clanswoman…' Genghis looked at the veiled face without a change of expression.

It could be a trick.

'….your wife,' the figure added.

His eyes brightened, 'Börte?'

'Yes. I am an Ongirad, though I am married to a Tangut.'

So, it is a woman, concluded Genghis.

She hastily continued, 'I can't say more. Be ready to climb down from this perch on the day the rain stops.' And she disappeared into the white sheets of water streaming from the dark sky, as if she had never existed.

Genghis Khan went back to his corner fingering the dry and blackened wishbone. He wondered, *can I believe her? Is she for real or was it a vision of my fevered mind? But this keepsake? Börte never parted from it. How could it reach this woman unless Börte gave it to her?*

He waited impatiently for the rain to stop. He would know then whether the mysterious woman would keep her promise. It was only by the evening of the third day that it reduced to a drizzle and finally stopped. Dark clouds still hung threateningly but drops did not fall.

Did she say day or night? Genghis racked his brains trying to recall the brief instructions.

The guards finally decided to throw in some food which Genghis wolfed down quickly. Not only was he hungry but he had a reason to build up his strength. That night, he lay close to the bars, his eyes raking the bridge gently moving in a breeze that had sprung up. After a time, his heavy lids dropped and he slept.

How long the slumber lasted, he had no idea, but something woke him up. Instantly, his eyes went downwards. In the empty yard beyond the wall, there stood a covered, wooden box-like litter. Slowly, Genghis sat up. From his vantage point, he observed the guards approach it. A conversation ensued between the litter bearers and them. As Genghis squinted at the group, he made out from the gestures that things were not agreeable between the two groups. Suddenly, the curtains of the litter parted, and a hooded figure stepped out. Some object was thrown with great disdain at the guards. It fell to the ground and the guards scrabbled in the dust for it. As Genghis watched, one of the guards handed over the long, large key to the barred door of his cell. Then they both walked away with rapid strides through the open gates leaving his cell unguarded.

The figure climbed the bamboo staircase and walked down the swinging bridge. Genghis Khan tightly held the bars as she leaned across to fit the key to the lock. It was not easy, and she had to match her efforts with each swing of the bridge that brought her closer to the lock. She struggled with it but finally the lock sprung. Immediately Genghis pulled the barred door towards him. He stepped out onto the ledge and looked down at the drop of twenty feet. A jump may cost him broken bones, but it was worth his freedom. The woman had already run down the stairs and was standing near the litter. Genghis jumped with his hands spread to clasp the swaying bridge. His fingers curled around the bamboo slats.

He hung there wondering if the gangway was resilient enough to allow him to bodily pull himself up and attempt the staircase. The bridge creaked. It was too fragile. So, he flung his legs in the air as hard as he could. The bamboo bridge began to swing to and fro. Repeating the ploy, he made the light catwalk swing out more and more each time. Finally, it began to arch across the wall that divided the yard from the guard enclosure. At the right moment, Genghis jumped and managed to fall on his hands and feet on the narrow wall. From there it was only leap of a few feet to the yard below, but he hit the ground in a tangle of arms and legs. Scrambling up, Genghis ran towards the litter.

The bearers were already in position as the hooded woman thrust him inside. She climbed in after him into the spacious interior and slammed the wooden doors shut. The bearers instantly picked up the litter on their shoulders. Genghis Khan could hardly believe that he was free. The litter quickly left the yard passing through the open unguarded gates and into the maze of streets. As he tried to prevent himself from falling on his companion in the lurching litter, he closed his eyes and thanked Khökh Tenger with all his heart. *Who else but the Eternal Blue Heaven could have sent him this saviour; Börte's clan sister in Xi Xia?*

18

The passing of time could not be measured because the adrenaline that had vitalised Genghis' half-starved limbs to make the audacious leap to freedom had drained away leaving him weak and shaking. His companion covered him with a blanket but did not converse with him. As it is he was too overcome by his sudden deliverance from months of torment and was content to snuggle into the warmth enveloping him. Still, it was quite a while before the litter became still, so Genghis assumed that they had left the main city. The blanket was removed, instructions were given and acknowledged in hushed voices before two pairs of strong arms held up the emaciated man to walk him into a building that loomed up in the darkness.

It did occur once to Genghis' befuddled mind, *am I being taken into another prison?* But when he was laid down on a soft, raised bed, he closed his eyes and gave in to his fatigue. What he didn't know was that for the next few days he was delirious with fever for he had caught a chill from the rain dampening his cell for days. In the few lucid moments he was conscious of the touch of gentle hands wiping the sweat from his brow. It took nearly a week for the fever to break.

The morning the fever left him, Genghis lay with eyes closed but acutely aware of melodious chirpings drifting from somewhere close by. A scented breeze softly played over his cooled skin. It was so heavenly that he was sure Khökh Tenger had taken his breath away. Slowly, he lifted his eyelids and then he was sure he was in heaven. A pair of brilliant, blue eyes looked down on him, limpid with tenderness. The face was round, smooth and as fair as the moon and just as serene. She could be none other than a goddess.

'Are you feeling better?' The husky voice brought back memories of a miraculous rainy day. He struggled to get up, but the lady gently pushed his shoulders back on to the feather-soft bed. Anyway, his head had begun to swim the moment he had lifted it, so he didn't need much encouragement. 'Please lie down,' she said. An infinitely sweet smile turned up the corners of a rose-bud mouth. Looking beyond him towards the head of the bed, she instructed, 'Bathe him and change his clothes.' Then looking down at him, she said, 'I will come later in the evening. Please rest now. You are still too weak.' Amazed, he watched the celestial being rise from his side and glide through a large, wooden door, turning to give him another angelic smile.

Genghis was insensible for the next couple of days, so he didn't know whether she kept her promise. Yet, half-consciously, he was aware of a gentle presence whose ministrations helped him recover gradually from his debilitating condition. When he finally became fully aware of his surroundings, he realised that he had been bathed, his hair and beard trimmed, and a soothing herbal ointment applied to the shingles on his skin. His wounds had scabbed over. For a moment, he cringed wondering if it was the lady who had carried out these intimate services, but he soon realised that there were two men and an elderly woman who were his daily caregivers. He was surprised to find that they conversed with him in his native tongue.

As he sat up to have his nourishing soups and meats, he looked around himself in wonder. He was in a large room with broad windows on two walls that definitely overlooked a garden for he could hear the birds singing and smell the fragrance of flowers. The bottom half of the walls were stone while the upper parts were polished wood with carved niches that enclosed painted images of a cross-legged saint draped in flowing garments, hair knotted atop his head, eyes closed, his fingers peculiarly bent, smiling beatifically. Genghis wondered, *who is this? Their Emperor?* He knew that the Emperor of Xi Xia was known as Burkhan meaning the 'Holy One', thus he assumed these were his portraits. However, his questions vanished in his fascination with everything around him, whether it was the fine garments on his own body and slightly ordinary ones on his servers, or the bed he was lying on with its soft layers or the metal and wooden platters, bowls and cups that he ate from or the smooth, stone floor under his feet. No doubt, his mind kept spinning around the identity of his divine benefactress but he hesitated to ask the servers. He would look for her every day, but she had not visited him since he had regained consciousness.

Eventually, another fine morning, Genghis was strong enough to be helped by his servers outside to a covered patio facing a walled garden. Sitting in a deep cushioned chair with long arms that supported his body, he gazed at the bright sunflowers waving their slender stalks while the blooming bushes at their feet attracted hordes of bees and butterflies. Warm and dappled, the sunshine fell on his limbs that had fleshed out a little now. He frowned at the violet, maroon, pink and white flowers on the bushes spread across the garden. Opening cup-like petals they released sweet perfume into the air. *What are these flowers? They don't grow on the steppes,* he was thinking when his ears discerned a female voice. He looked up eagerly and was rewarded by the sight of his saviour at the far end of the garden. She had just come through the small gate in the wall and was conversing with a man who carried gardening tools. Since the lady was absorbed, Genghis used the opportunity to observe her. She was taller than most women and looked stately due to her high chignon and the way she held up her head. Draped in rich, embroidered flowing gowns clinched by a wide belt around a tiny waist gave him a fair idea of her willowy figure. Her round face with its slanting, cerulean eyes, delicate nose and full, red mouth was familiar to him.

All of a sudden, she turned to look at him as if aware of his scrutiny. Instantly, he lowered his eyes but not before seeing her smile and wave at him. To his disappointment, she did not come over but left soon after. That night he plucked up courage to ask the old woman server about her.

'She is *Guunj* Gurbelchin, Sire,' said the elderly maid. 'She is wife to Prince Asha, the *Gambu*...the Imperial Commander of Xi Xia. A great lady.'

Genghis recalled his first meeting with her. 'But she is a Mongol, isn't she?'

'Yes, Sire,' nodded the maid.

'How is she married to the *Gambu*?' Genghis asked.

'You see, Prince Asha is the Burkhan's nephew.'

An image rose before Genghis' eyes of a sneering, richly dressed man who had ordered his cruel confinement. *Hmmm...Burkhan's nephew! No wonder he is so arrogant,* reflected Genghis.

He turned his attention back to the old maid's words. 'As a young man, the *Gambu* had wandered into the Mongol lands. There he glimpsed our beautiful lady, only a child of seven years, then. He had fallen in love with her and persuaded her father, the Chief of the Ongirads clan to allow him to marry her. Giving her father many gifts in return, the Prince had carried off his bride to his own country, Xi Xia. Her father, being rich, had also gifted his daughter a large dowry and we, her Mongol servers, were part of it. Prince Asha nurtured her like a precious pearl and ensconced her in his household here in Yinchuan, the capital of Xi Xia. That happened twenty-four years ago. Though, he is elder to her by many years, our Gurbelchin has always been the Prince's senior wife and his entire household bows to her. She looks after all his wealth and property that consist of several palaces and many riches.' She picked up the empty bowls of food and began to carry them off. At the door, she turned to say, 'This palace also belongs to the Prince.'

While her words solved one mystery for him, it brought up another one; a worrying question. If Prince Asha was the Burkhan's Imperial Commander, he was unlikely be a collaborator in this intrigue to rescue him from the captivity carried out on his own orders. Yet, he was cloistered in Prince Asha's palace. An extremely volatile situation to be in! *And,* mused Genghis, *what has prompted his beloved wife, Guunj Gurbelchin to play this dangerous game? Or are they both in league and for some dubious reason have confined me in this luxurious prison?* He passed a very restless night, tossing and turning. At the very crack of dawn, he sat up waiting for the old maid to come with his bowl of milk. He wanted to question her further.

While he racked his brains thinking of how to get information without raising suspicions, one of the male servers entered with a large bowl of milk on a platter.

'Where is the maid?' Genghis asked.

'She is cooking, Sire. How can I help you?' He was pleasantly humble, but Genghis hesitated to speak to him. *Who knows whether any of them are Asha's spies?*

Instead he asked, 'When is the *Guunj* coming?' *That is the best recourse; to confront the Guunj,* Genghis decided, *after all, attack is the best form of defence.*

'Probably sometime during the day. I am not sure,' he replied.

'Hmmm...please inform her that I need to speak with her,' he told the man who nodded.

Genghis prepared himself to wait patiently as he began to dress and take his morning meal. Somehow, as he donned the cream silk robe that clung to his skin and tied the sash, he had a passing thought about his appearance being suitable. Never had he worn such colours wrought in such elegant material or waited to meet such a refined, enchanting lady. Then he laughed at his own foolishness, *she is married to a prince, you fool!*

He couldn't pace inside his room anymore. So, he went for a stroll around the courtyard garden. Bees buzzed, dragon flies droned, and birds twittered amidst gaudy blooms and fluffy pinks of cherry blossoms overhead, but Genghis hardly saw any of it. When he reached the small gate, he leaned over it but balked at going beyond. His view was of a larger formal garden with a paved path leading to the massive doors of a splendid mansion. All at once, he heard the distant sing-song chant of litter bearers. Instantly, he rushed back to the patio and settled himself in one of the reclining chairs. He wanted to look relaxed though his heart was banging painfully in his chest. Possibly, it was a few minutes, but it seemed a long time before *Guunj* Gurbelchin appeared at the gate. Today she was dressed in a butter-yellow satin gown that swished as she walked towards him. He got to his feet and bowed low.

'You wanted to speak to me.' Her voice was low and soft.

Genghis Khan came erect and indicated the chair, 'If you please, *Guunj*.'

She sat down gracefully, and tilted her head to one side, waiting for him to speak.

Never had Genghis' throat dried up thus when speaking to a woman. *But this was no ordinary woman*, he thought. 'I wanted the opportunity to thank my saviour. You have taken great trouble in not just rescuing me but in giving me shelter, care and comfort. I believe I am alive only because of your efforts and I am eternally grateful to you, *Guunj*.'

The lady inclined her head elegantly, accepting his gratitude silently with a slight smile. Encouraged, Genghis went on in a lower tone of voice. 'Yet, I am perplexed as to why am I given this honour.' And he waited.

She lowered her lashes momentarily but when she raised them, her eyes had a determined glint. In her usual husky tone, she said, 'I was waiting for this question and you deserve to know the answer. As I had told you, your wife had sent me a message along with a memento that I must aid you to the best of my ability. My loyalty to our clan persuaded me to fulfil her request.'

She stopped speaking but Genghis softly said, 'And?'

The *Guunj* sighed. 'Yes. There is more. By now, you must have got to know that my husband is Prince Asha. He is not only the Burkhan's *Gambu* but his Chief Advisor. Over the last few years, I have been disheartened to notice that our ruler's policies are turning more and more against the Mongol nation. He wants Xi Xia to align with the Jin Empire. Despite being married to a Mongol for so many years who has given him no cause for any complaints, my husband is hostile to the Mongol people. It is a source of great unhappiness between us.'

'So, my rescue is a way to avenge his malice towards our nation?' Genghis asked, slowly.

Gurbelchin shrugged. 'Maybe. Maybe I have become tired of his steady decline into cruel practices against any Mongol who may fall in his power.'

'Hmm...,' mused Genghis Khan. 'Can I assume that Prince Asha is not aware that I am being hosted in one of his palaces?'

'That is right.' She permitted herself a small smile. 'In fact, he has been mad with rage since it was discovered his latest Mongol animal had fled the cage. At first, he went after the guards who had escaped across the borders to the Song Empire on that night itself. Then he ordered searches in each house and inn in Yinchuan but couldn't find his prey. He didn't think of searching the palaces especially his own. Now there is a ring of soldiers constantly patrolling the walls of the city. The gates have double guards who check thoroughly all who leave the city.' She smiled again. 'Well, this time he is outwitted.'

'But have you not put yourself in a risky position?' Genghis' voice expressed his amazement.

'I don't care anymore,' she blurted. Genghis saw the placid mask crack as a spasm of bitterness passed over it. 'Besides, we own six palaces. I run all of them. He has never taken any interest in their details or which of our guests are lodged where. As long as the feasts we give are well organised and the Burkhan is happy with our hospitality, he absorbs himself with virulent politics.'

Genghis was silent trying to assimilate the astounding reality.

She assured him. 'Don't worry. You are quite safe here. You must rest and eat well. I hope you are comfortable.'

'Yes. Yes. I am more than comfortable. Actually, I am thinking about your well-being,' said Genghis and then felt he had become too familiar.

But she smiled her usual sweet smile and stood up. 'You will have to excuse me. I have duties to look to.' Turning towards the gate with a dainty wave of her hand, she said, 'Don't think about me.'

Genghis bowed to her. When he raised himself, her yellow gown flashed for an instant at the gate and she was gone. *How can I not think of a noble soul like you,* thought he.

19

Turning right at the Sayram Lake, the carts, wagons and trebuchets, heavy siege weapons were hauled over the ravines and torrents of the new Pine Tree Pass military road, with its forty-eight wooden bridges, built by Chagadai, the Khan's son, for the Mongol invasion of the previous year. Enkhtuya trotting alongside Shigi took a deep breath of the cool air and looked around herself. On both sides of the rough gravel path, were forests of fruit and nut trees. She identified the apple or *alma* trees and noticed a few fat golden pears hanging from branches.

'What are those?' She pointed to a profusion of green balls spread beneath the green canopy of a towering tree. Some of them had cracked open revealing a brown interior.

'Oh! Those are walnuts,' replied Shigi nonchalantly.

'Walnuts!' Enkhtuya was delighted. 'I love walnuts. Can I pick some?'

'Umm…alright. But be quick,' warned Shigi. He moved his horse into the shade of the trees a little way out of the path of the rest of the riders. Enkhtuya did the same. He dismounted and helped Enkhtuya to her feet. He extended his hand for the reins of her mare as Enkhtuya slipped off. Quickly, she ran down the slope and began to fill her *deel* pouch above the sash with the round, green fruit.

'Come on! Come on!' Shigi urged her worriedly. He was not supposed to allow the *Guunj* so much liberty and sighed when she came running. But a grin spread across his face at the spectacle she made with the front of her *deel* bulging like a bag.

Enkhtuya frowned at him. 'What's so funny?' She snapped at him as he flung her on the back of her mare.

'You!' He guffawed as they cantered ahead to retrieve their places in the cavalcade. Enkhtuya made a face at him. As they trotted up the inclining track, Enkhtuya bit into the green skin, peeled it off and spit it out. Then she crushed the thin, inner shell with her teeth into two halves. Digging out the fissured nut, she chewed on it with gusto. It was delectable. Suddenly, she pointed upwards silently, her mouth full of walnuts. Outlined against the blue sky a mountain goat leaped across a chasm between the rocks. Snow-white and plump, its curved horns gave it the look of a flying devil!

'What a marvellous place!' Enkhtuya exclaimed after swallowing.

Shigi smiled. 'These are the Tien Shan Mountains. They are beautiful but not as grand as our Altai ranges.'

'Ufff...,' expostulated the girl, 'Now don't go on and on about your great Mongolia, please.' Shigi pressed his lips together, scowling at the troopers around him.

Snorts and a scuffling in the undergrowth made Shigi look towards his left and he shouted, 'Boar! Wild boar!' The soldiers looked longingly in the direction of his pointing finger. But nobody stopped to shoot an arrow in the anticipation of some succulent roasted boar meat during meals. Discipline while the army marched was paramount.

Enkhtuya screamed, 'Where? Where?' She bent this way and that trying to spy the animal but couldn't see a thing. Soon they had passed the spot.

'There are jackals, wolves and foxes too,' said Shigi with a wicked grin. 'They might enter your tent at night...'

'Humph...,' retorted the girl to his teasing.

For the midday meal, they halted on a grassy toll against the background of juniper forests rising up into snowy peaks. Far below, sunlight glinted on a cool, crystal lake. As Bolorma served Enkhtuya with apples, nuts, boiled eggs and some bread filched from an Almalik baker, a pair of roe deer came up to them on delicate toes. Erect ears pricked up against their small horns, short tails flicking and noses snickering, they were fascinating. Enkhtuya threw them some apple cores which they were content to munch but when she moved to touch them, they leaped in alarm. As they loped away into the trees, the girl sighed, *this place is really heavenly!* Somehow, the serenity of the mountain glades softened the ache she carried constantly in her heart.

When the sun had just begun to slide down from above their heads, they exited the mountains and began to traverse a stretch of gravel and boulders. After the cool heights, the sun's heat reflecting off the stones burned Enkhtuya's skin. The wool of the *deel* was prickly against her soft skin but she had to bear with it for a few more hours. Only when the sun began to sink behind what seemed like brown hills, did a small breeze spring up drying the sweat freely dripping down her face. In a couple of hours, Enkhtuya was glad of the warmth of her *deel* for now the breeze was distinctly chilly and stronger. The velvet dome above was pierced by a thousand pin heads, big and small and the only sounds were the jingle of harnesses as the procession wound its way through a hushed darkness. *What a strange, weird world...blow hot, blow cold,* thought the girl.

'There it is!' exclaimed Shigi. Drooping with tiredness, Enkhtuya raised her head and was stunned to see fairytale strings of lights emerging from the dark sea. As she stared at it, Shigi explained, 'This is Beshbalig. It is an oasis.'

'Oasis?' The Princess turned wide eyes at him. 'Are we in the desert?'

'Nearly. At least we will be in a couple of days,' he replied.

At Beshbalig, Genghis Khan was met by the Governor of the small town, one of the outposts of the Silk Road. After elaborate greetings, bows and small talk, the Khan and his commanders were led into the Governor's own residence. Shigi touched his mount and Enkhtuya's mare to canter behind the group. The governor of Beshbalig lived in an imposing two-storied structure sprawling across a large area though it was too dark to see and the girl was too wilted to observe much. Shigi went towards a side door where Bolorma was waiting. As Enkhtuya dismounted and nearly tumbled into her maid's arms, Shigi turned around and trotted away.

Helped by Bolorma, the Princess climbed a flight of wooden stairs to reach a room on the upper floor. A lone candle did not light up the far corners but outlined a low sleeping platform. Bolorma deposited the girl on it and went down to look for some hot food to revive her mistress. When she had scolded the kitchen slaves into giving her some hot broth and finally returned, the girl was curled up on the pallet fast asleep. Since none of Bolorma's entreaties pierced her utterly weary repose, the old woman herself quaffed off the broth she had wrangled with so much effort.

Dawn had hardly gleamed through the open windows before Enkhtuya stirred. It was her stomach repeatedly rumbling in hunger that had woken her up. For a few moments, she lay still trying to orient herself to the surroundings as the smoke cleared from her benumbed mind. Pieces of the previous day flitted through; riding amongst sapphire lakes, emerald forests, viewing unusual wild creatures and finally the hot stones. *Where am I now?* Enkhtuya scrambled up and the walnuts dropped from her *deel* thumping on the wooden floor waking Bolorma.

She inquired sleepily, 'My *Guunj*?'

But the Princess was leaning out of the window. Misty in the morning dew of the approaching autumn, vineyards stretched in long furrows fanning outwards from the mansion. Intermittently, oranges trees sprang up between them. On the horizon, an expanse of blue water sported flocks of wild ducks and a few one-legged cranes. It was idyllic and Enkhtuya breathed in lungfuls of the enchanting dawn. Without turning, she declared, 'I am so hungry, Bolorma. Please bring me something or I will crumble to nothingness.'

'I imagine so,' retorted the old maid drily, hastily getting up from her pallet. 'You slept on an empty stomach last night, my lady.'

The princess leaned further to the right and sighted around the corner a covered patio on the ground floor. She observed from above, a familiar figure emerge through the door. Genghis Khan looked to his right and nodded to somebody just beyond the girl's view. Then he climbed down the few stairs, turned right and walked away. After a few minutes, she heard thudding hooves. The Khan with four generals galloping behind him flew through the vineyards towards the lake and vanished in clouds of dust. *Can't he ever relax and enjoy a peaceful morning?* Enkhtuya shook her head, mournfully.

Bolorma entered the room with platters of large, luscious grapes, oranges and a bowl of goat's milk. Enkhtuya sat down at the low table beside the window and began to peel an orange, humming to herself. Somehow, the refreshingly pleasant morn had lightened the burden of sorrow that she had been carrying all this time. She savoured the juicy wedges and then popped a few grapes into her mouth. As she bit into them, the sweet juice spilled from the corners of her mouth. She wiped them with her palm, giggling at Bolorma. But the maid only looked at her grimly.

Conscious that the old woman was down in the dumps, she remarked, 'Another quarrel at the kitchen?'

'Worse.'

'Why? What is it?' Alarm flashed through Enkhtuya.

'We are not going to Mongolia,' said Bolorma in a flat tone.

'What? Where are we going, then?' The girl sat up.

'Nobody is sure,' the maid said dismally.

'Who told you this? How do you know that we are not going to Mongolia?' Enkhtuya demanded, her hunger forgotten.

'Well, what I heard in the kitchen was this: if we were going to Mongolia, we should have gone on the straight route through a patch of desert and then crossed the Altai Mountains. But the Khan has commanded the forces to turn south. That is why we are in Beshbalig,' offered Bolorma.

'But…but Shigi said this was enroute to Mongolia… no, he didn't,' the girl recalled. 'He only said Beshbalig is an oasis.'

Heavy silence reigned in the room as both women stared at each other. Finally, Enkhtuya asked, 'Did you get any…any hint as to where we are headed?'

'Some say that the Khan has veered off the course for he wants to advance into China and finish the incomplete business of taking the Jin government at Kaifeng under his control. Others speak of camp rumours that the kingdom of Xi Xia is the Khan's target. Apparently, it has a new emperor...called Xianzong who is too arrogant to submit as a vassal to the Khan. So, he needs to be taught a lesson.'

Enkhtuya's heart leaped. 'Xi Xia? My father's country?'

Bolorma gave her a quizzical look.

'What kind of lesson does the Khan want to teach my country's king?

'There is only one kind of lesson that the Lord knows,' remarked the maid.

'War!' exclaimed Enkhtuya. 'He means to go to war with Xi Xia. That means bloodshed.'

Bolorma shrugged.

'No! No...,' wailed the Princess. Instantly, Malikpur rose up before her eyes, its ghosts frozen in agonised postures...and her little son....

'Well, you cannot stop him.' Bolorma's tone was pragmatic. 'But war means our comforts will certainly disappear. Everything from food to transport will be dedicated to the war effort. Like...like your mare....'

'Our comfort is not the point here, Bolorma. It is the unjustified killing of innocents that has to be prevented,' declared the girl passionately.

Bolorma unfolded herself from the corner where she had been squatting. Picking up the unfinished platter of fruit, she said dourly, 'To me, our comfort is important for I have to beg, borrow or steal it, *Guunj*. So that you have the time to think about saving the world.' And she flounced out of the room.

After a hot bath, Enkhtuya was amidst the vines still trying to work out how she would convince Genghis Khan to not go to war or at the least wage a war where his soldiers fight only other soldiers; without killing, maiming or raping unarmed men, women or children. She tried out various speeches addressing them to the fat, large, purple and green bunches of grapes hanging from the trellis. They only swung gently to and fro. A clattering of hooves brought her up short and made her rush along the furrows. Panting, she emerged onto the path leading to the mansion just in time to see the Khan approaching it. Behind him the commanders galloped like obedient waves following a rushing river.

Enkhtuya lifted a hand and shouted, 'My Lord, I need to speak with you.'

The Khan's eyes were focused in the distance as if she was just an inanimate shadow in his way and he swept past her. His men also looked stoically ahead and cantered past. Dust rising behind the entourage covered the girl from head to toe leaving her coughing. She stared at the distant horsemen, perplexed at the deliberate snub.

20

'So where did the Tanguts come from?'

'Well, they were originally from the eastern mountains of the Tibetan massif but due to trouble with the Tibetans, many thousands of years ago, they moved further east. They came upon the Ordos plains, within the bend of the Yellow River. Later, the Tangut leaders built a new capital, this city called Yinchuan, west of the Yellow River and thrust further westwards over the Helan Mountains to establish an empire.' Princess Gurbelchin leaned back in her chair and looked across the walled garden. It was dark in the patio and the fireflies had begun to twinkle in the peony bushes.

'Is that how they took control of the fertile pastures between the Alashan Desert to the east and the Takla Makan Desert to the west?' verified Genghis. 'Smart!' he chuckled.

'Certainly!' agreed Gurbelchin. 'This is called the Hexi Corridor and is part of the main trading passage, the Silk Route. It made Xi Xia accessible to merchants from far off lands and brought fabulous merchandise into the country.'

'Who actually founded the kingdom of Xi Xia?'

'The true founder was Li Yuan-hao, an ambitious and talented ruler,' explained his companion. 'He declared himself emperor, defeated powerful neighbours and created the special Tangut script to record laws and translate Buddhist texts that the Tanguts had brought from Tibet. Our country's religion is Buddhism. He actually gave Xi Xia an identity. He called it The Great State of White and High.'

'Even the Tangut men are quite identifiable...,' remarked Genghis. 'I have noticed that they shave the top of their heads and only keep a fringe around the forehead and ears.'

'Yes. That was also commanded by Emperor Li.'

'But what is Buddhism?' Genghis was curious.

'Well, it less of a religion and more of a philosophy founded by Siddhartha Gautama from the Land of the Indus River. He said that one can attain Enlightenment by following the Eight-Fold path through the practice of the teachings of the Buddha in one's daily life. It develops a person's spiritual growth and insights into the true nature of the Universal Truth,' explained Gurbelchin.

'Interesting! I must find out more about it,' declared Genghis. 'In Mongolia there are only shamans with their roots, bones and corals. But I am sure there are more than one way to reach the Universal Truth.'

A companionable silence ensued each reflecting on the other's words. These were the conversations with abundant contemplative intellect that had drawn Gurbelchin and Genghis together. Often, they would relax after simple but fine dining to discuss matters, both erudite and theological.

'And today Xi Xia is a stable, prosperous kingdom with six major cities,' mused Genghis Khan. 'You have skilful weavers, leatherworkers, builders and metallurgists. I had never in all my life seen such furniture or paintings as I have found in this palace. It has a nationwide system of schools and even a college. An academy of scholars to write and store historical records. You even use coins to buy things instead of bartering them.' Genghis thoughtfully pulled at his goatee.

'And, our merchants trade across entire Central Asia to provide our wealthy with luxuries,' said Gurbelchin.

'And your army is dispersed across a dozen military districts, each contingent under the command of a member of the royal family while the *Gambu*, Prince Asha supervises it all,' added Genghis.

'Did you know that there is a system whereby at the time of war the Emperor can dispatch messengers with silver tablets to local generals carrying orders to conscript males between the ages of fifteen and sixty? So, within days, he can raise an army of 300,000 troopers!'

'Hmmm...impressive. And this Emperor is also regarded as a spiritual leader,' mused Genghis.

'His authority is dependent on the idea that by being a virtuous ruler, he will attain enlightenment,' added Gurbelchin.

'Xi Xia is a model of a nation that is worthy of emulation but there is a flaw,' nodded Genghis.

'And what is that?' His fair companion smiled.

'An army marches on its stomach. Your army is not supported by the countryside as our Mongol troops are. It is dependent for food provided by its farmers and city traders. What will happen when the army is fighting too far from its cities or is cut off from them? They will die of starvation!' laughed Genghis.

Gurbelchin smiled and thought, *he is dazzled by the splendour of Xi Xia yet is discerning enough to point out its vital weakness. It must be his hard life on the steppes that has made him so astute and wise.*

It was not just these informative chats that vitalised their friendship, but also revelations of personal nature. Gurbelchin would relate hesitatingly how her marriage has been ruined due to her husband's overpowering ambitions. Today, he was the man who held the reins of the kingdom. He controlled the Burkhan or Emperor. Yet he hardly acknowledged the existence of his wife. Maybe it was because she had not produced the expected heir in the twenty-four years they had been married.

'The Burkhan expects the *Gambu* to host all state feasts and state guests. That responsibility falls to me. If everything is taken care of, he is not bothered about what else I do. I am no longer a wife to him. I am just an official hostess,' she lamented.

Genghis felt like smashing a fist into the face of the arrogant Prince for his cruel neglect of such a fine lady. *Truly, he is a colossally stupid man for all his grand connivances.* But he listened with an impassive face to this attractive woman and observed how she tried to hide her sorrows beneath a dignified exterior.

And when Genghis would wax eloquently about his childhood travails, the care of his wise mother and his beloved steppes, Gurbelchin would wipe away the tears helplessly running down her cheeks imagining the little boy running alone in the wilderness with the *cangue* round his neck. When he revealed his aspirations both for himself and his people, she sat up and asked excitedly, 'So are you the Khan destined to make Mongolia one nation again?'

Genghis had laughed unpretentiously and refused to reply.

Gurbelchin had whispered in awe, 'Genghis Khan, Emperor of Mongolia.'

Unconsciously, the lonely man and woman began to feel a deeper chemistry than just platonic camaraderie. One night, Genghis woke up with a guilty start. He had been dreaming of kissing a sleeping Gurbelchin. He was aghast and walked over to the open window. Outside the tranquil moonlit garden was a sharp contrast to the heated turmoil inside him. His heart hammered not with the fear of indiscretion but with undisguised passion for this wondrously alluring woman with whom he spent most of his waking hours. As his heart beats slowed, he felt ashamed. *How can I feel like this? These are depraved feelings for a woman who is my saviour. She will hate me if she gets to know. What will Börte think?*

Recalling Börte was like a bucket of icy water upturned on his head. *How can I be disloyal to her? Börte, my true wife, who detected me in his far-off land by her shamanistic intuition and sent her clan sister to help me…this is a betrayal of her. I must control myself.* Thus, strengthening his resolve, Genghis went back to his solitary bed.

He did try very hard. But every time, he walked with Gurbelchin in the garden, desire would flash in his core as he observed the gentle sway of her hips above the impossibly tiny waist. When she laughed at something he said, flinging her head back, his eyes raked the soft swell of her bosom visible at the corner of her gown's neckline. Sometimes when her bluest eyes held teasing laughter, his hands trembled to hold the heart-shaped face within his palms.

The inevitable was fated to occur.

It was a particularly warm night. The couple had just had a sumptuous dinner of delicately spiced herb meat and flagons of red wine. Genghis had joked that the wine was as light as water compared to his Mongolian *airag*. He had gulped more wine than he usually did. Gurbelchin suggested a stroll in the garden. They had moved between the scented blossoms on bushes sparkling with fairy lights of fireflies. It was a new moon night, so the tiny, diamante lights were brighter against the dark forms. Genghis walked just behind Gurbelchin innocently breathing deeply the jasmine scent wafting from her.

The lady half turned her head to look up at him to observe his reaction to one of her comments. Her rosy lips were half open and temptingly close. He could not help dipping his head and gently brushing them with his own. To his surprise, she turned around and pressed her lips to his. He didn't know when his hands cupped her face and he was kissing her with all the fervour of his pent-up passion. The fact that she was responding with equal ardour only fired his blood more. In hardly some minutes they were on the floor of the dark patio, restless hands and limbs exploring feverishly.

The fact that Princess Gurbelchin was as enthralled with him as he was with her completely swept away all feelings of guilt and shame from Genghis' mind. Börte was a closed door he locked up securely. If his conscience ever pricked him, he would tell himself, *something that feels so good cannot be wrong. The love we have for each other is as pure as a mountain spring on a hot summer's day. How can it be wrong to quench our thirst at it?* Once when he had divulged his doubts about their relationship to Gurbelchin, she smiled and justified their sweet bond in similar terms. Thus, the lovers sailed on the enchanting river of new-found intimacy with nary a thought to the future.

Genghis never ceased to wonder at the magical essence of his bonding with Gurbelchin. In some intangible way, not just their bodies and minds but even their spiritual dimensions blended seamlessly. One night, after some torrid yet ardent love, Genghis moved Gurbelchin's long hair away from her nape. Around her slender neck, he wrapped a black cord and tied it behind. When she looked down towards her breast, she saw the curious pendant; the bony wishbone.

'But isn't this Börte's?' Gurbelchin raised inquiring blue eyes to Genghis' face.

'No. It is mine,' replied her lover. 'I gave it to Börte to keep against my childhood promise that I would return to marry her.'

Still, Gurbelchin's eyes held questions.

'This wishbone has been my talisman. Now I give it to you with the pledge that my soul will always belong to you in this life and forever.'

Gurbelchin sat up. Tears welled up in her eyes. She held the pendant in her hand and said in a voice choked with emotion, 'I shall wear it on my breast always; all my life, as long as I live. I miss you terribly when I am away from you. This token will be like your touch on my skin. It will keep me with you forever, my Genghis.'

The rest of the night passed as Genghis described to Gurbelchin the adventure through which he had acquired the talisman.

The servers at the palace kept the lovers' secret hidden from all eyes and ears. The old maid and two men were Mongols from Gurbelchin's father's home. Their first loyalty was to their Princess and not Prince Asha. So, they looked on silently and revelled in the happiness of the lovers. The prince had no inkling that the dangerous creature for whom he had laid traps all around Yinchuan was safely ensconced in his own palace happily in his wife's arms. Whenever this thought occurred to Genghis, he chortled at the sheer irony of it.

21

Everything conspired to create a many-splendoured bliss for Genghis and Gurbelchin. Summer days prolonged; mellow sunshine filtered through the foliage of their secret garden, perfumed by the blooming peonies and the constant symphony of buzzing bees and the delicate dragon flies droning idly as the lovers lazed on the patio between bouts of ardent togetherness behind locked doors. Mid-day meals of fruit for the lady and nutritious soups and meat slices for the gentleman accompanied by copious volumes of wine would bring on a delicious lassitude to their world. When they awoke refreshed at dusk, Gurbelchin would return to her palace for a few hours. She did not want her husband to miss her when he returned home from his official duties. Besides, there would always be some state event to arrange. Only maintaining a normal pace of life would conceal their secret.

If she was not engaged otherwise and her husband was busy with work, Gurbelchin would return to share Genghis' dinner. Consequently, they would saunter through the dark garden or surrounded by its beauty give vent to their desires. Late at night, she could slip unseen into the bedroom at her palace that was separated from her husband's by a several large rooms in between. These sleeping arrangements had been decided by Prince Asha a long time ago.

After the initial heady exhilaration had passed, it was not as if Genghis did not question his intoxication with Princess Gurbelchin. *What was it about this particular lady, lovely, charming though older than me, in whose presence*

I cannot think of any other being not even Börte? It is her, her and only her…in my conscious thought, unconsciousness, in my very spirit and soul. Why is it that the depth of my fascination with Gurbelchin only increases with each day? With Börte, Genghis' love was one of a callow youth giving way to dependency and domestic bonding, fatherhood; not this leaping fire of unquenchable desire each time he saw her. As he pondered deeply, he realised that not only did Gurbelchin satiate him physically and emotionally giving back as much as she received, but she matched his mental prowess. With her he could plumb the galaxies of pedantic queries on the meaning of life or the universe, whether there is an ultimate Truth that one should seek, what does peace of mind mean and so on.

Besides, Genghis never forgot his destiny. Here, he may be far from being the Khan that he had proclaimed himself but he was always looking for strategies and solutions to reach his final destination. He could discuss them fully and confidentially with Gurbelchin which he had never done with any other person. Often, she would give him another view to a situation or a shrewd comment to chew on. Thus, her companionship was not only delightful but involved much learning.

That they were sufficiently clever to go on with their liaison right inside the lion's den made them even more daring. When Genghis expressed a wish to see the wonders of Yinchuan with his own eyes, Gurbelchin organised a tour. She arranged a closed carriage on wheels pulled by horses. They could view the outside world by pushing up the blinds on the windows, but nobody could see them. Since it was common for ladies of noble families to go around in this manner, nobody found it strange that Prince Asha's wife should do so. Of course, they were unaware that she was accompanied by a very virile young man. It was a great risk but Gurbelchin was willing to do anything for her love.

They rolled through streets filled with stalls and shops selling pungent perfumes, wonderful scrolls, silks, ornate rugs and many more marvellous treasures. Peeping into pagoda monasteries, Genghis observed huge, sculpted and painted images being venerated with incense, bells and gongs and realised he had seen the same serene face in the icons in his room.

'Who is that?' he whispered to Gurbelchin.

'That is the Enlightened one; the Buddha whose teachings we follow,' she whispered back.

His neck ached craning upwards to squint at the tiled roofs of the numerous grand palaces and the stately government buildings. Genghis Khan was duly impressed by the wealth of the kingdom. But it was the elegant splendour of the Imperial tombs that he would always remember. After moving through numerous neighbourhoods, they travelled out of Yinchuan city gates. The guards stopped them but when they saw the wife of the Imperial Commander leaning out of the window, they waved them ahead. Soon the carriage was trundling along a high rugged wall of rocks. They had entered the Helan Mountains. After a short distance, just above the rows of roadside trees, loomed up eight monuments. Giant, grey towers that rose to rounded points, each was the tomb of an Emperor of Xi Xia. They looked like huge fingers pointing to the sky. Each of them stood in its own courtyard and had its own series of five roofs, curling up at the corners and rising up smaller and ever smaller in size. Glistening turquoise, red, orange, green and yellow in the sunlight, tiles in ornate designs covered each roof with stone carvings edging them. Their magnificence took Genghis' breath away.

'Look there! The tomb for our present Burkhan is being raised,' pointed Gurbelchin.

Genghis looked in the direction of her pointing finger and noticed workers and artisans crawling on one side. Half the pagoda had been raised. 'I suppose the grey tower will be built after he is buried,' he concluded. The lady nodded and ordered the driver to move on.

When they returned to the palace, Gurbelchin insisted that he listen to her favourite poetry. Though Genghis was not really in the mood for abstract ideas, he acquiesced. In reality, he was unable to banish the sights and sounds of the tour that still assailed his senses. He was content to lie back as Gurbelchin recited and visit them once again in his mind.

Summer was nearly drawing to an end when disaster struck.

Prince Asha was not as obtuse as Genghis or his wife believed. He had noticed the pink flush on his wife's usually pale face and believed the unusually warm weather was the reason. During state feasts, he had seen her glowing and animatedly chatting with the guests. He had been glad for he thought she was following his orders to be more caring of the state visitors. And he had his spies. It was another matter that it took those sly creatures several months to unearth the perfidy occurring right under his nose because Gurbelchin's Mongol servants were staunchly loyal to her. In fact, they were not the cause of the revelation. When, the Prince's palace cleaner discovered Gurbelchin's maid handing over basins of vomit every morning for a week, he decided to gossip in the servants' room and pass on the good news that the Prince was going to become a father. One thing led to the other and it reached the Prince's ears. He knew that he could not be the father. He called on his espionage system and berated them roundly for their carelessness. They got into an energetic mode and came back with the information that Princess Gurbelchin spent an inordinate time at the remote palace. The die was cast.

That night the moon was at its fullest hanging like a yellow, round lantern. Their enclosed garden was illuminated as though it was day, each leaf, each flower outlined. Fireflies had decided to stay away from the competition, but a nightingale sang among the branches of a peony bush. Honeyed yet anguished, her trills seemed to be about the waning of summer joys. Gurbelchin and Genghis lay quietly in their chairs listening to the sonata that brought an unknown sadness to their own hearts. Slight but with nippiness to it, a breeze sprang up and Genghis went inside to get a wrap for his lady. She smiled her thanks as he gently put it round her shoulders. Her cerulean eyes now inky blue searched his face.

'Yes?' he mouthed silently. She shook her head but kept looking at him as if she wanted to say something. Genghis waited quite aware that she would speak when she felt it was right to do so. *After all, we have no secrets,* he reflected.

Suddenly, a scream came from beyond the garden gate along with an urgent pattering of feet. One of the men servants burst through the gates, *'Guunj!* Flee! Sire, flee, flee. The prince has arrived!'

Both of them sprang up and for a moment, Genghis was confused. He had lived so many months here that he had forgotten to prepare for the crisis of discovery. Gurbelchin instantly took control. 'Get the horse to the gates,' she instructed.

'Horse?' Genghis asked stupidly, still stunned.

'Yes, I keep a horse tethered here always...for an emergency like this. Go now before they come,' she spoke without panic.

'No!' Genghis shouted, 'I cannot leave you here. You must come with me.'

'Don't be foolish. How far will you go with me behind you? Everybody knows me. But nobody knows you. I know you will slip between their nets.' True to character, she was being pragmatic.

'No! No!' shouted Genghis, still adamant.

'Go!' Gurbelchin gave him a little push. 'Remember you have a destiny to fulfil. I will be alright. I know how to handle the Prince.'

A shout from the gate showed the large shadow of a horse. At the same time, screams came from inside the rooms and a couple of men burst through the front door. They had stealthily approached the palace from behind to ensure they caught the culprits red-handed. Genghis sprang to the gate and flung himself on the saddled horse. The man handed him the reins as Genghis wheeled around looking for escape. Soldiers were flooding the grounds surrounded by the high walls of the palace.

There was only one way out. He turned around for one last look. The patio was full of men though Gurbelchin's figure was clearly visible in the moonlight. A tall man emerged from the crowd and swung his hand at Gurbelchin's face. She sank without a sound to the ground. Genghis choked on a sound that was half a sob and half an expletive, but he had no choice. He dug his feet into the horse's belly and his excellent horsemanship came to the fore. He bent and spoke encouragingly in the horse's ears forcing its face to the wall. When he was sure that he controlled the animal, he rushed at the wall on a gallop.

The horse and he sailed over the high wall like a falcon. That was the last that the beautiful Princess Gurbelchin saw of Genghis Khan, her eyes nearly swollen shut from the slaps dealt by her enraged husband. Content, she sighed and closed her eyes painfully.

Genghis evaded the Imperial Commander's soldiers, but it was not so easy to elude the strict security lassoing the city of Yinchuan. There were two gates, one on either side of the city, each guarded by a formidable cache of sentries. Even the closed litters of the ladies were searched by them as he had found out when Gurbelchin had taken him out for the tour. It was she who had responded to their queries having flung a veil over Genghis' head. Now, there was no way he could pretend to be a woman and pass through. Besides, one gate was closed at night and the security doubled at the other one. Genghis trotted along the city wall for it was a shady area inhabited by the poorer people of the city. Months of tender care, good food and the emotional serenity had given him back his strength. Toned muscles rippled under his silk gown. He was apprehensive that someone from the derelicts cooking their dinners over open ovens would notice his rich clothes and bearing. The difference between them and him may arouse suspicions or worse tempt them to attack him for robbery. He kept to the shadows of the wall avoiding the bright moonlight. Going over the city walls that were four times his height was unthinkable. Besides, there would be sentries stationed on the outside perimeter.

All of a sudden, an animated knot of people ahead caught his attention. He halted in the dimness of gloom cast by heaped grain sacks to observe them. To his surprise a man on a horse joined them but Genghis had not seen any rider come towards them from anywhere. *Where had this man come from, then?* As he watched the chattering group, the man was gone. A few more moments of acute observation explained the magical trick. Obviously, there was a crack in the wall and people were coming and going through it. He realised that a kind of liquor hooch had sprung up near the crack. It was selling moonshine to the people on this side of the wall as well as to the bored sentries outside it. *If I wait patiently for the night to progress, the crowds will go home, and I will get my chance,* he thought. Looking around, he realised he was standing near a grain storeroom and it was unlikely that anybody would come there during the night. He walked his horse closer to the wall of the building so that both were hidden from the view of any passersby coming along the wall. He prepared to wait patiently.

Ears alert and muscles stiff, he couldn't relax fearing that soldiers would appear any moment searching for him. He was sure Prince Asha had alerted his security system by now and wished he was in a less vulnerable hiding place. He knew that he would have to make the attempt to escape from the city tonight itself. Tomorrow the city will be locked down like a fort. It was well past midnight when the merry mob began to disperse. In a couple of hours only a lone drunkard lay propped up against the wall and now the narrow chink in it was visible. Very cautiously, after looking all around, he began to approach it. The moment he left the shadows, he expected to hear a shout and an arrow slamming into his exposed back. He was equally aware that going through the wall was not necessarily the means to freedom. He may just walk into the arms of sentries.

The horse sensing his tension moved very slowly. When Genghis was parallel to the part of the wall where a few bricks had crumbled, and others removed, he saw the opening was just enough for a mounted man to slip through. Though the temptation was great, he waited just inside it. Clattering hooves came around the outer wall face. *Sentries!* As they passed the crack, Genghis saw they were patrolling in pairs. *That makes it more difficult,* he surmised, waiting inside. The moment the sentries passed, he began to count in a measured pace. By the time the next pair of sentries came by, he had counted to hundred. This meant it took around a hundred count for each pair to come around to the chink. He will have to be fast. Thankfully the wall was not straight. It curved and sharply turned adhering to the margins of the city. As he waited for the next pair, he peeped out. A few feet away were dark fields of crops standing nearly to a man's height. *Hmmm…good enough for me.*

The next pair cantered by and Genghis got ready, his heels digging into the horse's belly but reins tightly holding it back. Counting to twenty, he gave the sentries time to move away from the opening, before approaching it. He walked the horse through it as silently as he could. He knew the sound of their own horse's hooves would cover any sound he would make. He looked to his right and saw the backs of the sentries vanishing into the night. But the next pair would come by soon. I *must be quick,* he thought as he walked his horse towards the thick mesh of tall, green stalks. His sharp ears caught the sound of thumping hooves and he loosened the reins allowing the horse to gallop into the standing crop. Once in, he instantly pulled the reins tightly and brought the horse to stillness so that the rustle of leaves disturbed in their dive did not catch the attention of the sentries. As soon as they went past, he gave free rein to his *aduu*. With long strides, the horse joyfully chased the wind across the cultivated fields carrying Genghis to freedom.

22

It was burning hot during the day. Enkhtuya would gasp breathlessly in her tent. Weak with the fiery heat that was frying her up, she could not even lift her head. Periodically, Bolorma untied the cords of the leather pouch of water and held it to her dry mouth. Sounds of water sloshing in it tempted Enkhtuya to take several gulps of the coolness but she could only sip a little painfully through chapped lips as much of it dribbled down her chin. Bolorma wiped her face often with a wet cloth but her skin would dry up immediately and start burning even more. She lay inert but sleepless. Her only hope from the torment was when the fierce ball in the sky set on the horizon.

Gradually, the sand cooled under her pallet and the open flap of the tent darkened. Enkhtuya dozed off by then. She woke to a hustle-bustle as Bolorma heaved a bucket of warm water into tent. 'Wake up, *Guunj*!' She called. The girl sat up and rubbed her hands over her body wondering that her skin had not scalded during the day. The old maid would urge her to wash herself quickly before the chill of the night descended. After a change of clothes and a quick meal, Enkhtuya felt more like herself but the fatigue remained with her. When she heard the soldiers calling to each other, she knew it was time. Leaving her tent, she emerged into the night. The dark sky roofing the earth glittered with a million gems and the glistening white sand below her feet stretched away to as far as the eye went. *It was all very lovely,* Enkhtuya sighed, *but for how long would this tortuous journey go on? And where am I going?* She stepped on the mounting block to fling a leg across the mare's back and settled herself in the saddle shivering a little despite her warm *deel*. Idly, she watched her tent being dismantled and packed on a wagon. Bolorma climbed in with their belongings. The Princess yawned waiting for Shigi to escort her to their place in the long caravan.

Soon, they were trotting through the desert. To Enkhtuya it looked like an endless expanse of sand; tan in the daylight and white in the moonlight. But they were actually only passing by the edge of the Takla Makan Desert. And her fatigue combined with the coolness of the night brought on drowsiness making Enkhtuya's eyelids drop. But tonight, she did not want to sleep. Last night, she had been unable to stay awake and had nearly tumbled from the saddle. Half-conscious with sleep, she had an impression that strong hands had broken the terrible fall. Though she was still not sure whether it was all a dream, she had heard loud laughter and a man saying, 'Let's put her in the wagon with her maid.'

Another voice refuted it; a familiar voice with amused undertones saying, 'No. No. Just tie her up to the horse. My father used to tie me to my horse as a baby so that I didn't fall out.'

Enkhtuya had wanted to indignantly say that she was not a baby, but the paralysis of heavy slumber was upon her. She could only squirm ineffectively. In the morning, she had been embarrassed to find herself trussed up like a pig to the neck of her mare. Quickly she had untied her sash to the grins of Shigi and the troopers around her. Tonight, she was not going to go through the indignity again. So, she kept her itchy lids widely open. And thus she encountered a unique phenomenon.

The night was not very old when a strange, low music began to curl around the caravan. Enkhtuya looked to her right and left wondering who the singer was. Mounted soldiers trotted slowly and Shigi looked straight ahead. It did not seem as if they were hearing the low, wavering tune.

'Who...who is singing?' Enkhtuya asked hesitantly, wondering whether she was being stupid.

Shigi turned his head and putting a finger to his lips, whispered, 'Ghosts!'

But the girl was not having any of it. 'Don't be silly, Shigi!' she snapped, 'There are no ghosts and I am not a little girl.'

'Aren't you?' he countered and grinned. Enkhtuya knew he was referring to the previous night and bit her lip. Shigi enjoyed baiting the girl whose arrogance he deplored.

Then he took pity on her and pointed into the distance. The Princess looked that way and drew her breath in sharply. Out of nowhere, a row of hills had sprung out of the flat sands. 'Those are the Singing Sands,' intoned Shigi.

'Singing...? Do you mean to say that sands sing?' Enkhtuya frowned at the giant. 'Don't tease me. Tell me the truth.' She was shouting now for the wordless, mournful dirge was quite loud.

Shigi shouted back, 'That is the truth. Some kind of wind blows through those sand dunes making music. Nobody knows why.'

'How strange!' mouthed Enkhtuya.

'Better you cover your face and eyes with your sash for the wind also carries sand grains that will cut your skin,' shouted Shigi, pulling out his own sash.

Quickly Enkhtuya wrapped her sash around her face leaving only the area around her eyes open. All around her the men were doing the same. She hoped somebody had warned Bolorma, too. Now they were nearly on the dunes and she saw not one but rows of dunes one behind the other. Horses had lengthened their stride so that they could move through this natural wonder as fast as possible. Her ears deafened with the wailing that rose and fell as if a woman was singing a sorrowful song, Enkhtuya closed her eyes as gritty sand brushed against her face and bare hands. She pulled her sash over her eyes and rode blind into the flurries of sand. Her mare was clever and steadily followed the other steeds. Little by little, the stinging grains became lesser and lesser, the gusts of wind turned gentler and the music weaker. When her face no longer smarted, Enkhtuya raised the cloth from her eyes. They were through the Singing Sands! The dunes were behind them and their musical lament only wafted in the air. It drifted further and further away till it was heard no more.

After a couple of hours, a cheer went up and down the lines of troopers. Enkhtuya, who had fallen into a kind of stupor, roused herself to look around. When she raised her brows at Shigi, he explained, 'The mountains are close.'

'Mountains!' Enkhtuya raised herself in the saddle to glimpse this welcome respite from the sandy wilderness but could see nothing ahead.

'No. You cannot see them. You can smell them,' laughed Shigi.

Instantly Enkhtuya took a deep, snorting breath and her nose filled with sand flying from the hoofs of her horse. She sneezed and sneezed as Shigi guffawed. However, she constantly kept peering into the darkness to sight the mysterious mountains. Only when dawn broke, did she finally see the grey, uneven outlines of highlands on the horizon.

'There! There!' she shouted excitedly, as the caravan slowed to a halt for the morning break.

Bolorma arrived with her platter of fruit that she had acquired from Beshbalig and carefully preserved in a wet cloth during the day heat. Just the sight of the cool mountains had revived Enkhtuya and she hungrily consumed the pears, grapes and figs. As she drank deeply from the leather pouch, her eyes fell on Shigi, some distance away. Sitting on a rock, he was absorbed in his script. Not for the first time, the Princess was struck by Shigi; a fighting man by profession, his real interests lay in reading and writing. As she observed him, Enkhtuya wondered if she could force some information about their destination from him. *Why not try?*

She stood up brushing away the crumbs from her *deel* and strolled towards him. He looked up from the paper in his hand as she came near.

'Shigi...,' began the girl.

The giant frowned. *She is out to get something out of me.*

'Shigi,' repeated Enkhtuya, 'Where are we going?'

Instantly, his eyes went opaque. For a few moments, he stared at her silently. Then his eyes dropped, and he went back to his script.

'Peculiar!' snapped the girl and flounced away from him. She frowned at the clutches of men chatting and laughing over their meal until she noticed their ruler at the far end. For once, he was not surrounded by his commanders. Genghis Khan had found a flat stone that accommodated his cross-legged seating. On it he sat as if sculpted from the rock, eyes closed, a pipe clamped between his lips. Smoke drifting from it was the only sign of life in the stillness. Suddenly, the Princess made up her mind and with purposeful strides began to wend her way through the scattered groups.

Diffidently, she asked, 'Can I sit here?'

A slight inclination of his head.

Taking it as a positive reply, she sat on a boulder near him wondering how to begin. *Best not to mention the slight he accorded me the other day,* she reflected. Not knowing how else to retrieve what she wanted and acutely aware of the expediency of the time, she decided to be direct.

'You have been busy meeting your generals. So, are you planning another campaign?'

He only grunted.

'Who are you going to attack this time?'

No answer.

Enkhtuya ploughed on. 'Are you planning another massacre of innocent people? Isn't that what you consider a great victory?'

Oh no! This is not going the way I want it to. Why am I needling him? As she desperately cast about her mind for the right question, she nearly missed his abrupt reply.

'I am not responsible for the deaths of sinners.'

His words pierced a raw wound. 'Sinners? Hundreds of thousands of men, women and children, yes children, your Mongol army killed children...killed on your orders. Were they all sinners?'

He took the pipe out of his mouth and opened his eyes; black, hard and shining like onyx. They considered the girl, the stormy eyes in a young face. Then he spoke languidly, 'Maybe they were not the actual sinners but the leaders they sheltered were sinners. And rallying to these leaders was their sin.'

'What about your killings? Were they not sins?'

'Killing all the people in the cities of Khwarezm, Ortar, Merv, Bukhara, Samarkand...'

'And Malikpur,' cut in Enkhtuya.

'...was a principle of strategy. It was a technique to terrorise other rulers and people of other cities. And it worked. Citizens of many kingdoms opened their gates to my forces. You see?'

'No, I don't see,' she snapped. Then she swallowed. Bringing a studied sweetness to her words, she entreated, 'Please! Is there no way that the innocent can be spared in your new campaign? After all, they are not armed or soldiers. Let soldiers fight soldiers. Let the ordinary people be safe. Please, please consider this.'

The Khan just stared at her, his face expressionless.

Encouraged by his non-committal stance, she went on. 'I am a mother who is tortured day and night by the sight of her child's horrifying death.' Her voice choked as she articulated her terrible pain in words, but she went on, 'I don't want any other mother to face this great sorrow. Besides, the ordinary people can help you in many ways after the war is over. They can build houses, cut roads, grow food, make weapons, create things, trade and do so, oh...so, so many things.'

She looked at him, an impassioned plea in her large, blue eyes reflecting the blue morning sky.

The Emperor gave a short laugh and shook his head. 'What you ask for is impossible. We cannot shoot our arrows telling them to only pierce the chests of soldiers when we shower a city with them. Besides, what will I do with so many human captives? Sheep, goats, horses are more valuable than humans especially those who do not accept my absolute sovereignty. It is better that they die.'

'You and your army are murderers,' shouted the girl, her eyes filling with tears.

The Khan sighed. 'Enkhtuya, you are being unreasonable. Remember, what I told you. I am the punishment that the Eternal Blue Heaven deals out to those who break His laws. If they had lived by His laws, Khökh Tenger would have protected them and nothing. . .not even I could have hurt them. But that is not so. They deserve to die.'

'You are abominably arrogant,' declared Enkhtuya bitterly. 'Do you really believe that you are God's weapon doling out death to sinners? What an idea!'

The Khan puffed on his pipe a couple of times. Then he removed it from his lips to say, 'No, *Guunj*. This is not my pride. It is a truth that I discovered long, long ago when I was still a youth. I saw it written in the skies, the mountains, the grass, the animals and birds of the steppes.'

Wide, blue eyes contemplated the man as Enkhtuya racked her brains for another way to convince him.

The Khan knocked out the ashes of his pipe against the rock and declared, 'My destiny was written by Khökh Tenger when He freed me from the Tanguts. Now Xi Xia has to pay its debts to me.'

'Xi Xia?' Exhilaration made Enkhtuya forget everything. Shrilly, she asked. 'My country? Really? Are we going to my country?'

Genghis Khan's eyes, cold as pieces of black ice, regarded the ebullient girl impassively. Finally, he shrugged, 'Maybe.' He stood up and walked away. The girl stared after him, an indefinable lightness in her heart. *It's been a long, long time.*

23

The fertile banks of the Yellow River were cultivated expansively. Crops stood tall in the fields ready for harvest. Consequently, there was a lull as cultivators let the last days of bright sunshine ripen the wheat. Nobody worked in the fields now. They would come back at harvest time. Genghis would lie low in the fields during the daytime feeding the horse and himself with kernels of wheat. At night, he began to ride along the river until he found a series of sandbanks to cross over. Summer had reduced the level of the fast-flowing water yet his horse and he were nearly swept away by the swift currents in the river. Finally, he was across and began his progress towards the northern border of Xi Xia. Avoiding all cities, he remained in the wheat fields during the day and trotted through them after sundown. From the branches of a tree, one day, he fashioned a rude bow and used the plaited leaves of the wheat to string it. Sharp stones squeezed into thin, hard but straight sticks split open on one side became arrowheads. Now, he had a few arrows for his bow. It was not much of a weapon and would hardly sustain him in a real battle but would serve well to intimidate a curious farmer. At least he did not feel so defenceless with a bow slung across his back.

While he was confident of finding his way out of Xi Xia, he was constantly troubled by what he had left behind. He felt guilty that Gurbelchin, his ethereal companion and soulmate, was bearing the brunt of his freedom. He vowed to return to take her away as soon as he was able to. At night, when he lay back in his soft bed of wheat leaves, the *aduu* contentedly munching beside him, he would relive the last moments they had had with each other. Her lovely, serene, blue eyes shining with love at him as he wrapped the shawl around her haunted him. Somehow, he felt that she had been about to divulge something to him, but they had been interrupted by the raid on the palace. *What could she have wanted to say?* He asked himself repeatedly, a thousand times. He would try to recall whether there was a matter that they had wanted to discuss but nothing came to mind. Most nights he would sink into sleep frustrated with these thoughts. Next day, the same thoughts would propel him to try and reach the borders of Xi Xia, cross them and return to his own country. Once he had regained his power among the Mongols, he would return to rescue his beloved Gurbelchin.

He did not count the days but quite a few of them went past before the fields petered out. One morning, sleeping among the green stalks, he discerned gusts of wind bending the wheat. As he sat up, his face was stung by grains of sand. He realised that he was close to the desert and a sandstorm had sprung up. He curled himself into the ground and dragged the horse down beside him. Though the storm played havoc with the wheat above his head, they remained safe among the thick undergrowth. When the storm blew over, Genghis began to prepare for his route across the desert. Gurbelchin had had the foresight to include saddle bags and a blanket to the harness on the horse. Not for the first time he silently thanked his lady for she had thought much ahead of his needs if he had to flee.

That night, he filled the saddle bags hanging on both sides with wheat heads. He filled a small leather pouch with clear, cold water from an irrigation canal. Then astride his horse, he began to ride out of the fields. Once he was free of them, he gave rein to the horse who rushed into the sandy tracts with giant strides. Exuberance filled Genghis' heart as the night wind played in his hair and the desert opened up before him. He was in his element; a nomad on a fast horse in the wilderness.

He was aware that the desert formed the northern borders of Xi Xia and the further he advanced into it, the farther he got from Prince Asha's clutches. Before dawn, he calculated he was far enough and turned right. Now he was riding along the Jin kingdom and needed to be careful. While soldiers may not be patrolling in the desert, there could be smaller bands of desert robbers waiting to attack a lone traveller like him. That Genghis had no valuables was no deterrent, even the wheat and water in his bags was incentive in the desert. But when dawn broke, he had met nobody, and he rode on until the sun was too hot. Then he dug himself and his horse into a deep hole in the sand in the shelter of a dune, closed his eyes and tried to sleep away the fiery heat.

After sundown and munching wheat kernels for a meal, Genghis was once again on his way. By the time that night ended, he would have turned north and by midday reached the Ongirad's settlement. But he had gone only a hundred *alds* before he saw a group of horsemen riding hard towards him. When they came close he realised that they were Keraits, clansmen of his father's old friend Toghril. After much backslapping and whoops, they told him that Toghril's younger brother, with the help of the Naimans clan, had deposed the older man. Genghis was relieved to have met some friendly Mongols. As they rode on together, he told them the story of his insurrection and escape from Xi Xia. On the other hand, they informed him of how the clans had scattered once he had disappeared and how powerful Jamukha had become during the past couple of seasons. As Genghis had planned, by the next day, the entire band was at the Ongirad's camp being fed heartily by Dei-Tsetsan.

Once the Mongols knew that Genghis was back, they came in hordes to join him. Genghis was again the Khan and revelled in his reclaimed leadership and power. He related all that had happened to him in Xi Xia to his family though understandably certain things remain unrevealed.

When they were alone in their *ger*, Börte clasped her arms tightly around him. 'I have missed you terribly,' she whispered, her voice choking.

Genghis felt a pang at her words. His arms went around his wife as he murmured into her hair, 'It was your intuition and resourcefulness that rescued me, Börte. I will never forget that. It is my good fortune to have a wife like you beside me.'

A pair of serene, blue eyes gleamed in the gloom.

His wife smiled up at him through her tears and then pulled him down on their pallet. Next morning, it was Börte who reminded him that doubtlessly his providential escape was the result of Khökh Tenger's blessings. Genghis agreed that truly he was indebted to the Eternal Blue Heaven.

One wintry morning, when snow encrusted the slopes, Genghis went back to the *ovoo* he had made on the slopes of Bukhan Khaldun. Like the earlier occasion he knelt on the snow, bowed his head and closed his eyes to express his gratitude to the Eternal Blue Heaven. Arrayed in glittering silver fur, the steppe wolf once more meandered through the clearing unseen by the bowed figure. Genghis prayed:

Oh, great Khökh Tenger, I bow before you.
Give me strength to unite the Mongols.

The Mongols need laws.
I will make them obey even if I have to kill half of them.
Our laws will be simple.
Do not kill women or children.
Don't forget your debts.
Fight enemies to the end.
Never betray your Khan.

Thunder crackled overhead as dark clouds heralded a storm. Genghis was content for Khökh Tenger had heard his prayers and given His assent.

It was in 1204 CE, when Genghis Khan, risen like a phoenix, was ready to smash the consolidated might of the Naimans, Merkits and of Jamukha who had aligned with them. Gathering his forces, he began marching along the Kherlen River towards the Khenti ranges where the enemy under the leadership of Prince Tayang of the Naimans was holed up with a vastly superior force. When Genghis' army encountered the enemy, the Mongol horses were exhausted. Spying out the opposition troops, it was decided that Genghis' army would camp below the hills over the night to regain strength. One of the commanders suggested that each man light five fires to deter the enemy from attacking them during the night. It would also give the impression that they were more in number than they really were. Naiman guards posted on the heights reported to their Prince that the Mongols had 'more fires than stars'.

Tayang began to have second thoughts about taking on such a huge force but was forced into battle by his allies. In the first skirmish, Genghis' vanguard routed the outlaying Naiman troops. When Tayang asked why his men were fleeing, Jamukha reminded him that Genghis has 'four hounds'; the generals Jebe, Jelme, Subdei and Khubilai who have been raised on human flesh.

Their foreheads are of hardened copper,
They have chisels for snouts,
And awls for tongues;
With hearts of iron
And swords for whips,
They advance feeding on dew
And riding on the wind.

Tayang was panicky and wanted to retreat into the hills but was now trapped on the battlefield facing the Mongol host. It almost seemed Khökh Tenger was an observer behind the dark clouds that piled layer on layer above their heads. As both sides with bristling spears and flashing blades began to approach each other, lightning flashed and thunder rolled. The men were facing each other when the storm struck, and heavens opened up in a heavy downpour. Giving in to the age-old Mongol superstition, men from both sides instantly crouched on the ground, their shields over their heads to hide themselves from Khökh Tenger's rage. All except Genghis Khan.

He alone stood erect, rain lashing him on the battlefield, among men cowering in abject terror. His general, Subdei peeped from under his shield and observed his leader. Nothing harmed Genghis though the storm raged around him. Subdei stood up too and soon all around him, Genghis' army rose like nemesis. With whoops and war cries they fell on the still crouching foes and cut them down to the ground. Many of the enemy soldiers believed it was the Eternal Blue Heaven's forces sent to decimate them and fled into the mountains in disarray. Genghis' clever thinking won him the battle even before it started.

Later in the day, Jamukha's two generals rode into Genghis' camp. They had caught and bound Jamukha. By bringing him captive to Genghis, they expected to be accepted into the Mongol army and rewarded for their deed. Genghis summarily ordered the generals be thrown into a cauldron of boiling water for turning against their clan ruler. He had no use for traitors.

Genghis gave Jamukha a chance to recant. He did not want to abandon the ties of sworn blood-brotherhood but Jamukha knew that he was finished. He knew he had been a traitor to his brother. So, he replied to Genghis, 'Now that the world is at your disposal, of what use would I be as companion to you? On the contrary, O my sworn friend,

I would intrude into your dreams in the dark night,
I would trouble your heart in the bright day,
I would be a louse in your collar,
I would be a thorn in the inner lapel of your coat.'

He condemned himself, saying:

Let me die swiftly
Let them kill me without shedding blood.
When I lie dead, my bones buried in a high place,
For ever and ever I will protect you
And be a blessing to the offspring of your offspring.

Genghis granted Jamukha a princely death. He ordered his men to strangulate him rather than spill his blood. He was gifted the Mongol tradition of a dignified death usually accorded to royal personages. Jamukha's body was not left to lie exposed to the elements but buried as befitted one from a noble family.

Circumstances of this great victory over the joint forces of the Naimans, Merkits and Jamukha elevated Genghis to a mythical stature; a legend that only grew with time. Genghis was now the absolute master of all Mongolia, the man who had 'unified the people of the felt-walled tents'. He was the true Khan of the Mongols. In 1206 ce, the national assembly of the Mongols or *khural* proclaimed him leader of the newly united nation and confirmed the investiture of his title, Genghis Khan.

This was the moment Genghis' loyal companions had been working towards, fighting and waiting for. Plenty of rewards were conferred on those who had stood by him. It was announced that the especially favoured would be forgiven for up to nine crimes. Boorchu, Mukhali, Borokul and Chilagaun became Genghis' 'four warhorses' while Jebe, Jelme, Subdei and Khubilai his 'war hounds'. Sorkan-shira, who helped him escape the Taychuits, became a royal aide and quiver bearer, as did each of his sons. His own brothers and sons, including Shigi comprised his immediate circle for he needed his close family around him on whom he could depend without question.

These appointments marked a revolution in the hitherto nomadic imperial administration. In the past, tribal rivalries had undermined Mongol unity. Genghis' own childhood had been blighted by them. So, Genghis did not give appointments based on tribal hierarchy but on services rendered by people. Loyalty was the key. Like Sorkan-shira and his sons, many who had been herders, shepherds, carpenters or blacksmiths were raised from obscurity. Out went tribal regiments and in came regiments that owed loyalty to commanders. Switching regiments was a capital offence and commanders who failed to measure up were fired. Genghis formed his own elite bodyguard of 10,000 men who had special privileges. Very cleverly, he included the sons of his commanders in the bodyguard so that their rank was equal to their fathers'.

If any of his commanders entertained thoughts of disloyalty, he would recall that his son was a hostage to the Khan and treachery would need to involve both of them. Personal loyalty superseded tribal bonds weaving a new and enduring social texture devoted to only one purpose; conquest.

A new society especially of this size required new laws. By now around 950,000 households were dependant on Genghis Khan. Possibly the female influence throughout his growing years made Genghis especially benevolent towards the fair sex. He bestowed women with equal rights as men so that they were respected as matriarchs of their families. Property of widows remained with their families. Thus, his men went into battle with an assurance that their families will not be deprived on their death. Genghis encouraged women to train in warfare and often during his campaigns they were given administrative roles in his army when the men were busy fighting.

Genghis, himself illiterate, realised very early that his empire needed written rules and laws for efficient administration. From the Naiman captives, he acquired a Uighur who used to keep Naiman records using the Uighur script. Genghis ordered him to do the same for his new government and to teach the scripts to the younger princes. He chose Shigi, his adopted brother to oversee the chancellery. 'While I am setting in order the entire nation under the protection of the Eternal Heaven, you have become my seeing eyes, my hearing ears,' Genghis told Shigi. 'Divide up the people of the felt-walled tents... punish those who deserve to be punished...record the division of possessions, the laws and the judgements.'

Genghis established his capital at Avraga, beyond Kherlen's flood plains, a place that guarded the route into northern mountains, the Mongol stronghold. He built there an Imperial palace, administrative buildings on platforms of mud with huge, square tents erected on them. These palace-tents or *ordon,* were much more spacious and stronger than the *gers* but nothing close to his memories of the grand buildings of Princess Gurbelchin's nation. A small town and ironworks sprang up around the *ordon*. Thus, Genghis Khan became the architect of the first Mongolian city.

Old ways had been broken and new ways forged but what was the goal? Once all the conquered tribes were absorbed, men allocated to regiments, women distributed, all the silks, goblets, saddles, horses and herds shared out, the warriors looked to their Khan with new expectations. The nomadic nation was not a money economy. Troops could not be paid in anything other than in kind. Genghis Khan began to look to more sources of wealth; to the limitless riches of the settled lands to the south of the Gobi.

The Mongols knew their neighbours quite intimately through trade and diplomacy. The nations to their south must also have been observing Genghis' revolution with great interest wondering what the Mongols' new Khan was going to do with all his men, horses and blacksmiths forging new swords and arrowheads. What nobody, not even Genghis Khan, fathomed was that the acquisition of wealth, while vital, was not going to be enough; that conquest would mean a much more grandiose idea that had been ordained by the Eternal Blue Heaven leading to the Mongol rule going much beyond the wastelands of the Gobi Desert.

At Avraga, Genghis Khan already began to plan his first campaign that would be followed by so many more that over the next twenty years they would change the world order drastically.

There were three main kingdoms in the neighbourhood—the Jin, the Song and Xi Xia, nation of the Tanguts. The Jin Empire was a tough nut to crack. It was already allied with the Song kingdom, ruled its citizens and defended its cities well. Comparatively, Xi Xia was guarded only by the Gobi Desert that the Mongols could cross in days. It had a smaller army and fewer cities. In a prudent strategy, Genghis decided to first secure the weak and then go after the strong. Besides he had a strong personal reason to attack Xi Xia; the rescue of his beloved Gurbelchin.

In 1209 CE, Genghis' army marched 500 kilometres southwest from Avraga, down the Ongi River to reach where the Altai Mountains petered out into a 20,000 square kilometre oval of peaks, canyons, high pastures and gravel. Known as the Three Beauties, it made a perfect staging post for an army on the move. The Mongol cavalry moved fast across the hard, open Alashan desert and seized a fortress town. The Tanguts appealed for help to the Jins which never came. Driving southward with the desert to their right and mountains to the left, the Mongols came upon another fortress. It defended the only pass leading through the mountains to the Tangut capital, Yinchuan. After a two-month stand-off, Genghis knew forcing through this point was impossible. He pretended to retreat with the larger part of his forces leaving only a small contingent to act as a lure. When the Tanguts attacked, this little group kept retreating allowing the Tanguts to push them out of the pass. The moment the Tanguts were out on the stony plains, Genghis pounced on them and won a stunning victory. The way to Yinchuan was open.

However, Genghis now faced a problem. Yinchuan was a well-guarded city, and nobody knew it better than him. The Mongols were fast-moving, nomadic cavalry men. They had no concept of how to besiege walled cities.

They had no triple-bow siege bows that could shoot arrows as long as small tree trunks, no large-scale catapults, no incendiary bombs filled with low-grade gunpowder and no experts to teach them the techniques of siege warfare.

As he racked his brains looking for a solution, Genghis remembered from his journey the canal system that irrigated Yinchuan's fields. He ordered that the dykes in the surrounding fields to be broken. He assumed that the city would flood and bring the King to his knees. Unfortunately, the ground around Yinchuan, where the Mongol army was camped, was at a lower level than the city, itself. Consequently, the palaces and buildings of Yinchuan stood clear of the flood while the Mongol army's tents, horses and carts were awash. With no idea about the geography of the area, the Mongols had flooded themselves. Nevertheless, the Tanguts were also in a quandary. Their enemies surrounded their city walls, their crops had been ruined and the Jin emperor was not going to help them. Finally, the Tangut Emperor, the Burkhan, submitted to Genghis Khan sending him women, camels, falcons and textiles as tributes. Convinced that he now had a compliant vassal from whom he could requisition troops or demand tributes when required, Genghis ordered his army to withdraw.

But there was something specific he needed from the Emperor; a safe passage for Princess Gurbelchin, wife of Prince Asha. When the army was laying siege to Yinchuan, Genghis had given Shigi the responsibility of finding out about the well-being of the said lady. He was sure that the crack in the wall would have been closed but Shigi had garnered Tanguts who had defected and recruited them to his system of spies. They were able to dupe the guards at the city gates to let them enter Yinchuan. Just the night before the withdrawal of the army, Shigi's spies returned to say that no lady of that name or title could be found in Yinchuan. As evidence, they had captured a Mongol servant of Prince Asha. When Shigi gave this disappointing news to Genghis, his Emperor insisted on speaking with the servant. A trembling man was dragged into the Khan's presence. Genghis recognised him as Gurbelchin's man servant. He was the man who had warned the lovers of the Prince's attack on that fateful night.

'Leave this man alone with me,' Genghis commanded Shigi and the soldiers.

'Please let me live, my Lord. I will serve you faithfully,' wailed the terrified man who had also recognised Genghis.

'Don't be afraid. Answer my questions truthfully and you will live,' assured the conqueror. The man nodded vigorously.

'Where is your mistress, Princess Gurbelchin?'

'I don't know, my Lord,' he shook his head. 'After you left, the Prince in a fearsome rage locked her up in the palace. Nobody was allowed to meet her. Whether she was given any food and drink, I don't know.'

'Then?'

'After a few weeks, the palace was reopened on the Prince's orders. But the Princess had vanished. Where she had gone or if she had been killed, nobody knows. All we know is that our mistress disappeared overnight.' The man was wringing his hands wondering if Genghis' anger at the bad news he had revealed was going to be wrecked on him.

Genghis narrowed his eyes and regarded the man for a long time. Then he discerned that the man was speaking the truth. He clapped his hands and the guards rushed in.

'Take this man to the kitchens and feed him well. Then let him go.'

It was usual practice for all Mongol rulers to take women as plunder from defeated foes. Some even became concubines. Genghis was no different. Later, many vassal rulers offered him their daughters in marriage. For Genghis, these were political, never emotional alliances. Despite all these women thronging his life, Börte remained his true wife, his helpmate, always at the helm of his life. Besides, she was the mother of his heirs. But Gurbelchin was much more. She had become his soulmate. Their love had been spiritual, sublime and seraphic, isolated from the grind of daily life. His heart was unable to come to terms with this dire loss.

For some days, Genghis Khan remained in his tent. He hardly ate or drank, nor did he speak to anyone. He did not wish to reveal his close ties with the wife of the *Gambu* of Xi Xia to avoid any misconceptions. Shigi wondered what could have laid his ruler so low. The Emperor of Mongolia was desolate. Besides, guilt overwhelmed him. He could not stop accusing himself. He had sacrificed his beloved at the altar of his own safety and to realise his own aspirations. Though the recouping of his power had been ordained, he had spent too much time in establishing himself. Meanwhile, the noble Gurbelchin had suffered vilely. He had come too late to her rescue...his dearest Gurbelchin had gone beyond his reach. He felt as if a part of his heart, nay his soul had been cruelly cut off. All his life his remorse and her deprivation would bleed him.

24

Back in Avraga, after the Xi Xia subjugation, Genghis turned his attention to the Jin kingdom. He was disdainful of the new Jin emperor who ruled an insecure state weakened by famine and economic collapse. The Ongut tribe who straddled the zone between the Mongol grasslands and the Jin farmlands was ready to allow the Mongols open access to the Jin kingdom. Besides, Muslim merchants, grateful for the security provided by Genghis' expanding empire brought him information about the Jin defences.

In spring 1211 CE, Genghis struck. His planning of the invasion of the Jin Empire was meticulous and audacious. The nomadic army advanced across the Gobi in waves in order not to drain the scattered wells and pools on the desert route. They were linked by fast-moving messengers. As the Mongol army approached the pass called Huăn ér zuĭ or Young Badger's Mouth that led to Beijing, the capital, the Jin commander of its army sent an officer to discuss peace terms with Genghis. The officer promptly defected with the information that the Jin army was waiting at the other end of the pass. When the Mongol army charged, the Jin cavalry, packed between ridges, was so overwhelmed with the shower of arrows that horsemen turned and trampled their own infantry. Bodies piled up like rotten logs lay scattered for 50 kilometres along the valley. Even ten years later, travellers would see the stacks of bones on the escarpments. Follow-on skirmishes captured several major cities and forts driving Jin generals back to Beijing leaving the Mongols free to loot and raid at will.

Next, Genghis headed southward for another 300 kilometres to the Yellow River. At the same time, his general, Jebe travelled east and captured the Manchurian stronghold of Mukden. Content with these victories, Genghis withdrew north to the borderlands between the steppes and the Gobi. Though victory meant only booty, destruction and asserting dominance rather than occupation, Genghis had entered a new kind of warfare…the taking of cities and he would need to mould his tactics to it.

The second assault came in 1213 CE. The Jin army strewed the kilometres around the two fortresses around Young Badger's Mouth with caltrops which are iron balls with spikes to hobble horses. But Genghis' generals, Jebe and Subdei, rode above the pitted ground, all along the mountain crests. They seized the forts and opened the road to Beijing. The Jin Empire faced a catastrophe. Thousands of soldiers had died, and the rest of the people were starving for the Mongols were like locusts eating away all the food as they advanced. No food supplies came into the forts where people resorted to eating human flesh. By then Beijing had lapsed into deadly political turbulence. Nevertheless, it was not that easy for the Mongols to take the capital city, Beijing for it was surrounded by three strong fortresses.

Genghis' army was still nomadic and still did not have siege weapons. He conceived a different strategy. He sent off his troopers to ravage the countryside and seize the small Jin cities. By the thousands Genghis' forces gathered together prisoners and then put them at the head of their assault forces. When people, inside the walls of the forts, identified their relatives in the sieging hordes, they could not kill their own people and submitted to the invaders. In the regions north of the Yellow River, all the Jin cities were ruined.

Still Beijing, the capital, held out. Its defenders used a variety of formidable weapons such as double and triple bows shooting three-metre arrows, catapults and wagon-mounted trebuchets that flung boulders, fireballs and fire arrows from the walls. Naphtha in pots or bottles thrown from heights at the enemy took care of scaling ladders and assault towers used by the Mongol forces to come over the walls. Tubes filled with distilled petroleum would be ignited and squirted on the enemy below. Such means held the Mongols off but also taught them useful lessons; that these devices were essential when taking cities. Their manufacture and the skills to operate them will have to be mastered by the help of prisoners and turncoats from the enemy.

The siege of Beijing went on for a year and it was a hard winter for the Mongols who suffered from epidemics as well as starvation. Eventually, Genghis had to withdraw his forces but only after the Jin Emperor paid him the tribute of one princess, 500 boys and girls, 3,000 horses and 10,000 bolts of silk. But the moment Genghis Khan went back to the grasslands, the Jin Emperor shifted his capital all the way south to Kaifeng. Many Jin generals mutinied because they believed this move exhibited the cowardice of the Jins. Thus, many Jin commanders went over to Genghis' side. Infuriated by the unexpected escape of the Emperor from Beijing, Genghis came back to besiege the city until it starved, and its inhabitants capitulated. His men ransacked the city, burning palaces and killing by the thousands.

Genghis' conquest of Beijing reputed for its strength sent out ripples of disquiet. The Shah of the far-off kingdom of Khwarezm found it incredible that the mighty and well-defended Beijing could fall to a mere nomad. His ambassador reported back that the city had mountains of bones of those killed and the ground was still slippery with human fat.

The Mongols now controlled most of the Jin kingdom. Between 1214–16 CE, nomad general Mukhali and Genghis' brother, Kasar swept across Manchuria, seizing its significant city Pei Ching by pretending to be its new Jin commander. By 1216 CE, they raced 300 kilometres further right to the shores of the Pacific Ocean pursuing thousands of Jins across the Yalu River into wealthy Korea. After killing and capturing many Jin soldiers, a Mongol emissary went into the court of the King of Korea to announce brashly that the Mongols had just saved Korea from the Jins and so they deserved to be compensated for this great deed. Among other things, 100,000 of Korea's best and largest sheets of paper were part of the demand!

Genghis now launched an attack on Kaifeng with the help of Tangut forces. In the autumn of 1216, they advanced 1,000 kilometres, riding an astounding 13 kilometres a day, through regions bristling with fortresses and against vastly superior forces right to the outskirts of Kaifeng. There the Mongol army fought four major battles in two months. Eventually, the Jin emperor sued for peace.

But the war with the Jins would go on until the Mongols had attained complete victory over them.

However, before he could plan out the next assault on the Jins, Genghis' attention was drawn west to the Islamic kingdom of Khwarezm. It was an important and wealthy kingdom that controlled the vital cities of Bukhara, Urgench, Khojend, Merv and Nishapur that fell along the Silk Road. These places were critical as trading and business centres in Asia. Watered by the melting ice of the Pamirs, Khwarezm had rich farmlands, pastures, mineral deposits and trade goods. It was ruled by an abominable despot, Sultan Mohammad Shah. In 1217 CE, three merchants from Bukhara, eager to exploit the routes opened up by Mongol advances into China, arrived in Mongolia. When they returned to Khwarezm, Genghis Khan sent with them a hundred trade delegates. He wanted to trade with Khwarezm. His traders wanted to acquire the 'wondrous wares of those regions' and establish relations between Mongolia and Khwarezm. Nothing could be farther from an announcement of war, but Mohammad Shah intentionally regarded Genghis' gesture as such. At Otrar, on the Syrdar'ya River, these delegates were mercilessly put to death by its governor. Genghis was appalled but decided to give the Sultan one more opportunity. He gave Mohammad Shah the benefit of disclaiming the heinous act and handing over the culprit. The Sultan killed the envoys who carried Genghis' message to him.

When the news reached Genghis, it was said that he flew into a whirlwind of fury, the fire of wrath driving the water from his eyes so that it could only to be quenched with blood. He went up to Burkhan Khaldun and offered up prayers:

I am not the author of this trouble;
Grant me strength to exact vengeance.

Though Genghis would have preferred not to undertake the assignment of subduing a dominant power so far away from home, he had no choice. Not only had he been humiliated, he had been challenged. If the threat was not met, he could become a victim of the Sultan's ambitions to expand into China's rich lands. Before planning this complex campaign, he put the administration of the conquered Jin lands into the hands of the well-read, spiritual and able Chucai from the Khitai royal family.

Next, he demanded troops from his vassals; from the borderlands of Mongolia, Uighur lands, Northern China, Manchuria and Xi Xia. When he had conquered Xi Xia, the Burkhan had promised him troops and tributes but now came a stinging slap to the Mongol face. Its *Gambu* or Imperial Commander, Prince Asha refused, saying, 'If Genghis is really that weak, why did he ever bother to become Khan?'

At that time, Genghis was too preoccupied with the planning of the campaign against Sultan Mohammad Shah to give a fitting riposte. But he vowed, 'If I am protected by the Eternal Heaven, then this certainly deserves a reckoning in the future.'

In 1219 CE, Genghis marched his army west, swatting minor tribes on the way. Around 100,000 to 150,000 soldiers each with two or three horses, the Mongol army retained the fast-moving, hard-riding flexibility of traditional nomadic armies with divisions that could cover 100 kilometres a day, cross deserts, swim rivers, appear and disappear as if by magic. It also implemented lessons learned in the sieges of Chinese cities. Tied to horses and camels, dragged in wagons or their own wheels were battering rams, scaling ladders, four-wheeled mobile shields, trebuchets with their variety of fire and smoke bombs, flame-throwing tubes and huge double and triple bows that could fire arrows as big as ship masts to punch holes in baked-earth walls a kilometre away. This formidable combination of siege weaponry and nomadic cavalry had never been seen before in history.

Till now, whenever nomads won a war, they would kill the men, rape the women and enslave the children. Taking and keeping prisoners, en masse, hampered the flexibility of the war machine. However, Genghis' army had learned to use captives in three different ways; as a slave-labour force of specialist artisans; as soldiers in non-nomadic contingents; as cannon fodder. The last was a dreadful technique of taking fortified cities with frightened civilians driven ahead of the army to fill moats around forts, take the full force of the defensive fire and possibly blunt it as the defenders refrained from killing their own people. Genghis' army was a juggernaut, a cumbersome beast that required the building of bridges and roads across the mountains and rivers. With every city taken it increased in size.

Reaching Ortar on the borders of Khwarezm, Genghis faced resistance from the governor who had executed the conqueror's first delegates. He wanted to catch the culprit alive and hang him publicly. Therefore, the siege lasted for five months. The governor of Ortar was finally caught and executed as he was trying to cravenly escape leaving his town to the mercy of the invaders. After hanging the governor, the town of Ortar was flattened to rubble.

Meanwhile, Genghis divided his army into two attacking forces. He sent his general, Jochi northwards to sweep across Khwarezm in a vast curve while he led the other arm of the pincer across the freezing Kyzylkum desert towards Bukhara. On the way, towns were given the ultimatum: resist and die or surrender and live. None of them took much time to make the wise choice. When cities decided to surrender, usually the Mongol army would destroy the citadel which comprised their military strength, then a contingent of young men was forcibly recruited into the army and the rest of the citizens allowed to go home.

In 1220 CE, when, on his cleansing drive across Khwarezm, Genghis Khan approached Bukhara, a garrison of 20,000 defenders came out of the city to attack his forces. The Mongols quickly blotted them up on the banks of Amudar'ya river. The townspeople, unwilling to be killed, opened their gates and Genghis rode in through lanes lined on both sides by wooden houses and imposing palaces right into the inner city. For the first time he was in a city rich in ways he had never known.

Five hundred years ago the Arabs had spread Islam over Persia, Syria, Iraq, Egypt, North Africa, Central Asia and even Spain. Now trade linked all these regions. Along with other goods, a lucrative trade in slaves, whether African, Turkish, Slav, Mongol or Indian also flourished. Sponsored by the staggering wealth of their rulers and merchants, the arts and sciences spread over these Islamic lands. Brilliant scholars and their written word were venerated, architects built domed mosques, stuccoed and frescoed ornate palaces were the style. Mathematical tools were provided by using Arabic numerals gleaned from the Land of the Indus River. Scientists were experimenting assiduously to discover the 'philosopher's stone' that was said to transform any metal into precious gold. The ancient Persian cities of Samarkand, Bukhara, Merv and Urganj reflected this erudite culture. Apparently, Bukhara's royal library had a suite of rooms, each dedicated to a different discipline! These traditions were Khwarezm's inheritance that Genghis knew little about. But of its wealth, he had heard about more than enough.

In Bukhara, Genghis Khan addressed its merchants and wealthy people: 'O people, know that you have committed great sins, and that the great ones among you have committed these sins. If you ask me what proof I have for these words, I say it is because I am the punishment of God. If you had not committed great sins, God would not have sent a punishment like me upon you.' It had the required effect. The rich of the city filed into Genghis' tent to hand over their wealth; cash, jewellery, clothing, fabrics so that more 'punishment' was not meted out to them. Genghis then turned to the citadel of Bukhara where the Sultan's troops were still holed up. He filled the moats around it with the local citizens and bombarded the defences with flaming naphtha. For days the battle raged until the citadel was battered and burned to submission, its defenders dead. The Mongols then went through all the males in the city slaughtering all those 'who stood higher than the butt of their horse whip'. Of the survivors, the young men were forced into military service, women and children made slaves and skilled workers such as blacksmiths, carpenters, goldsmiths added to the numbers of Mongol artisans.

After that, Genghis marched to Samarkand, Sultan Shah Mohammad's new capital, a paradise of a city. Around 110,000 troops defended its moats, city walls and citadels. Herding prisoners, taken from Bukhara and other cities, before them, every tenth captive waving the red–and-yellow Mongol flag, Genghis' army gave the appearance of massive legions of invaders. Mohammad's foolish arrogance did the city in. He fled from Samarkand and advised everyone to get hold of their goods and flee, too. Nevertheless, the merchant princes and clerics of Samarkand sued for peace and suffered just as terribly as the citizens of Bukhara.

To castigate Sultan Mohammad Shah with punishment due to him, Genghis and his generals pursued the man across the regions to the shores of the Caspian Sea. With the Mongols only a day behind him, Shah and his entourage along with his son, Jalal-ud-din holed himself up in an island in the middle of the sea. Though far from Mongol hands, the tyrannical and cowardly Sultan was meted his just dues dying of shock and despair on the island.

By then the other pincer arm of the nomadic army under General Jochi came around and joined Genghis' contingent. Together, the forces took Urgench, another city on the Silk Road. Within three months, Merv, Nishapur and Herat were all taken, their people killed, and the towns ploughed over. It is worth mentioning that the final assault on Nishapur was led by Genghis' daughter whose husband had been shot down by an arrow just a few days ago. Merv made the mistake of resisting and suffered immensely. In 1221 CE, when 800 Mongols attacked it, they were chased off. Some sixty Mongol soldiers were captured, paraded through the town and then executed. This ensured a terrible fate being allocated to Merv. About 7,000 Mongols besieged it for six days. Even though the defenders were around 18,000, they had to finally submit. But the Merv leaders had resisted Genghis Khan and knowing the penalty of fighting him, its citizens were hypnotised by fear. The Mongols entered the city and ransacked it. Palaces and buildings were mined, libraries ruined, and books burned. Then the killings began.

It is said that when his soldiers began the executions by beheading a single human at a time, Genghis became impatient. Walking up to five captives, he seized in one hand bunches of their hair so that their necks were forced together. Then with his sword in the other hand, he slashed off five heads together. His troopers applauded his efficiency and since then, this became the Mongol mode of carrying out large-scale executions in the shortest possible time.

Though not verifiable, the genocide at Merv according to an eminent cleric of the times, was a staggering one million three hundred thousand lives! In the two-year course of Genghis Khan's invasion of the Muslim empire, perhaps three million people had been massacred by the Mongol army. No doubt this was a holocaust on an unprecedented scale!

Just when it seemed that Genghis' massive campaign of Khwarezm, had been a conclusive success story, the Mongol army suffered a defeat; its first.

Jalal-ud-din, Sultan Mohammad Shah's son rallied the surviving Khwarezm forces and retreated south pursued by Genghis. In 1221 CE at Parvan, he defeated the Mongol army incidentally commanded then by Shigi, Genghis' adopted brother. Trying to preserve the resistance, Sultan Jalal-ud-din kept retreating another 400 kilometres through the Hindu Kush Mountains onto the hot plains until the Indus River brought him up short. His army was finished but not so the brave Sultan. He jumped into the swift-flowing, vast river with his horse and struggled to the farther bank. In astonishment, Genghis stared at the man lying wet and tired on the other side and exclaimed, 'Every father should have such a son!'

Genghis was about to follow him into the churn but exactly then a strange creature rose from the waves of the river. It looked like a cross between a horse and a fish, but it vanished before a closer look could be taken. The men around him breathed in awe, 'A unicorn!' Genghis felt it was not a good omen and decided against taking the plunge. Later, the shaman in his camp advised the Mongol Emperor to never cross the Indus River for failures awaited him beyond it.

Nevertheless, a few days later, he did permit Shigi with a small band to make the risky river crossing. His brother, smarting under defeat at the hands of Jalal-ud-din, believed he would be able to seize the Sultan and drag him back across the river. However, Shigi returned with no Jalal-ud-din; he brought with him only the Sultan's wife as one of the captives. It was then that Genghis decided to call off the adventure and turn homewards.

During 1221 and 1223 CE, Generals Subdei, Jebe and Jochi went on an astonishing expedition 7,500 kilometres beyond the Caspian Sea. They overran Georgia, made allies of the Venetians, fought off the tough Polovtsy tribes on the steppes north of the Caucasus Mountains and tricked the overwhelmingly strong Russian forces to a defeat. They were beaten off by the nomadic Volga Bulgars and backed away, vowing to avenge themselves the coming year. Then laden with riches, they rejoined Genghis with detailed information of the lands, resources and opposing forces beyond the Caspian Sea. With proper planning, Genghis would pursue his destiny by expanding his kingdom onto the rich plains of Hungary and the wealthy cities of Europe.

25

Flurries of loose snow whirled outside, visible through the slight opening in the thick skin covering the narrow door of the tent hut. Enkhtuya turned her head as Bolorma, a steaming bowl of broth held in two hands, entered.

'Come *Guunj*, sit up. This will warm you.' She persuaded the girl who lay on the wooden bed covered by layers of furry bearskins.

'Is it snowing today?' Enkhtuya wanted to know whether she would be cooped up for another day in the gloomy hut with only despair to give her company or would it be a good day for riding out.

'The storm has abated and the thin snow on the ground is melting,' replied her old maid, 'But clouds are shifting. Maybe later in the day, there would be sunshine.'

She went outside to get hot water for the Princess' toilet as the girl considered the thin slice of outdoors that she could glimpse. She shivered a little as the fire in the ground pit had reduced to glowing embers. *All in all, despite the cold and snow of the last months, it has been a relief to not jog on horseback day after day. Besides, this has been a good place to reflect,* she thought.

When the nomadic army had begun to rise from the wastes of the deserts into the salubrious highlands called the Three Beauties, Enkhtuya's spirits had risen with it. She recalled how despite the constant sorrow in her heart, her faith in herself had strengthened and she had vowed that she would convince the Khan to be compassionate towards the ordinary citizens of the cities he was planning to attack. But their conversation on the way up had brought home to her as to how futile her hopes had been. However, the charm of her surroundings once they had wended their way up through high green pastures, forested tracks and bubbling brooks had swept Enkhtuya's misgivings away.

Genghis decided to set up camp on a flat, grassy patch overlooking the ravines crowded by juniper. *Gers* were assembled, and kitchens opened. The Princess expected the usual calls to dine but the Khan had been busy in meetings with his generals. Sometimes, she glimpsed him riding away at full throttle, his commanders grouped around him, to unknown destinations. All of it made her suspect that he was planning an important campaign. I *wonder, whether it is my own country Xi Xia that he intends to attack,* Enkhtuya thought, *his words that morning had been too vague.* The fact that she was so close to the lands from where her mother had come and to which she presumed her father belonged thrilled her in no small way. She kept imagining what Xi Xia, its cities, its people were like and the cool, natural beauty around her encouraged her to daydream.

With Bolorma to care for her daily needs and no tight restrictions on her movements here, Enkhtuya had ridden and walked through the verdant slopes as much she wished. They were meditative journeys. Memories of her little son as a baby would bring on storms of weeping. Sometimes a black rage would creep on her inducing an overwhelming desire to do something to avenge her baby's death and so lessen her grief...*even...even stab to death with my knife the men who killed him...or kill that callous, barbaric Khan*, she would rant. Then a grey despair would cloud her. *Foolish of me...I would be finished off before I could do anything so drastic,* she would rebuke herself. *But...but the idea of using this knife to inflict pain on the brutes is so deliciously tempting,* she would contemplate and finger her little knife.

There were moments when she would long for the security of her *Eej's* arms. Her face streaming with tears, she would complain of her misery to her mother pleading with her, aloud at times, 'Take me away from here, *Eej,* please. I can't bear it anymore.' The junipers would whisper softly in answer to her mournful pleas until she once again regained a measure of calmness.

At times, she would brood about her husband, the Sultan. *Had he returned to Malikpur? Had he searched for her? Had he found their son's body and given him an honourable burial?*

Whenever her mind went back to the days she had lost forever, she would think how unimaginably life had changed over the last few months. How much anguish and hardship she had suffered! From a beloved princess, she had become a destitute captive always fearing for her life and safety. *I had been so vulnerable and naïve then. And now? Now I have seen how hard life can be…how carefully I must tread its ups and downs….*

These pensive jaunts had always been solitary for the girl had observed that all the other Mongols in the camp avoided her. If she passed by them, they looked through her as if she was an unwelcome ghost. *Well, I have no use for murderers either,* Enkhtuya would retort silently. Shigi, despite being brusque, was the only one who had acknowledged to her other than the Khan. But Shigi was hardly seen after they had reached here. *Probably holed up somewhere scribbling away in that outlandish script,* sniggered Enkhtuya to herself.

Autumn had been in full swing when they had set up camp. There had been a sharp nip in the air which whetted her appetite after her walks or rides. She would return with a rumbling stomach after riding hard along the tracks in shady glades. Often sitting on a knoll, she had watched the mountain sheep gambol in the pastures. Once while riding out she had seen the maimed body of a dead sheep, evidence that there were wolves around. And Shigi had warned her that snow leopards slinked in the forests and so she should avoid going too deep into them. Enkhtuya had fingered the sharp knife permanently residing in her pocket and nodded. Probably, it was too small to really help her in an animal attack, but it gave her confidence.

One day, she had been witness to the nomads from the camp hunting wild asses. The horsemen had indentified a group of asses and isolated them from the herd. Then they surrounded the group and shot arrows into each ass. The slaves had brought back the carcasses which were served in meals for days. The Princess had been openly disdainful of the way the beautiful beasts had been cut down. 'That is hardly hunting,' she had remarked to Shigi who had given one of his rare appearances to watch the event. 'Where is the risk of killing these harmless animals?'

Shigi had only shrugged. He had begun to wonder why this girl, whom he himself had gifted the great Khan, was being given such special benefits. Then he had chastised himself for questioning the Khan's intentions. *Possibly she is an exclusive concubine and had demanded these facilities,* he told himself. *Still she is only a concubine. Why does she give herself such airs?*

Autumn had chilled into winter with its roaring storms of sleet and hushed snowfall. Though they were sheltered against the rock face behind the *gers*, it was bitterly cold in the felt tents. The Princess had noticed some hustle-bustle of a building venture taken up by the Muslim builders.

In a few days a neat circle of mud and log huts with felt roofs had sprung up on the grass. She moved into one of the tent-huts. As the snow piled against the mud walls, Enkhtuya could not have enough furs to cover herself. Besides her reflective forays into the mountain glades ceased and she was forced to live with her dark thoughts in the dark hut.

One morning, Bolorma informed her that many of the troopers had left the camp.

'What? Are they leaving the Khan's army?' Hope suddenly sprang up in her heart. Without his fighting force, Genghis Khan may call off his campaign.

Bolorma snorted, 'What a thought, *Guunj!* Who will leave the Lord? The men are going home to stay with their families for the winter months. After all, the roads are frozen, and their weapons, mantled with snow, are useless until the thaw sets in.'

Enkhtuya had snuggled into her warm bed and wondered if this was the time to seek out the Khan. If she could have enough time, she would be able to wear down the Khan's resistance to her ideas. At least one of her aspirations would be fulfilled. She could be the saviour of many lives. However, soon she realised that either the Khan was not in the camp or he was busy with his generals. Still, during the howling snowstorms of the past months, Enkhtuya would sit inside her furs and deliberate. She would stare into the lively flames of the fire burning in the central pit and weave various plans of approaching the 'saving lives' project differently and argue to justify minimising collateral damage during the Khan's next war. She would speak out, her voice echoing off the hut walls, and then counter herself as if she were the Khan. Bolorma, the only witness to these passionate dramas, would sometimes laugh and sometimes shake her head. There was a time when she tried to tell the girl that it was all going to be a waste of time, but it is difficult to divert a zealous novice.

To bolster her confidence and win the debate with him, Enkhtuya convinced herself that at heart Genghis Khan was not an oppressive bully. *Look at all that he has done for his own people! He has brought in radical social changes still not observed in the civilised world. Besides his belief in God or Khökh Tenger or whatever, whoever…is very deep.* 'There has to be a core of goodness in him,' she told herself again and again. 'I will appeal to that aspect of him.'

Day after day, she would inquire if he was available or if he had been seen around the camp. She wanted so badly to talk to him. Every time, Bolorma would return with a message from Shigi saying that it was not possible for her to meet the Khan. In this manner, the winter months gave way to a frosty thaw declaring spring was around the corner while Enkhtuya had begun to feel that she would now burst with all the arguments fermenting within her. The last winter storm had now passed them by a week ago. Though the ground was muddy, the air was not as freezing as before. Enkhtuya decided a walk through the forest tracks would clear her mind and she set out in the weak, afternoon sunshine. Though she had to wade through puddles of mud, it was good to breathe the sharp, fresh air after being cooped up in a smoky hut for days. On her return to the camp, she observed logs of wood being piled up in a deep pit in the centre of the circle of huts. Usually, it was the site of outdoor camp gatherings but that had been discontinued in winter. She told Bolorma to find out the reason for this sudden exertion.

Bolorma came back with the information that the Khan wanted an outdoor meeting, as the weather had turned pleasant. Enkhtuya rubbed at her frozen face and blew on her hands speculating about the Mongol idea of 'pleasant weather'. However, she wondered whether she could catch the Khan at the event. So, when the sound of voices began to penetrate her hut, she peeped out from behind the fur curtain. The generals were settling down around the roaring bonfire, chatting to each other. All conversation was hushed as Genghis Khan strode into their midst. All of them bowed down to him until he commanded them to sit. Soon, bowls of *airag* were being passed around by the slaves. Enkhtuya decided quickly. *Now! Before he gets too drunk. Though,* she mused, *I have never seen him drunk.*

She emerged from the hut, her cream *deel* gleaming in the cold moonlight, walking casually towards the gathering and then halting as if surprised to see them. The voices died down, as the men noticed her. In the firelight, she looked directly at the Khan who turned his usual inscrutable profile towards her. Then he gave her a casual wave inviting her to join them. Gracefully, she moved to sit on a stool near him. Instantly, the circle of men, including Shigi, turned their faces away from the couple granting them some privacy. They continued with their discussions in low voices.

The Emperor offered Enkhtuya a bowl of *airag,* which she refused with a shake of her head. 'There is no wine,' he said softly. It was almost an apology and encouraged the Princess to broach the topic that had been spinning in her head all through the winter.

'My Lord, I have some notions as to how civilian casualties can be minimised during a war. What if we send spies into the cities a few months before attacking them? Couldn't they warn the non-fighting citizens to leave the city? Or...,' her voice faltered as Genghis Khan looked skywards. She turned her head upwards too, wondering what had caught his eyes. She could see nothing specific other than noting that the clouds had completely vanished leaving behind a canopy of luminous stars against an ocean of blackness. Some were dull, merely flickering into existence every now and then, but there were adequate numbers of shimmering diamonds to illuminate the moonless night. Puzzled, she looked back to his face, but it was still upturned to the celestial dome.

The Khan seemed lost in his thoughts. The silence between them grew longer punctuated by the low tones of the men. Slowly, it began to smother her, and she cleared her throat to continue with her exhortations. All at once, he spoke up. In low, hushed syllables, he said, 'My father taught me to read the stars when I was only as tall as his knee. By the time we began to hunt together, I knew the star signs so well that I never ever got lost on the steppes at night. I wonder if he knew intuitively how important stars would be to me when he was gone. In my childhood and youth, several times I could travel safely only by night to flee my enemies. Each time, these stars were my friends and guides.'

It was then that Enkhtuya knew for sure that her project of saving lives was lost forever. The Khan was not even going to hear her proposals, let alone act on them. Fierce, red anger inundated her, but she could not display even a flicker of it. Dully, she stared up at the sky. 'My mother used to say that our fate is written in these stars,' she pronounced astonishing herself. *Where did that come from? Had Eej actually said that?*

'Your mother? Gurleen? Did she really say that?' The Khan sounded amused and the girl gave him a sharp look. But the firelight didn't show his lips smiling.

'Yes.' Enkhtuya said briefly, annoyed with herself for letting the arrogant ruler laugh at her. She tried to bolster her dead mother's belief by adding, 'Well, the Muslims study the stars and then etch human fates on paper with their help.'

'So, I have heard,' nodded her elderly companion. He didn't sound amused now. 'In fact, Börte told me once that the stars had told her that I would certainly return from Xi Xia. Later, when I finally wanted to announce my leadership of all Mongolia, the shamans surveyed the stars to know the right moment to do so.'

'Do you mean to say that among the Mongols, there are those learned enough to study the stars?' Enkhtuya's query had a prickly thorn but the Khan ignored it.

Instead, he replied a trifle solemnly, 'Certainly. Did you think all Mongols are like me, unlettered?' His rhetorical question made Enkhtuya blush, yet she remained defiantly and unapologetically silent. He continued, 'Some of my people are so scholarly that they have engaged themselves in penning down the history of the Mongols, their unification and the rise of this great empire.'

So Shigi was telling the truth, thought Enkhtuya but before she could reply, thudding hooves from the edge of the camp drew everyone's attention. A guard stumbled into their midst and announced that the envoy had returned.

'Bring him, at once,' ordered the Khan, his tone curt and abrupt.

The envoy walked in, bowed from the waist.

'Tell me, Man. What did the *Gambu* of Xi Xia say?' Genghis Khan asked impatiently.

'My Lord, the *Gambu* said, "If you Mongols say, 'Let's fight!' then turn towards the Helan Mountains and come to me. Let us fight there!"'

'What?' shouted the Khan.

His commanders muttered darkly. 'Such arrogance!'

'What did the Burkhan say?' Genghis demanded.

'My Lord, the Emperor of Xi Xia said nothing. He is afraid of the old *Gambu*,' said the envoy.

'Let us fight then. Even if we die, let us challenge their boasts! Eternal Heaven! You be the judge!' exclaimed the Khan, waving the envoy away.

As the generals raged among themselves, the Khan raised a hand to silence them. Once the hubbub died down, he said, 'Shigi, how do you think we should approach them?'

Shigi bowed his head acknowledging the honour. Softly but confidently, he said, 'My Lord, we should break the back of the horse at its weakest point. Let us attack the border fortress in the north, the Khara Khoto.'

'Alright,' said the Khan slowly, 'And then?'

'Lord, if Prince Asha must send a force to aid Khara Khoto, it would have to cross the Yellow River and then the desert to reach the north. That would take considerable time. Besides, their army would be quite worn out by then. After all, they are city-bred and not nomads like us. By that time, Lord, our army will have conquered Khara Khoto. We will have enough food, fodder, prisoners and weapons to march on to Yinchuan. But we would go to the capital from the opposite direction to the Helan Mountains. Prince Asha will not expect us to come that way.' Shigi paused to take breath.

'That is an excellent suggestion,' assented their leader, 'What do you think?' He addressed the other commanders.

They heartily cheered the proposal. Jebe spoke up. 'If we divided and a branch went west and another to

Yinchuan, then we would throttle Xi Xia by pressing it simultaneously between two hands. Their forces would not be able to fight on both fronts and will be easily defeated.'

'Agreed!' exclaimed the Khan.

Forgotten by the men, Enkhtuya's eyes went from one speaker to the other in growing horror as she listened to plans of destroying her birth country. *I had been right,* she surmised. She looked aghast, her face pale and eyes goggling. Shigi's eyes fell on her terrified face and he exclaimed loudly. All the men turned as one to stare at her. Genghis Khan shouted an order and the guards loomed up instantly as if appearing out of thin air.

'Take the *Guunj* away,' commanded the Khan. 'See that she is kept under strict scrutiny, henceforth.'

The guards surrounded Enkhtuya. She was forced to rise and make her way to her hut. Seething with fury and distress, she ran the last few steps into the hut and flung herself on the bed giving way to a deluge of scalding tears.

Next morning, the camp in the Three Beauties began to break up. The nomadic army was on the march.

26

Finally, it was in 1224 CE that Genghis could focus back on Xi Xia, the Tangut kingdom that had refused him reinforcements five years ago. The refusal had been a contemptuous snub. An unforgivable insult from a vassal state and a threat to the new empire's existence. Xi Xia was the key to Inner Asia and to Genghis' future expansion into China. Xi Xia had to be destroyed.

Now Xi Xia had a new ruler, Xianjong, who wanted to balance on a tightrope between two strong neighbours; the Jins and the Mongols by signing peace treaties with both. Genghis wanted an assurance and Xianjong promised to send his son over as a hostage. The Mongol ruler whiled away the waiting period hunting wild ass at the Three Beauties, but no royal hostage arrived. Genghis sent Xianjong his envoy wanting to know whether the hostage will be sent. Confident of support by the Jins, the Burkhan of Xi Xia refused him outright. Prince Asha, the old but powerful Imperial Commander, sent Genghis an arrogant challenge inviting him to war. Xi Xia's fate was sealed. In spring, the nomadic army, now skilled at siege war advanced on Khara Khoto, the northern fortress of Xi Xia.

Enkhtuya was held captive at a camp on a nearby hill. Since the ridge was quite high and difficult to access and there were enough guards, she was not locked up. She could move freely about the camp which could be likened to an eagle's nest on top of the peak. However, she had full view of the battle of Khara Khoto. Stunned and fuming by turns, the girl along with Bolorma observed the development of the siege. Genghis Khan and his generals were strategising the entire operation from a high ground behind the troops. First, the Mongols surrounded the fortress and set up their deadly devices. Next, at a sign from the Emperor, catapults began to throw gunpowder-filled bombs over the citadel walls. Flame throwers and multiple bows sent a rain of deadly arrows and fire into the city finding targets indiscriminately; civilians or soldiers. Smoke billowed from the inside the fortress walls as the bombardment went on day after day, from dawn to dusk. Each morning the generals would shout orders to their troops relaying Genghis Khan's commands to make the assaults even more deadly and bloody. The Princess watched all of it helplessly losing all hope of any survivors in the terrible devastation.

'Those are my people being killed, Bolorma, and I can do nothing to help them. That Khan is an animal. He is a bloodthirsty monster. How I hate him!' Enkhtuya would gnash her teeth, smash her fists against the stones, crying out, 'How I wish I could kill him the same way as he is snuffing out thousands of innocent lives!' She would scream invectives at the Khan again and again. Unawares, tears streamed down her cheeks as the old maid would try to console her.

Still Khara Khoto did not open its gates to admit the Mongol troops. Enkhtuya prayed every day for her brave people. In vain, she would scour the valley for Tangut reinforcements, but none appeared. The final attack on the hapless fort came with the launching of the new 'heaven-shaking thunder' bombs. The sound of the explosions came up all the way to her prison camp. She ran to the escarpments and saw powerful conflagrations lighting up several parts of the citadel.

Her hand pressing down her lips, Enkhtuya was too dazed to even utter a word, as Bolorma spoke in awed tones, 'They say everything within the area of this explosion is blown to pieces. And they have sent in so many bombs. What will be left of the people in the fort?'

Finally, when the smoke cleared, they saw the gates of the fort slowly being winched up. Enkhtuya gave a sob of despair. The Mongol troopers rushed inside the citadel. The Princess sat down on a stone and refused to leave the spot even for meals. From her viewpoint, she could see into the fort but not into every lane and home. She could only imagine the killings, rapes, brutality going on inside for she knew the penalty for those who resisted Genghis Khan. Once again, the forcefully repressed scenes of Malikpur's tragedy rose up before her eyes. She saw her son dying again. The tears just would not stop and the black rage filling her up made her feel sick. By evening, she saw the survivors...prisoners of the Mongol troopers being driven out of the gates like cattle. Mostly women and elderly people, they looked dazed at the calamity that had befallen them. That there was hardly a man or a child among them told its own tale. Many stumbled as if blind. Even from her distant watch, she saw several women carrying babes in their arms. They were led to an open ground and segregated into groups. Genghis Khan and his commanders watched from an elevated ledge. Enkhtuya was puzzled as to what was happening but not for long. At a shouted command from the Khan's general, each group was approached by a Mongol soldier with a bare blade. He held to two or three persons by an arm around their necks. One mighty slash and heads rolled down the grassy knoll. The girl gave a choked cry and covered her ears. Indistinctly, she heard the cries of those not yet killed; saw them trying to run but in vain. The circle of soldiers cut them down. Finally, the grass was wet and darkly red, clumps of bodies marked the ground and no captive remained alive. The soldiers rode away. High above them, the Princess collapsed in a faint.

That night Bolorma informed Enkhtuya that they would be marching again and so the Princess must sleep early. *As if I could sleep at all,* Enkhtuya thought, deep, black sorrow weighing her down. Her dry eyes burned into the night and her mouth kept filling with the bitter bile of hatred against the monster responsible for the destruction of her people.

Thus, Khara Khoto was seized. Its conquest ensured that there would be no military reserves with Xi Xia when the final offensive came. Prince Asha had not supplemented the defenders of Khara Khoto by sending troops across 500 kilometres of desert from Yinchuan. The Tanguts preferred to fight from within city walls and not on open grounds. It suited Genghis perfectly. Augmented with Tangut prisoners and defectors, supplies and weapons, the nomadic army moved 300 kilometres south. Over the two months of its journey, it mopped up smaller towns on the way. At the Quilin Mountains, short of Yinchuan, Genghis divided his army. Subedei went west to attack the distant cities of Xi Xia while Genghis led the main force towards the core of the rebellious kingdom. On the way, many cities like Kan Chou and Wuwei surrendered rather than face death and destruction.

Enkhtuya saw a great deal of the suffering of the Tangut people as the Mongol invasion rolled through the country. She heard enough tales of horror to make her sick with grief. She stopped eating. Whatever she ate would be forced back through her gullet and emitted out as acidic vomit. She could not even drink water. Despite feeling lightheaded with weakness, she sat upright on her horse, moving with the cavalcade. She observed the green pastures, the cultivated fields, the majestic temples and thought, *finally I have come to my land and what a beautiful land it is!* She stood by and watched the magnificence of her land trampled underfoot by the barbarian Mongols. She recalled the tales her mother told her of this land and lamented, *it is my misfortune to witness the splendour of my country and its people crumble to dust before my own eyes.* Whatever little respect or regard she had begun to feel for Genghis Khan crashed into that dust and a deep anger against him corroded her insides.

It occurred to her that the duality of Genghis Khan's personality was not a schism between opposing facets but contradictory aspects in conflict with each other. Yet, these multifarious characteristics so apparent to her did not affect the man himself. He was quite comfortable in his own skin and did not seem to have any qualms exhibiting his innate incongruities as, when and whatever the situation demanded. *Strange!* Above everything else his foremost priority was the advancement of the Mongolian Empire. Further, he truly believed Mongols to be a race superior to all others. Despite all the civilised peoples that he had met on his trail of conquests, Genghis believed that nothing could match the lifestyle of the Mongols. Thus, to him as to all his soldiers, an *aduu* was more valuable than a human life, especially if that was not a Mongol one.

However, just as Enkhtuya had earlier believed that there was a little goodness in Genghis Khan, now she considered him evil through and through. To her any justification for the shocking mass murders she had viewed were just excuses. The real purpose of the Khan's annihilating conquests, she believed, was to quench his thirst for a bloody and fearsome domination over people who were non-Mongol. *I wonder*, she mused, *is it possible that in times to come, this same lust to dominate fellow humans through fear and death may incite powerful men to create excuses such as the right religion, nobler blood, fairer colour or simply safer borders to rain atrocities on other countries and their people?*

As they rode out every day covering enormous distances, she would search for the terrible Khan's erect figure among the masses of horsemen with a vague idea of wrecking her anger on him at least through a burst of vitriolic words. But somehow, she did not see him throughout the entire journey into Xi Xia.

Finally, the army reached the Yellow River, a broad kilometre-wide waterway, thick with mud and silt. Cavalry would be able to swim across but what about the wagons and heavy weaponry? Tangut defectors came in handy. They found boatmen from a nearby river town. Sheepskin and cow skin floats were tied together and spanned by wooden platforms. Wagons and weapons were trundled onto these platforms and several rowers manned them across the river. Thus, the entire army was ferried across the Yellow River and began to approach Yinchuan from the southwest, diametrically opposite of Prince Asha's proposed route. By then the Tangut Emperor, Xianzong, had died and a clansman, Xian was reigning.

Mere 30 kilometres out of Yinchuan, at a place called Ling-wu, the Tangut army finally made a move. Enkhtuya stood on the roof of a supply wagon to see the battle. That morning, the winter chill had settled in and she could see that the network of irrigation channels was frozen and gleaming in the sunlight. She saw the Tangut troops, pennants bright against the blue sky, canter forward along the far bank of the frozen river. Her heart was bursting with pride as she waited for them to rout the rag-tag Mongol forces. Suddenly, a movement from her own side caught her eye. The Mongols, not waiting for the enemy to reach the battlefield, broke ranks and galloped across the frozen river. The Princess clearly saw the Tanguts halt in surprise and a wave of anxiety ripple down the rows of warriors. Before they could even put arrows to bows, the Mongols were upon them, slashing and cutting through them.

'Oh no!' exclaimed the girl, 'That is deceit. The Mongols have no sense of ethics. How can they attack the enemy still not prepared to join battle? That is not fair!'

'Hummph!' snorted Bolorma, beside her. 'In war everything is fair. It is the winning that matters, not how one wins.'

Infuriated, Enkhtuya watched the demoralised survivors of the shattered Tangut army turn and flee towards Yinchuan while the triumphant Mongols returned. It was clear to both sides including the raging Enkhtuya that the Tanguts were finished.

A ring of siege was laid around Yinchuan but Genghis and Subedei veered off to the east with another force. Enkhtuya was forced to go with them. They wanted to secure the smaller cities and advance through the Jin borders. The idea was to cut across a narrow strip of Jin territory to effectively prevent Jin troops from coming to rescue their Tangut neighbours. Enkhtuya, sullen and boiling silently with anger, was once again accompanied by Shigi who glanced at her once or twice and then thought, *good she is silent for whatever reason. Her chattering makes my head ache.*

As they cantered along the valley of the southern Qing Shui river, the wagons followed slowly across wooden bridges over streams that cut into layers of dark, red earth. The cavalry rode ahead scouting the land for best routes and food. They suggested that the army go down a tortuous track along the steep sides of the Si Kou or

Temple Mouth river. As the track, looping along twisted red sandstone rocks, went around a bend, an astonishing sight met the eyes of the travellers. They gaped at a red cliff face honeycombed with hundreds of holes.

'Cells of Buddhist monks praying and meditating,' replied a Tangut guide to Shigi's query, 'It is called Xumi Shan or Treasure Mountain.'

Even Enkhtuya was roused from her self-imposed isolation to stare open-mouthed at the breathtaking sight. 'What a place to seek enlightenment!' she exclaimed and then pursed her mouth up as if she had tasted a bitter lemon when Shigi looked at her with a cocked brow. Truly, it was a remote, austere place yet radiating an abiding beauty, overlooking the reds and greens of sandstone ravines and grass-pimpled uplands. Despite squinting up at the cells as they rode past, Enkhtuya could not see any of the venerated monks or signs of life in them. However, she was aware of a presence here; an Omnipresence.

When they had gone a little further, she perceived why she had that strong intuition. Looming upwards to the sky was a Buddha, enshrined by the rock from which it had been sculpted. The half-closed eyes and the formal robes signified a traditional image of serenity and wisdom. Although in a sitting posture, it was the sheer size of it, more than 20 metres tall, that made each person crane his neck to look up at the spectacle. The entire column halted at the spot enraptured by the sublimity of the figure. Possibly, they felt humbled in the presence of such immense declaration of faith.

Enkhtuya reflected, observing the ear lobes of the deity, *each one must be at least 3 metres long. I hope the Khan is looking at this statue too. I hope the insight comes to him that it is faith that survives the onslaught of Time and not savage killings.*

Possibly standing at the same spot, Genghis had also considered posterity. How would History remember him? It was also possible that he would have shrugged at the huge Buddha, contemplating, *monuments, temples and tombs will eventually crumble. Only if I can make people worship me, can I live in the hearts and minds of humanity forever. And that is real power.*

Six months of hardships and disease due to the siege had taken such a toll of Yinchuan that Emperor Xian was more than ready to surrender. All he asked for was a month's time to prepare suitable gifts for Genghis Khan. Hoping to survive as a loyal vassal, he agreed to meet the Khan in the Liupan Mountains from where the Emperor of Mongolia was directing the campaign. Now the Khan's revenge on the traitor state as well as on the perpetuator of his own torment, the arrogant *Gambu,* was complete.

In the meanwhile, the Jins also sent him emissaries to sue for peace. Genghis met these envoys with warmth. He told them about an unusual conjunction of five planets a few months ago that had inspired him to end all killing and plundering. In the presence of the envoys, he instructed his generals, 'But in my haste I failed to authorise the order. Now, let it be announced far and wide, at home and abroad, and make sure these ambassadors know my royal command.'

But an end to killing and plundering did not mean peace. The progress of the Mongol forces through Jin lands continued. Genghis, himself, began to advance north. As before, Enkhtuya travelled with his cavalry. Shigi, the benign yet alert sentinel, escorted the silent, glowering girl.

27

Emperor Xian of Xi Xia hoped for clemency and a long reign as a vassal of the Mongol Empire, but he did not know that the Khan had no intention of granting him either. However, Genghis did not want the Tangut Emperor to know that he was planning to be utterly ruthless with the head of the twice-deceitful Tangut nation. He did not trust the Tanguts at all and so, there was no basis for any understanding between them. The Tanguts had insulted him, broken promises, refused him soldiers, resisted him in most of the cities and finally destroyed his beloved Gurbelchin. Ethnocide was the only solution; nothing but a complete decimation of the entire Tangut nation along with its society, heritage and civilisation. The first step to that was the death of the Tangut ruler. The Khan agreed to Xian's capitulation at the Liupan camp but kept his plans to himself.

Emperor Xian's grace period was nearly over when the forces under Genghis Khan reached Guyuan, a city perched on the same Silk Road that led to Samarkand and Bukhara. Guyuan fell to the Mongols in 1227 CE without a murmur. Conquering it put the Mongols in total control of the main trade route that joined China to Europe. South of Guyuan rose rolling hills mantled in grass and cultivated terraces against the backdrop of the emerald ridges of Liupan Mountains. A pass led to a high, flat grassland through which swirled a mountain river. Genghis Khan had decided to pitch his camp there. The plateau, now carpeted with the verdant summer grass, yellow buttercups and blue gentians, was large enough for his army to practise their drills. So, the tent-huts were erected encircling the main one that was the Emperor's. Enkhtuya's tent-hut and Bolorma's smaller tent were placed a little away from the circle. The wagons, carts and weapons were positioned strategically depending on what they carried.

Glad of the respite from the saddle, Enkhtuya took a long and luxurious bath the first evening. The chatter of the slaves preparing the night meal filtered through the felt walls. Their talk irritated the Princess. *What are they so chirpy about? Xi Xia has been defeated and its Emperor was on his way to submit to the tyrannical, bloodthirsty Khan. Does one celebrate the fall of a nation…my nation… any nation?*

The more her thoughts dwelt on the architect of this tragedy, the more her outrage spilled over bringing nearly a physical ache to her guts. She tried to subdue her fury knowing that she could not vent it and it would only lead to a spate of painful retching. But just the mental image of his dispassionate, cool, cruel face made her burn up inside. No remnants of the little empathy that she had once felt for him existed. It had been purged by the atrocities committed on his orders that she saw daily now. She hated the man with a deep, sharp, burning, almost vicious antipathy.

Bolorma came in with a fresh change of tunics and remarked, 'The water must be cool, *Guunj*. Come, let me dry you.'

As the old woman rubbed her skin till it tingled, Enkhtuya idly inquired, 'So what is the news?'

'They say that Emperor Xian comes tomorrow to surrender. Everyone is excited,' she revealed.

'What are they excited about? As if the Emperor is bringing them gifts!' Enkhtuya tossed her head.

'But they say that he is. Scouts have seen a hundred horses and mules wending their way up from the plains,' Bolorma said.

'Hummph,' snorted the Princess. *Why should a defeated ruler bring gifts to the barbaric Mongols?*

That night as Genghis Khan ate with his generals, he commanded them, 'While I take my meals, you must talk about the killing and destruction of the Tangut, and say, "Maimed and tamed, they are no more".' Genghis' commanders discussed among themselves before taking their scheme to their Emperor who put his seal of approval on it. But the Princess knew nothing of it.

The next morn, as birds sang, and cicadas chirped, Xian's caravan reached the Mongol camp. Like everyone else, Enkhtuya watched with astonished eyes as an endless line of animals heaved onto the plateau bearing large bags bulging with treasures. A huge marquee had been erected to one side with white, silk curtains enclosing the interior. Apparently, Genghis Khan was inside but he was concealed behind the curtains. Standing behind the tent-huts on a slight slope, Enkhtuya observed the Emperor of Xi Xia, also known as the Burkhan or the Holy One, dismount. Arrayed in splendid robes, embroidered in gold thread and pearls, he looked every inch a king. The Princess' heart was bursting with pride for the monarch of her wealthy country, and then ached to see him brought down to paying obeisance to a wicked nomad.

He looks quite young, she mused as she observed him. Xian was accompanied by a retinue as magnificently garbed as he. Shigi dressed in a *deel* of bright yellow, the royal colour of the Khan, approached the Emperor. He bowed and announced, 'The Lord sends his greetings to the Burkhan and confers on him the title of Sidurgu or the 'Faithful One'. Xian bowed at the honour not knowing the irony of the Khan's gift. Then the entire entourage waited for Genghis Khan to appear.

And they waited. And they waited. And they waited.

Shigi had disappeared. The curtains of the pavilion remained tied. Nobody went in and nobody emerged from it. Enkhtuya watched in perplexity. Bolorma whispered, 'What is happening? Where is the Lord?'

As the sun climbed higher in the sky, the day turned quite warm. The Princess noticed sweat trickling from under the jewelled headdress of the Tangut Emperor in rivulets down his anxious face. After considerable time, it was quite definite that Genghis Khan had no intentions of meeting Emperor Xian. After a whispered conference with his aides, the Burkhan gave an order. Slaves began to unload the gifts for the Khan and laying them out on the grass in front of the curtained marquee. First row was taken up by nine golden Buddhas. They were followed by rows of golden and silver bowls, bolts of silks, jewelled ornaments all in the propitious number of nine. There were nine boys, nine girls, nine geldings, nine camels and so on. Enkhtuya could hardly believe her eyes at the opulent gifts that tumbled forth. The Mongol soldiers goggled, too. Everything was laid out correctly according to colour and form. Finally, the Burkhan flanked by his nobles, went down on his knees before the closed silk curtains. Laying his sword on the ground before him, he bowed his head and declared, 'With this sword, I hand over the Kingdom of Xi Xia to you, my Lord. I and my heirs become your faithful vassals hitherto.'

No acknowledgement came through the curtains. As the Burkhan knelt in the bright sunshine, Enkhtuya observed Tolun, one of the Khan's generals, saunter into the clearing. He came up behind the kneeling Emperor of Xi Xia, shouldering aside the royal nobles roughly. Dreadful apprehension rose like bitterness up the girl's throat as a thin rope suddenly sprang into Tolun's hands like a poisonous viper. In a blink of the eye, he had pulled up the monarch's head with the garrotte around his throat. Tolun gave a tug and there was sharp crack as Xian's neck broke. Before his shocked nobles could utter even a sound, Mongol soldiers fell on them. Within minutes, the ground was filled with bodies and severed heads. The green plateau darkening with spilled blood was churned up by hooves as the mules and slaves were led off. It was a business-like, efficient execution that took hardly a few minutes. However, it was structured to ensure that not a drop of the Burkhan's blood was spilled. After being honoured by the title of the 'Faithful One', the Burkhan was accorded a dignified death. For, did not Mongol traditions decree that after his demise, the virtues of a noble enemy would exercise a beneficial influence on his victor? In that way, the dead Burkhan, a former foe would become a protective spirit and watch over the Khan.

Screams of sheer terror and shock were about to burst from Enkhtuya's lips but Bolorma's hand instantly clapped down on the Princess' mouth. The maid dragged Enkhtuya away to her tent-hut as soon as the Burkhan's body tumbled to the ground. Thus, she only heard the screams and clash of swords while the rest of the systematic murders were carried out. But the sight of the submissive monarch being killed in cold blood was enough to make her moan in anguish. *Why? Why? Why?* Repeatedly, she whispered to her maid who only shook her head. *How could they kill an unarmed king who had come to submit to the Khan?* After bouts of crying and vomiting, gradually sleep overcame the agonised girl.

When she woke, it was already dark outdoors. Bolorma came in with some fruit to satisfy the gnawing in her starved belly. As Enkhtuya nibbled, the maid said in flat tones, 'There is to be a feast tonight to celebrate the victory on Xi Xia.'

The girl did not reply. She lay down and stared up at the felt roof with vacant eyes. She thought of the stories her mother had related about the beauty of Xi Xia; its palaces, temples, streets and gardens. *Will these savages destroy everything just as callously as they had killed the Burkhan this morning? Probably*…Then a stunning thought occurred to her. *Was it possible that her father had been part of Xian's entourage and was murdered with the rest right before her eyes?* It brought fresh tears to her burning eyes. I *wish I had known my father, even for a short while,* she lamented. *Now I have nobody…no father, no mother, no son, no husband.* She felt like a lost soul compelled to wander the earth alone drifting like an autumn leaf.

The night was as noisy as only an enthusiastic feast of victory could be. Enkhtuya pulled tighter the sash that she had wound around her head to muffle the cacophonous drunken songs and laughter.

Suddenly Bolorma burst in, 'Get up, *Guunj*. Quickly!'

'Why?' The supine girl groaned making no effort.

'The Lord has asked for you. Get up, please!' Bolorma pleaded.

For a moment Enkhtuya's heart missed a beat. *After so long? I thought he had forgotten me.* Then she recalled all that had happened since and her heart hardened with black wrath. 'No!'

'No?' Bolorma could not believe her ears. 'You won't go?'

'No. I won't go,' affirmed her mistress.

'Then be ready to be dragged out and…and…maybe killed.' She sounded as if she was speaking to a child. 'Do you want that?'

'Why not?' Enkhtuya countered, sitting up and throwing aside the covers. 'After all, what do I have to live for?' She added as Bolorma hid a smile and began to unwind the sash from her head.

It was due to Bolorma's skill that hardly in a few minutes, the Princess was ready in a fresh *deel* and trousers, her hair piled up becomingly on top of her head. While she was being dressed, a vague plan began to form in the girl's mind. When the maid gave a final pat to her cheek, Enkhtuya stood up and stepped to the bed to grab the small, sharp knife that went everywhere with her. Bolorma shook her head, indicating the redundancy of the small slicing knife. Then the women stepped out. A sentry outside indicated the marquee that shone brightly in the moonlight. Enkhtuya walked gingerly towards it expecting her slippers to squelch in the bloody grass. But the ground was hard and dry under her feet. No smell of blood came to her in the cool breeze laden with the scent of summer flowers.

The white, silk curtains were untied and fluttered as she went through. Inside, the large space had only a dais with two chairs and a table between them. A fire burnt in a pit casting long shadows on the tent walls. Nobody occupied the chairs. Enkhtuya peered into all the corners before slowly stepping up to occupy one of the chairs. Till now, every time he had asked for her, the Khan had been waiting for her. This was the first time that she was waiting for him. But not for long.

Footsteps came up to the marquee. Curtains were thrust aside as Genghis Khan strode in. Enkhtuya stood up uncertainly. Everyone bowed to him, but she kept her back erect. He came up to the dais with a slightly unsteady gait. The Princess guessed he was a little inebriated. But his voice was rock steady as he declared, 'Ah *Guunj*! Seeing you after a long time, isn't it?' He settled himself into a chair, digging into his pouch for the ubiquitous pipe and tobacco. He gestured to her, 'Sit down, Girl! Don't loom over me like prescience.' And then chuckled at his own jest.

Enkhtuya sat down on the edge of the other chair and waited.

'It is late, but I wanted to meet you. You have been hounding me for long about my killings.' He squinted at her through the smoke curling from his pipe. The girl said nothing, but her eyes turned stony. 'Did you hear what I have announced?'

He kept looking at her so that she was forced to shake her head. 'Well, I have vowed to the Jin envoys that there will be no more killing and plundering. Does that meet the *Guunj's* approval?' The last words were heavy with sarcasm.

The girl still kept silent. Wrathful hatred ran like poison in her blood. She wanted to slit his lying heart open, but she just could not make herself attack him in cold blood. After being terrified of a rapacious attack by the Khan for so long, at this moment, paradoxically she wished with all her heart that the vile man would molest her.

*I would be forced to defend myself, then, won't I? And in the passion of it, I would get the impetus I badly need to drive my knife into him. I will smash it in right up to its hilt. That will end his cockiness and inflict a deep enough wound…maybe even a fatal one…*were the angry thoughts running through Enkhtuya's head.

Unperturbed, the Khan puffed away at his pipe looking up at the silk ceiling.

Eventually, Enkhtuya said in a voice taut with anger, 'Were this morning's murders a practice of your vow?'

'Ah, now the *Guunj* speaks!' The Khan exclaimed. 'This morning…' He halted, and the girl waited. 'This morning was ordained a long time ago in the stars.'

'So, now you read the life and death of monarchs in the stars,' said Enkhtuya, biting every word.

'*Guunj,* Xi Xia has been treacherous too many times. I forgave them their arrogance and deceit each time. They took my patience for granted but outdid themselves this last time. Not only did they refuse to follow my orders but every city, especially Yinchuan, resisted me. But why am I telling you all these boring details?' He put a hand on her knee. 'Tell me how have you been?'

Disregarding his concern, Enkhtuya jumped to her feet. 'Did Khara Khoto resist you because their men, women or children were arrogant? Did the people of Yinchuan deceive you? Did the Emperor of Xi Xia come unarmed to surrender so that your men could murder him?' She was shouting at him, shaking with agitation.

'*Guunj!*' Genghis Khan put up a hand to match his conciliatory tone.

But Enkhtuya's suppressed anger bubbled up and spilled like hot milk from a cauldron searing her. She did not care anymore for her own safety. Eyes blazing fire, she screamed, 'How dare you think you can get away with killing the monarch of my land?'

'Your land?'

'Yes. The land my mother came from. The land of my father.'

'The land of your father? *Guunj…*'

'Yes. Yes. My father's land…my forefathers' land…my beautiful land. You have ravaged it…broken its temples, burned its cities, raped its women, killed its people by the thousands. What vow are you talking about?' She gave a bitter laugh. 'Your oath is like the wind…here one day… gone the next day. Today you make a vow to not kill… tomorrow you kill.'

'*Guunj…*' He stood up placing a hand on the agitated girl's shoulder.

'Don't touch me!' She screamed shrilly and jumped off the dais. Turning her back to the man, she ranted on. 'I used to believe that there is a little good in you but now I know you are the Devil riding Death. Nobody forgives a devil who only brings sorrow and grief with him. Punishment is waiting for you. Your Khökh Tenger will strike you down. I hate you. I hate you…' She broke down sobbing.

The Khan stepped unsteadily down from the dais, came up behind her and put his arms around the weeping, trembling girl to console her. 'Enkhtuya…' he began. The girl whipped around, and her hand thrust upwards in a metallic flash.

The Khan grunted staring with disbelief at a bright, red patch appearing on the front of his *deel*. It spread rapidly, gleaming wetly in the firelight. Cursing, he tore open the neckline of his *deel* to get to the wound. Enkhtuya's eyes were wide with apprehension. She knew the penalty for attacking the Khan.

As the neckline of the *deel* dropped from the Khan's left shoulder, Enkhtuya gasped sharply. She stared at a small, red circular spot on his skin with a fainter pattern like a sunburst around it.

'But…but…that is exactly like…' she murmured, bewildered. The Khan was still reeling on his feet, his hand trying to reach the deep wound in his gut, but he looked up at her words.

He saw knowledge dawning in a pair of confused blue eyes. He nodded tiredly at her. 'Yes *Guunj*.' His deep voice was tinged by infinite sadness. 'Yes Enkhtuya, I am your *Aav*. Princess Gurbelchin was your mother and this tyrant, Genghis Khan is your father. Not…' He coughed up a spurt of blood. '…not some dirty Tangut traitor as you believe.'

'*Aav?*' The girl whispered trying out the word on her tongue. She stepped forward to the suddenly crippled Khan. Giving him her shoulder, she took his weight on her slim frame as he stumbled to the nearest chair and dropped into it. The sentries outside had clustered around the marquee entrance, anxious about the loud voices from inside but not daring to intervene. Amassing his waning strength, Genghis Khan clapped his hands. Instantly, they rushed inside. Choking on his own blood, he muttered, 'Call Shigi. Take away the *Guunj*. Tell them to keep her safe. I wish to sleep.' And the conqueror slid into unconsciousness.

28

Behind the darkness of closed eyelids, white light flashed intermittently accompanied by thuds of a hammer. Enkhtuya kept her eyes closed trying to identify the root cause of this punishing torture. *Who is bashing me up?* After a couple more of agonising implosions, she realised that it was her own head that was thrashing her to bits. She tried to lift her lids, but they were stuck to her eyes with mucus. Slowly, she pried loose her upper and lower lashes. She was supine, she knew looking around. She could feel a hard, wooden floor under her back and when she tried to straighten her legs, the feet hit a wall. She was in a very small, enclosed space. A small, barred window near the low roof allowed a little light to filter in. Everything was shadowy, at first. When her eyes adjusted, she could make out the outline of a tightly closed door on the wall beyond her feet. She struggled to sit up, but nauseating waves of pain coming faster and stronger made her lie back again. She moved her hands and saw that she was not bound. Gingerly, she felt around her aching head. There was no wound or a tender bulge yet the torment inside it was excruciating. As she slowly tried to focus beyond the pain inside her, she became aware that the room was swaying. Her prison was moving and now she heard the slow creak of wooden wheels over the pounding in her head. *Where am I? This seems like one of the closed wagons. Where is it going? Where am I being taken?*

Amidst the white explosions, a face swam up...a familiar face...her mother's face. Enkhtuya had been dreaming of her...over and over again. The face had the familiar expression of abiding sweetness just as it used to when she was alive. However, her eyes were different…her eyes had…a sadness in them so acute, so real, that the girl's own eyes became misty. Once again, tears spilled over. Her cheeks already had caking dry, salty smears for she had been crying without awareness, without control for a long time now. 'No *Eej*! No!…I didn't do it on purpose… please believe me…no, no, no…I didn't…I didn't,' she mouthed to her mother's face swimming before her eyes. She pulled up her knees and turned on her side to sob into palms covering her face. But her mother still looked at her with sorrowful, blue eyes while the hammer continued beating in her head. Inside her chest, a hollow cavity was pulsating dully. *Is it my heart?* She puzzled.

Events of the recent past came back to her like frescoes painted on walls. She knew why her mother did not take her into her arms and comfort her. Enkhtuya knew she was lying to her mother…her intentions had been full of purpose. She had wanted to wound the great Genghis Khan mortally…fatally, if she could. 'But I didn't know, *Eej,* I didn't know…that…that it was the Khan…that he was my father…that he was the brave warrior you told me about…*Eej!*…How would I know, *Eej*…You didn't tell me his name, did you?'

Her mother's lips moved but Enkhtuya couldn't hear the words. Inside her head the hammer began to beat in tune with a chant 'You should have known…You should have known. Who else but you? Why else did he devote himself to your comfort, your food and your safety? Who else would trust you so much? You should have KNOWN…YOU should have KNOWN….' The sound of the incantation rose to a crescendo…shouting, screaming, screeching….

The girl held her head with both hands, face scrunched up in anguish and rolled from side to side, sobbing,

'No, no, no, no....' Her body shook as if in an ague. The legs knifed up in air trying to ease the affliction in her head. She tried to quell it by grabbing and tugging her hair hard with both hands. She was in a torturous trance from which she could not break free despite her desperate efforts.

She was not aware that the wagon had stopped moving until she heard her name, '*Guunj? Guunj* Enkhtuya?'

The girl slowly removed her hands from the sides of her head. *Is that Eej calling me?*

Again, the whisper came, '*Guunj?*'

It was a known voice though she could not place it in a mind fenced in with pain. Then it occurred to her... *Eej would not call me 'Princess'*. She lay still and listened carefully.

'*Guunj?*'

Yes.Yes. I know...it is Bolorma. 'Bolorma?' Enkhtuya mumbled, her voice hoarsely cracking.

'Oh *Guunj!*' came an elated whisper. 'I thought they had killed you with the herbs that the shaman put into the milk. I saw them forcing it down your throat two nights ago.'

Painfully, Enkhtuya sat up and dragged herself below the barred hatch. Hands pressing on the wooden wall of the wagon, she stood up on trembling legs. But only by standing on her toes could she see just above the edge of the window. Bolorma's kind, wrinkled face bobbed up. She smiled showing all the gaps in her teeth. 'Thanks to our Lord, *Guunj,* that they did not harm you,' she intoned.

'The Lord?'

'Yes. I heard them say that the Khan had ordered that you be safe,' she whispered.

The Khan? The man I wanted to kill? Guilt and misery began to fill the hollow in her chest.

'What do you mean by saying that the shaman made me drink herbs in milk?'

'Oh my poor *Guunj!*' exclaimed the old woman. 'Has it affected your mind? Do you remember nothing of the happenings of two nights ago?'

'Well!' Enkhtuya muttered uncertainly, 'I do…remember stabbing…the Khan.' Her voice broke on the last word while she swallowed tears rising up in her throat. 'Then… then what happened?'

Bolorma looked around, fearfully. 'They will kill me if they see me speaking you. Nobody is supposed to even come close to this wagon.'

'What happened, Bolorma?' Enkhtuya persisted.

'The Khan called Shigi and his generals to the marquee. You were screaming when they dragged you out…' Bolorma frowned. '…something about it being a mistake, that you didn't know and something else…I couldn't understand it all…you were just babbling.'

'It was a mistake…' the Princess whispered, though the old woman did not hear it.

She went on, 'Shigi slapped you once, then again and you fainted. Throwing you into my arms, he ran inside the marquee. The guards would not let me take you away to your hut. They shouted at me that you had attacked the great Lord and you must be punished. I heard the generals yelling inside and then the shaman also rushed in. Many people were inside the marquee. From outside, we heard a lot of voices speaking through the closed curtains. Only the Khan's voice was not heard. Even the guards had noticed it. They gave you baleful looks though you were unconscious. I heard them growling to each other, 'What has happened to the Emperor? Is our Lord dead?'

'Is the Khan dead?' Enkhtuya echoed.

'I don't know,' whispered the old woman. 'Nobody knows.'

'How did I reach here?'

'I waited with you outside the marquee before Shigi came out, his face furious. He ordered me to take you to your hut. He held your legs and I took you by the shoulders. Both of us carried you inside the hut and laid you, still senseless, on the bed. You looked so frail lying helplessly on the bed. But the Khan's brother saw none of it. His face was like a thunder cloud, scowling with rage. He returned to the hut with the shaman. They asked me to quickly bring some warm mare's milk. When I told them that you took goat's milk not the mare's, they took no notice. The shaman was busy grinding dried herbs to powder. When he poured it into the bowl of milk I had brought, the white liquid turned deep purple. I was sure that they were poisoning you. I begged them to spare your life. Shigi just roared at me. He told me to shut up. He also said that he wished he could kill a traitor like you but unfortunately, he had to obey the Lord's orders and he had desired your safety.

The shaman did explain that the herbs were not deathly. They would only cause deep sleep for a long period of time. I kept sobbing and pleading with them. When they tried to open your mouth to make you drink the milk, your jaws were clamped shut. I held you in my arms to shield you from them. Shigi picked me up and flung me out of the door. Crouching on the ground, I watched Shigi pinch your nose. As soon as you opened your mouth to breathe, the shaman poured the purple concoction down your throat. When the bowl was empty, they threw it at me and left. After a while, Shigi was back with slaves carrying a large piece of felt. On his instructions they rolled you in it and began to take you out. I followed them crying for them to let you go. I saw them throw you into this wagon and lock the door. A guard has been posted outside. And Shigi warned me to clear off. He said that if I came near this place, he would slash my throat.'

Enkhtuya said, 'This wagon was moving some time ago. Are they taking me to a prison?'

'We are again on the move, but I don't know,' replied Bolorma. 'In the kitchen, the slaves were saying that we are going to the Burkhan Khaldun.'

'Burkhan Khaldun? What is that?' Enkhtuya's weak voice betrayed the strain of hanging on to the ledge of the hatch. *How much longer will I have to bear this? I will break down, I know. Still, I must know my fate,* she thought, forcing her body to remain upright.

'It is a lofty, glittering mountain,' replied the old woman. 'They say Khökh Tenger lives there and so it is the sacred mountain of the Mongols. Right now, the cavalry and the entire train of wagons, carts and weapons are moving very fast. We crossed the Yellow River yesterday and have been travelling night and day. The commanders seem to be in a great hurry to reach wherever we are going.'

'Where are we now?' Enkhtuya wanted some kind of bearings.

'We are on the banks of the Kherlen River. We have halted for lunch. *Guunj,* I stole some food for you.' Two gnarled hands thrust a package through the bars. Wrapped in soft grass, it rolled down to the girl's feet. 'Some tender meat for you, *Guunj,* my dear. You must be very hungry. Eat it, *Guunj.* You have to keep up your strength. I must go. They must not find me here. I will come again.'

Enkhtuya exclaimed, 'Wait, Bolorma. Where is this Kherlen River? Where are we, now?'

'We are in our own land…the land of the great Mongols, well within the empire of our Lord, Genghis Khan. I must go now, *Guunj*. Don't worry. I will come again. Now, eat the food. You must be strong for whatever is coming. I think there is a pot of water in the corner of the wagon. Drink from it.' And Bolorma vanished leaving the girl bereft and once again in torment.

Enkhtuya lay down on the wooden floor releasing her legs from the burden of holding up her body. She looked up at the tiny patch of eggshell blue sky which was all that she could see through the bars. In it a dark speck flew weaving ever widening circles. If she strained her ears, she could hear the gurgling of water. *It has to be the Kherlen,* she thought.

In her mind, she reiterated the information that Bolorma had divulged. From her words, it seemed that she was alive because Genghis Khan was alive. *But for how long?* Despair overwhelmed her once again as tears began to drip making moist marks on the wood; tears of remorse for her own perfidy, tears for a father she had longed for and would never know, tears of terror for the pain and punishment awaiting her.

All of a sudden, her mind recalled all the kindness that the Khan had accorded her. It was not that the memory of his cruel deeds was erased but the terrible anger she had felt towards him was gone. Her own guilt overshadowed everything else. Her self-accusation was caustic. *What was I thinking? That I am an embodiment of justice for the people who were killed by his soldiers? That by killing him I could liberate the world from Genghis Khan's autocracy? How foolish I was! I only succeeded in wrecking my own chances of the little happiness I could have savoured.* In these corrosive words, she castigated herself repeatedly going round and round in circles wishing she had had some sense…sense to see the truth.

As time went by, in a strange, convoluted logic, she seemed to find plausible reasons for his tyranny…even for the bloodshed. All scenes of her personal interactions with him rose up before her eyes. She remembered how he had arranged for food suitable to her taste even when the army was marching through unfriendly territory, the clothes he had sent for her, his courtesy…only when she remembered his justification for killing her son…whom he had known was his own grandson…she faltered. Then, feeling a strange loyalty, she murmured, '…but he had not killed my baby…his soldiers had murdered him…'

*He had known all along that he was my father but did not let me know. Why? If he had revealed that I was his daughter, what an enriching experience we would have had. And now it would never happen…*She remembered the bloody patch on the front of his *deel* growing and growing, leaking away all his strength, rendering the mighty leader too weak to even stand on his feet. *All because of my foolishness… if they kill me for my dastardly act, I deserve it, I deserve it. How can an offspring deserve to live after attacking her own loving father?* Once again, the heartbroken girl collapsed in a storm of weeping. Her head throbbed as tongs seemed to crush it from both sides.

It was a very long time, before she felt like sitting up and checking the food package, Bolorma had brought her. She opened the package and found strips of roasted meat. Suddenly, her stomach rumbled. Her grief could not keep hunger at bay. She nibbled on one strip. Its soft skeins suggested it was the flesh of a bird or a marmot but whatever it was, the meat was delicious. After all, she had not eaten for three nights. She wolfed it all down and looked around. Sure enough, there was a small, wooden pot in the corner. She tilted it at her open mouth and drank deeply of the cool, clear water. As her stomach filled, the hammering in her head lessened but the painful hole in her heart did not fill. She lay back weakly on the wooden boards. *What is in store for me? Horrible death? How would the Mongols punish the one who had attacked their great leader?* She recalled the manner in which many innocent citizens of Khara Khoto, Yinchuan and Malikpur were slain; some beheaded, some ripped from throat to groin and left to slowly bleed to death. She shuddered. It was better to die instantly than be left to die over painful hours.

29

Enkhtuya was roused from her anguished torpor by the shaking floor boards of the wagon. They were travelling again. After a while, she felt the violent tremors of wooden wheels rolling over stones die down. Now, the wagon was still but they were still moving! *Is it floating?* Enkhtuya wondered. *Is it crossing the river?*

Bellows from men navigating rafts carried across to her. She had earlier experienced the movement of rafts with loaded wagons floating across the Yellow River. Thus, she was sure that the same mode was being used to cross the Kherlen. Loud splashes against the wagon's sides confirmed her guess. Nearly an hour later, the wagon began to quiver violently again. *So, my wagon is across! But where are they taking me now?*

Straining her ears, for she could see nothing but sunlit skies through the hatch, she faintly heard the murmur of the river. The rumbling of wheels over the stones was so loud that they drowned the river's song. She assumed that they were moving along the river bank. Enkhtuya passed the rest of the day in a dazed confusion lapsing repeatedly into delirious nightmares as the effect of the herbs still played in her body. Sleep brought up her mother's form pointing accusing fingers at her or a tall, strong, male figure swinging her as a little girl up to his shoulder while she plunged a knife into him again and again. His dark eyes would continue to smile at her, but his mouth would well up with blood spilling all over her. She would begin drowning in a river of blood and wake up gasping, screams choked in her throat. There was no way that she could escape the melancholy distress that assailed her and the anguish of her guilt-ridden heart. Disconsolately, she wondered how long this torture will go on for she was about to tumble down from the edge of sanity. Even death was better than these terrible, dark depths of hellish self-reproach she was sinking into with every passing hour.

By night time, the wagon had halted. Shouts and calls told Enkhtuya that the camp was being set up. She waited restlessly for Bolorma. Desperately, she wanted news of the Khan. *My father!* She held the bars of the small, high window and tried to haul herself up to see beyond, but her limbs were too weak and the wooden walls too smooth. As the sun went down, a murmur rose in the air, like the passing wind wailing ominously…as if for an inconsolable grief. Enkhtuya began to pace the small enclosure beside herself with anxiety and fear. A long time passed before she heard what she was waiting for; a whisper, *'Guunj?'*

'Yes.' Enkhtuya rushed to the window. 'Yes Bolorma! How is the Khan? Tell me. Tell me everything.'

Bolorma's low voice cracked with fear. 'Nobody knows. The shaman is calling out to the forces of earth and sky. Can you not hear it?'

'Eiiiyaah!' Enkhtuya cried out.

Instantly, Bolorma warned her, 'Don't cry so loudly, *Guunj*. If they find me…'

Enkhtuya's hand covered her open mouth. Through her fingers, she whispered to herself. 'Oh Khökh Tenger! Oh Allah! What have I done? My hands are stained… wretched me…with the blood of my *Aav*! Will I ever find peace? Even if I die this sorrow will not leave me…Is there anyone more hapless than I? Oh God! I will never be forgiven for this heinous crime. Oh God!' She turned to Bolorma and sobbing loudly, declared, 'Then the Khan must very unwell. If the shaman is praying to the powers, his medicines must have had no effect on the Khan. Or is he praying to obtain their blessings to make his medicines potent? Do you think, it could be that?' Plaintively, the desperate girl clutched at straws.

'*Guunj,* I do not know. Nobody is allowed into the Lord's tent palace. And *Guunj,* I have news for you.' She paused as Enkhtuya held the window bars, her blue eyes suddenly luminous in the gathering gloom.

Bolorma's words murmured like the summer breeze rustling through the steppe grass. 'They…the generals are furious. They believe that you have betrayed the Lord's trust. They say you have committed treason. They are angry that you are still alive. When they were dining around the campfire, I heard them mutter that you are safe till now only because the Lord has wished for it. If it had been left to them, you would be dead by now. They were saying that if you die, your spirit will work towards hastening the Lord's recovery. I heard Shigi declare that if they killed you without shedding blood and gave you a respectful burial, your spirit will protect the Khan and probably revive him.' She stopped speaking for the information to sink into the girl's mind.

'Kill me to revive the Khan?' Enkhtuya was perplexed. 'How?'

'Mongols believe that if enemies, especially of noble lineage, are killed and buried honourably, their spirits benefit their killers. Did you not see how they killed the Burkhan of Xi Xia? He was strangulated and none of his blood was shed…'

Both the women mulled over the dreadful memory of the execution of the Emperor of Xi Xia.

Then Bolorma whispered urgently, '*Guunj,* listen. The fact is I fear for your life. I don't trust Shigi and the generals. They may try to kill you just so that your death benefits the Lord. I am absolutely sure that if the Lord goes to the Eternal Blue Heaven, there is no doubt that they will come after you, *Guunj.* And Mongol rage can be terrible.'

Enkhtuya's eyes grew larger and larger as Bolorma was speaking. She gulped down the panic that rose in her heart. Grisly images of women with breasts sliced off or horsewhips pushed up their private parts during the retribution of Yinchuan swam before her eyes. No doubt, she was depressed enough to welcome death to release her from her unbearable agony but to be punished the Mongol way before that respite turned her legs to jelly. Bolorma's last words compelled her fingers to claw at her neck as if a noose was tightening around it.

Her loyal old maid continued whispering, '*Guunj,* I have a plan. This wagon has been placed a little far from the other huts, *gers* and the camp centre. I have seen that they have kept only one guard on duty here. They probably think that you are still unconscious from the herbs. They don't know that you have recovered. I will request the guard to let me in to wash you and change your clothes. Once he unlocks the wagon door, I will see to it that you escape. It is a good plan, isn't it?

The girl's hushed sobs filled the enclosure.

'Don't cry, my *Guunj,*' consoled Bolorma. 'Just wait till the moon is high in the sky. I will come and free you. Oh! Here is your dinner. I nearly forgot to give it to you.' Her thin hands pushed another grass-wrapped package through the bars. Enkhtuya took it and laid it aside. 'Wait, my *Guunj*. I will be back.' And Bolorma was gone.

Enkhtuya lay herself down on the wooden floor. Her limbs were trembling with anxiety and fear. Guilt and grief for her father…a father whom she had only accused and never sought to understand was eating her up. *If my death will bring Aav succour and health, I will gladly embrace it for I have nothing to live for, anyway,* thought the girl, deeply despondent. However, Bolorma's words also overwhelmed her with panic and dread at the prospect of a horrible death at the hands of her father's Mongol aides.

Her entire body began twitching as if hundreds of spiders crawled over it. *What will happen to me? If Shigi and the generals decided to kill me, they may hand me over to the soldiers to persecute me as they wished before the final slash across my throat.* She shivered and broke out in cold sweat. Her ears were alert for sounds of people approaching her prison. She forgot to eat or drink as the evening went by in terrifying apprehension. Once again, the hallucinations started. Suddenly, she was gasping for breath, her hands were dripping blood and the small knife that had been her secret companion for days dancing before her eyes, gleaming silver in the rays of the setting sun beaming through the bars.

Eons went by before she was woken by voices and a rattling. Somebody was at the door of the wagon. Her eyes wide with terror, Enkhtuya dragged herself to the farthest, darkest corner of her prison. The door opened. A rush of cool night air wafted in and then it was quickly cut off. '*Guunj?*' whispered Bolorma. Enkhtuya whimpered in her corner. 'Stand behind me,' instructed the woman. 'When I step out, slip out behind me and run towards the river.'

Enkhtuya managed to stand though her legs were shaking violently. She feared for her strength. *Will I be able to run?* Holding on to the walls of the wagon, she came up behind the old woman whose stout form was now visible in the slim crack of the door. Quickly, Bolorma opened the door. The guard sitting on the steps leading down from the wagon door was nonchalantly humming, sublimely ignorant of what was occurring just above his head. Raising the wooden pot full of water above her head, the old woman brought it down hard on the head of the guard. Soundlessly, he toppled off the steps on to the ground. Enkhtuya slipped out from behind Bolorma into the inky darkness. She was free.

Underfoot, the grass was soft and springy as only summer grass of the steppes can be. Sparkling stars sprinkled the dark sky forming the vast dome of Earth's pantheon. In the lap of fleecy, misty clouds swam a full moon; large, yellow and serene. Enkhtuya saw none of this. Ears attuned to the gurgling of the Kherlun, she ran swiftly towards it on bare, silent feet. Tall grass glistened as the chorus of the river grew louder and she came upon the swirling waters of the Kherlun. Standing on the slope of its banks, she paused to take in the sight; crystal waves gleaming with silvery reflections of a thousand moons.

And she saw her at once.

Standing upright among the singing waters, she was there for Enkhtuya. Floating white robes billowing on ripples around her, braided hair piled high on the head in an elaborate coiffure, soft, blue eyes brimming with love, her mother stretched out her arms out to Enkhtuya, silently promising to wipe away all her pain. Her *eej* had always been like this whenever she would fall or hurt herself as a little girl. Enkhtuya would run into her arms and be at once clasped to her breast. Immediately all pain and fear would melt away in a heavenly peace that would inundate her to the very soul. She had missed her *eej*. She had missed for so many months the bliss of being surrounded by love and security.

Enkhtuya kept her eyes on *Eej* swaying with the churning, foaming Kherlen. She began to slowly wander down the slope. In her mind, she was again the little girl, her thick, black hair braided into long plaits hanging to her knees, festooned with beads and ribbons, ankle-length robes flying in the breeze. *Eej* used to always line the rims of Enkhtuya's eyes with smoky-grey kohl making her blue, uptilted eyes turn aqua with green flecks. Her fair, round, flawless face, flat nose, small, pink rosebud of a mouth had made her an unusually beautiful child and everyone in Malik's palace remarked on her looks. Even when she married Jalal-ud-din, the Sultan, she had made an exquisitely, bewitching bride. No wonder that she had become his favourite in the harem and he would spend every night with her to the envy of his other wives. He would listen indulgently to her chatter and then love her passionately. He had been so proud when she had gifted him a son within a year of her marriage '...son! Oh my son! How cruelly he was killed...the pain, *Eej,* the pain of seeing my own child murdered is too sharp...too terrible, *Eej.*' By then, Enkhtuya had reached the edge of the river. Her mother still floated in the middle of the eddies where the Kherlen swept around a couple of boulders. Enkhtuya's hand went to her chest where her heart was bursting with intolerable agony. The other hand she extended beseechingly to her mother.

The agony caused by her son's murder, her own captivity, the shocking massacres and her own appalling guilt finally cracked the last vestiges of sanity. Her heart convulsed with acute grief as she recalled how callously she had responded to her father's loving embrace. '*Eej...*

my father had been my greatest hero…always…your tales about his bravery made me so proud…I was proud I was his daughter…I…I wanted to be like him. I hoped to meet him when I reached the land of the Tanguts not knowing he was already beside me all the while. I am an unfortunate daughter, *Eej,* that I did not know him. I was born under a cursed star. I have lost everyone I loved. But the worst is the affliction I carry within me. I have assaulted my own father. I cannot bear it any more, *Eej.* Can you take it away? Can you take me away, *Eej?* Hold me, *Eej,* hold me as you did long ago. Your arms will wipe away my torment…take away my guilt…drown my sorrows. *Eej! Eej! Eej….*'

Swirls of the Kherlen sucked at her long *deel* as the girl waded towards her mother, hands outstretched. A powerful current snatched at her feet and she toppled into the froth. Enkhtuya's fingers had just about touched her mother's hands when she felt herself drawn into her embrace. Foaming waves lovingly hugged the girl in their cool arms. As the Kherlen filled her mouth and nose, the blue eyes looking at the cold stars through the blue-green flood finally turned tranquil as the terrible angst inside the Princess was erased by the cool, streaming tide.

Bolorma had also run as fast as her old legs could carry her. She had hidden for a few hours among the trees dotted with new green leaves and buds. She knew that once the Princess' escape was discovered, she would be the first suspect. Panting and out of breath, she had jogged through a long, circuitous route to reach the river. By the time Bolorma was standing on the elevated plain overlooking the river, pink streaks were being etched on the grey sky. Light filtering from the golden orb still below the horizon picked out the wildflowers thickly strewn across the dewy steppes. Blue, pink, yellow, white blossoms opened their petals and nodded in the morning breeze. Gurgling and meandering through this carpet of many patterns, the Kherlen played hide and seek between clumps of tall grass. From her high viewpoint, Bolorma noticed another flower floating amidst the frolicking waves; a sky-blue *deel* spread around a form like petals of a huge gentian, loose strands of hair being its sepals and the open blue eyes its stigma.

Bolorma gave a piercing cry and slid down the knoll to the waters. Negotiating the slippery rocks, she managed to clutch Enkhtuya's *deel* and pull her ashore. She held the girl's head and breathed into her mouth repeatedly, but it was too late. Guided by the old woman's loud laments, the Mongol soldiers from the camp reached the river bank, too. They saw the girl lying among the flowers, her head on the old woman's lap. Bolorma's tears fell thick and fast on the girl's unconcerned face. An orange sun beamed golden rays on the alabaster profile lighting up its winged brows, slight nose and slightly open rosebud mouth in the beginnings of a smile. What struck the onlookers was the serenity of the face; Princess Enkhtuya seemed to be sleeping contentedly. In death she finally embodied the name given by her mother; Light of Peace.

Gradually, Bolorma became aware of a soft buzz around her. Lifting her wrinkled face grooved by continuous tears, an astonishing sight met her eyes. The rough Mongol soldiers were on their knees. Bowing their heads, they were offering their respects to the dead girl. Words floated to her ears, '...she went to her death willingly...to serve the Lord...it was her penance...redeemed her life...she is honoured...she is an honourable lady...she is a boon to our Lord...' More soldiers rushed up, saw the dead princess and knelt. Even the Khan's crusty generals when they came upon the sombre spectacle. . .even Shigi, slowly got down on their knees.

Thus it happened, that in death, Princess Enkhtuya earned a place of honour among the very Mongols who had reviled her when she had lived.

Epilogue

There is no doubt that Genghis Khan was the first world conqueror, and nobody has yet ruled such a mammoth empire as he did. By the time of his death, the Mongolian Empire was four times the size of Alexander's and twice the size of Rome's. It was larger than any nation today except possibly Russia. And it was only half complete. By 1300 CE, his descendants had doubled it adding what is now known as China, Tibet, Korea, Pakistan, Iran, most of Turkey, Georgia, Armenia, Azerbaijan, most of habitable Russia, Ukraine, and half of Poland. They had explored breaching the borders of western Europe, Egypt, India, Vietnam, Indonesia and Japan. One-sixth of the world's land area was the Mongolian Empire. The fact that Genghis Khan's grandson, Kublai was the master of this vast region is one of history's amazing truths.

Yet another strange fact is that nobody knows when and how Genghis Khan died. His death is a matter of great speculation. It is generally agreed that the year of his death was 1227 CE. Rumours have given rise to various versions of the manner in which he 'ascended to the Blue Heaven'. His death remained a matter of state secret probably on the orders of the Khan, himself, so that his enemies may not take advantage of his demise.

Where was he buried? Nobody knows for there is no grave. The Mongols believe that a secret grave exists across the Kherlen, at the foot of the sacred Burkhan Khaldun in the Khenti Mountains. There is a legend that says that those who buried him wanted to ensure nobody disturbed his remains. However, they wanted to remember the spot themselves. Aware that female camels had excellent memories, they searched for a camel whose baby was still being fed mother's milk. They killed the baby and buried it next to the Khan's grave. Thereafter, every spring they would release the mother camel who would return to the spot where her baby was buried. That is how his people would know where to venerate their Lord every year. Eventually, the mother camel grew old and died and the location of the Khan's grave disappeared from posterity.

He named his third son, Ogedei as his heir with all four sons, the others being Jochi, the eldest, Chaghadai the second and Tolui, the youngest, ruling their own divisions and areas of the Empire. As foreseen by Hoelun, with the suspicion of illegitimacy upon him, Jochi was given the farthest region beyond the Aral Sea. Tolui traditionally inherited his father's 'hearth' which comprised entire Mongolia. It gave him and his descendants a power base making them eventually the true heirs of Genghis Khan.

The great Mongolian Empire, a symbol of male dominance, owed a lot to the remarkable women of Genghis Khan's family. The contributions of his mother, Hoelun, his wife Börte and later his daughter-in-law, Sorkaktani are immeasurable.

Sorkaktani was a Keriat and a Christian. After the death of her husband, Tolui, she took over the administration of his region. She was astute and liberal as a ruler and also Ogedei's advisor. She believed in continuing with Genghis Khan's tolerant approach towards all religions and let them flourish in the Empire. It is recorded that she built a beautiful mosque in Bukhara and was much venerated for it as it was unprecedented for a Christian to build a mosque during those times.

Her son and Genghis' grandson, Kublai Khan consolidated the great Empire. Having been tutored and guided by his mother, the wise Sorkaktani, he became Genghis Khan's true heir. His conquest of the Song kingdom finally brought the entire Chinese nation into the Empire and he is known to have formed the foundations of modern China. In China, Kublai built roads, canals, trade, efficient taxation, postal-relay system and even introduced paper money.

From Avraga, the capital city of the Mongol Empire moved several times. First, Kublai made Karakorum the imperial city which English-speakers know better as Xanadu from ST Coleridge's poem that begins with these lines:

In Xanadu did Kubla Khan
A stately pleasure dome decree,
Where Alph the sacred river ran
Through caverns measureless to man
Down to sunless sea.

Later, Kublai Khan shifted the capital to Beijing so that he could control the Chinese part of his Empire better. After his death, family squabbles, clan wars, inept emperors began to break down the foundations of the Empire. Rebellions from its vast reaches ate into the peace and prosperity wrought about by Kublai Khan. Finally, in 1368 CE, the last Mongol Emperor, Toghon Temur fled from Beijing as the forces of the Ming Dynasty took over. In a lonely outpost in Inner Mongolia, Toghon died of despair.

The Mongolian Empire may have crumbled to dust, but Genghis Khan continues to remain an enigma to modern generations. Wherever he may be buried, provision had to be made to remember his greatness. He had to be honoured, his possessions had to be preserved, and a place had to be provided for his worship. Eventually, Genghis Khan fulfilled his aspiration of being ensconced in the hearts of men and thus become immortal. If you visit Mongolia today, in the green Ordos valley, you can visit Edsen Khoroo or the Lord's Enclosure. It is a mausoleum dedicated to Genghis Khan and is housed in three magnificent pagoda-like domes. Inside the main room, you will see his bow, saddle, clothing and yak tail standards. Of the other two tents, one is dedicated to Börte, his first wife and the other…?

That is Genghis Khan's untold story.

The explanation offered to you by the keeper from the Darkhat tribe, descendants of Boorchu, is that the third tent is consecrated to Gurbelchin, the Tangut princess who sacrificed her life for the Lord!

Actually, the truth of the third tent has been shielded carefully by the very few who knew about it, on the express wishes of the great Genghis Khan. It had been camouflaged so well and guarded so strictly that its certitude has been lost in the dusty mires of history.

The best-kept mystery of Genghis Khan's life is this:

Princess Enkhtuya was his daughter, the fruit of his undying love and passion for the beautiful Princess Gurbelchin of Xi Xia.

The third tent in Edsen Khoroo is dedicated to Genghis Khan's love child, Enkhtuya, who sacrificed herself to bring benediction to her father.

Author's Note

The range of figures from world history that one could write about is infinite. But there some whose appearance on the global stage incites deep curiosity. And to delve deep enough to satisfy that inquiry requires a great deal of passion. That is what happened between the writer in me and Genghis Khan—a personality so vilified by historians that one wonders whether he actually existed. Inquisitiveness instigated me to research into his life. What I discovered was a treasure beyond belief. I studied contemporary academic works as well as recorded history by people from his own era and a translation of *The Secret History of the Mongols* actually commissioned by Genghis Khan, himself. Soon the man, his people, his nation, his habitat, his traditions and the events of his life revealed themselves to me. It was like peeling off one clove after another from the wild garlic dug out of the steppes. Fascination with this gigantic persona and what created it easily turned into passion.

The Legend of Genghis Khan, Untold Story of the Conqueror was born from this ardour like a slim thread of fiction weaving a delicate motif into the robust fabric of established facts and truths from the conqueror's life. It is a story created with fervour and admiration along with the expectations that I am able to raise the same sentiments in you, my dear reader.

Of course, no procreation is a solo effort. Thus, I take the opportunity to express my appreciation to all those who have helped to make this book see the light of day. I have been extremely fortunate in having Dr John Man, British historian, Mongolist and travel writer, as my mentor who has guided me immensely right from the beginning. It was not just the explicit yet poetic descriptions in his books that painted an animated picture of Genghis Khan's life and times but also his constant advice on how to go about the project that have been invaluable.

I was at a loss to validate the Mongol vocabulary used in the book until Dr Vikas Singh, Assistant Professor, Zakir Hussain College, Delhi, one of the very few people to have studied Mongolian language at the Jawaharlal Nehru University, came to my help. I am boundlessly grateful to him for not just the accurate glossing but also presenting the words in the original script.

My heartfelt gratitude goes out to authors, Ms Vasudha Chandna Gulati, Ms Harshali Singh and Ms Sanghamitra Bose for their endless patience to read and analyse my manuscript. My telling of the tale has become refined only due to their constructive, relevant and beneficial comments. In this respect, I must mention that it is my editor, Ms Indrani Ganguly who has really polished this book to a gleam and my thanks go out to her every moment. I am grateful to Ms Rima Kar Ghosh for her helpful editorial comments.

For the gorgeous cover design, I am grateful to the creativity of Mr Sourish Mitra, artist and designer par excellence.

Mr Dipankar Mukherjee of Readomania, my publisher, remains my staunchest support and encouragement. Without his faith in my passion, *The Legend of Genghis Khan, Untold Story of the Conqueror* could not have gone out to you, my dear reader.

My thanks for the extracted verses in the book taken from *The Secret History of the Mongols: A Mongolian Epic Chronicle of the Thirteenth Century* translated by Igor de Rachewiltz, The Australian National University.

Sutapa Basu
2018

About the Author

Sutapa Basu is an author, poet and publishing consultant with a thirty-year-old professional career as a teacher, editor and publisher. While holding senior managerial positions with Oxford University Press, India, and Encyclopedia Britannica, South Asia, she has designed and published nearly 400 books.

In 2016, her short story 'Braveheart' was awarded the First Prize in the Amish Tripathi contest of the *Times of India*'s nation-wide *Write India Campaign*.

She has authored *Dangle*, a psychological thriller as well as a historical fiction, *Padmavati, The Queen Tells Her Own Story*. *The Legend of Genghis Khan, Untold Story of the Conqueror* is her second historical fiction and third novel published by Readomania.

Her short stories have been published in anthologies: *Crossed & Knotted* awarded 'India's First Composite Novel' by *Limca Book of Records*, *Defiant Dreams*, *When They Spoke* and *Write India Stories*. Her poems appear in *Kaafiyana* and *The Dawn Beyond Waste*, two poetry collections. She has edited *Chronicles of Urban Nomads*, *Crossed & Knotted*, *A Window to Her Dreams* and *Rudraksha* published by Readomania. Her work is showcased on her website Storyfuntastika.com and Readomania.com.

References

Text Resources

John Man, *Genghis Khan, Life, Death and Resurrection*, St. Martin's Griffin (1st ed), 2007.

John Man, *The Mongol Empire, Genghis Khan, His Heirs and the Founding of Modern China*, Bantam Press, 2014.

Urgunge Onon (trans), *The Secret History of The Mongols, The Life and Times of Chinggis Khan*, Routledge (1st ed), 2011.

'Ala-ad-Din' Ata-Malik Juvaini, *Genghis Khan, The History of the World Conqueror*, JA Boyle (trans), University of Washington Press, 1997.

Igor de Rachewiltz, *The Secret History of the Mongols: A Mongolian Epic Chronicle of the Thirteenth Century*, The Australian National University, 2015. Shorter version edited by John C. Street, University of Wisconsin—Madison. Books and Monographs. Book 4.

Online Resources

https://www.biography.com/people/genghis-khan-9308634

https://www.livescience.com/43260-genghis-khan.html

http://www.history.com/topics/genghis-khan

https://quizlet.com/117033654/genghis-khan-vocab-glossary-flash-cards

https://www.mapsofindia.com/history/mongol-dynasty.html

https://www.forbes.com/sites/ryanholiday/2012/05/07/9-lessons-on-leadership-from-genghis-khan-yes-genghis-khan/#3885d29c6996

http://www.coldsiberia.org/monwomen.htm

Glossary

Mongolian	English
Aav (аав)	father
Aduu (адуу)	horse
Airag (айраг)	a drink made from fermented mare's milk
Ald (алд)	the distance between the outstretched arms of a man or roughly 1.6 metres
Anda (анда)	blood brothers
Deel (Дээл)	caftan-like, ankle-length padded silk robes lined with sheepskin for the winter and tied around the waist with a sash like belt
Eej (ээж)	mother
Enkhtuya (Энх тайвны гэрэл: enx taivnie gerel)	name for a female meaning 'Light of Peace'
Ger (Гэр)	round tents made with felt stretched over circular wooden rafters and struts
Guunj (гүнж)	princess
Gutal (гутал)	embroidered leather knee boots with thick soles and upturned toes
Ovoo (Овоо)	an altar or shrine to Khökh Tenger, the Mongolian Supreme Being
Ordon (ордон майхан: ordon maixan)	palace tents
Sumo (сумо)	refers to people who come from Central and West Asia
Temur (Төмөр)	iron

Chinese	English
Cangue	a collar made of a pair of thick, wooden planks each with half-circle to fit around the neck and bolted together

Tangut	English
Gambu	imperial commander